Peace and Conflict Studies Research

A Qualitative Perspective

A volume in
Peace Education Series

Volume Editor
Edward J. Brantmeier, *James Madison University*

Peace Education Series

Jing Lin, Edward J. Brantmeier, and Ian Harris, Series Editors

Peace and Conflict Studies Research

A Qualitative Perspective

edited by

Robin Cooper
Nova Southeastern University

Laura Finley
Barry University

INFORMATION AGE PUBLISHING, INC.
Charlotte, NC • www.infoagepub.com

Library of Congress Cataloging-in-Publication Data

A CIP record for this book is available from the Library of Congress
http://www.loc.gov

ISBN: 978-1-62396-691-1 (Paperback)
     978-1-62396-692-8 (Hardcover)
     978-1-62396-693-5 (ebook)

Printed in the United States of America

CONTENTS

CHAPTER 1

INTRODUCTION

Exploring Qualitative Approaches to Researching Peace and Conflict

Robin Cooper and Laura Finley

QUALITATIVE RESEARCH IN THE FIELD OF
PEACE AND CONFLICT STUDIES

Peace and conflict studies—so much is encompassed by this term. Mediators, arbitrators, and negotiators are active in the practice of resolving conflict outside of traditional legal systems. Ombudsmen and group facilitators help to manage conflict in the workplace. Sociologists and political scientists examine sociological and political factors contributing to intergroup and international conflict. Social psychologists, therapists, and conflict coaches seek to understand and ameliorate interpersonal conflict as well as the effects of trauma caused by conflict. Peace activists engage in work on the ground in communities to overturn forms of injustice and oppression and to participate in peacebuilding in the aftermath of violent conflict. Peace educators strive to address structural and cultural violence and empower the next generation to contribute constructively to a peaceful and just society. While these various scholars and practitioners may differ in terms of the focus and context of their work, all in one way or another address issues of conflict and violent or peaceful means of resolving conflict. The phrase "peace and conflict studies" is thus used in this text as an umbrella term meant to reflect the shared focus of all these scholars and practitioners on issues of peace and conflict.

The fact that more and more professions and disciplines relate in one way or another to conflict resolution is reflected in the growing number of graduate programs in this field. According to the website gradschools. com, there are currently some 272 graduate programs in peace and conflict studies. Graduate programs (both in this field and others) typically require that students take one or more research courses, depending upon the level of studies. Such courses enable students to understand the studies presented in scholarly journals as well as to be prepared to conduct their own research. Graduate students are expected to be able to appraise and to conduct both quantitative and qualitative research in their given field, and this includes students in programs in peace and conflict studies.

Historically, the emphasis of published research has been on quantitative studies, and this is reflected in the dominance of quantitative research reports in such journals in the field as *The Journal of Conflict Resolution*, the *International Journal of Conflict Management*, and the *Journal of Peace Research*. Over the past several decades, however, the rise of qualitative methodologies in the field has also been reflected in the growing number of journals, such as *Peace and Conflict Studies* and *Conflict Resolution Quarterly*, which welcome and publish reports of both quantitative and qualitative research.

The term "qualitative research" encompasses a wide array of methods and perspectives. Broadly speaking, qualitative research is the study of people and phenomena in their natural setting and reflects an emphasis on the meaning people find in their natural social life. Flick (2008) observes,

> Qualitative research uses text as empirical material (instead of numbers), starts from the notion of the social construction of realities under study, is interested in the perspectives of participants, in everyday practices and everyday knowledge referring to the issue under study. (p. 2)

While there is significant diversity within the world of qualitative inquiry, these observations describe some characteristics of qualitative approaches to research.

It is beyond the scope of this book to provide a history of the development of qualitative research. Vidich and Lyman (2003) describe the progression in the fields of sociology and anthropology from early ethnography prior to the 17th century, through colonial ethnography in the 17th–19th centuries, metropolitan and small town ethnography of the 20th century, to the postmodern and critical forms of ethnographic research of the late 20th and early 21st centuries. Yet ethnography is but one thread in the history of qualitative inquiry—a field which encompasses multiple methodologies and multiple disciplines. Denzin and Lincoln (2011) mark what they refer to as "at least eight historical moments" of qualitative research (p. 3), from the start of the 20th century to the present. They define these moments as including "the traditional (1900–1950), the modernist or golden age (1950–1970), blurred genres (1970–1986), the crisis of representation (1986–1990), the postmodern, a period of experimental and new ethnographies (1990–1995), postexperimental inquiry (1995–2000), the methodologically contested phase (2000–2010), and the future (2010–), which is now" (p. 3).[1] According to this timeline, the moments accelerate from a span of 50 years, to 20 years, down to periods of four or five years. Other authors highlight the role of feminist and critical race theorists in pushing the boundaries of qualitative inquiry to address issues of equity and the importance of narrative (e.g., Butler-Kisber, 2010).

While the timelines and labels associated with the history of qualitative research can be debated, typically there are several important features of qualitative research, including a naturalistic context for research, researcher reflexivity, honoring the voice of participants, and issues of evaluation within qualitative research. Regarding the context for research, Flick (2008) notes,

> Qualitative research is intended to approach the world 'out there' (not in specialized research settings such as laboratories) and to understand, describe and sometimes explain social phenomena 'from the inside'... Qualitative researchers are interested in accessing experiences, interactions and documents in their natural context. (pp. ix–x)

This emphasis on a naturalistic approach to research is highlighted in the following chapters, which provide examples of how the site for data collection in a qualitative study may be a particular community, organization, or family home.

In addition to a natural context for research, another common feature across the various qualitative methodologies is an acknowledgment of the importance of reflexivity on the part of the researcher. Qualitative researchers recognize that not only do the participants in our studies make meaning out of their experiences and interactions, but also that researchers themselves are making meaning out of the information gathered through interviews, observations, and analysis of documents and visual artifacts. Noting that even novice researchers have a "research identity," Butler-Kisber (2010) points out, "clearly we all bring beliefs, even unarticulated ones, to the research process" (p. 19). In light of the fact that in qualitative research the researcher is the primary instrument, researchers seek to be transparent about who they are, their positions and contexts as researchers, and to take steps to address and manage their biases and beliefs in the research process. The following chapters will discuss this feature of qualitative research and provide examples of how researcher reflexivity is practiced according to various qualitative methodologies.

Another common characteristic of qualitative research is the emphasis on honoring and representing the voices of participants. Typically, qualitative research reports include verbatim quotes from participants. Such quotes contribute to the quality of the research report in several ways. In terms of the issue of researcher reflexivity noted above, the inclusion of the participants' own words helps to assure that the researcher is not merely presenting his or her own perspectives. Such quotes also support the trustworthiness of the findings, as they serve as exemplars to illustrate the researcher's conclusions. Beyond the functional contributions, the words of participants included in qualitative research reports also honor the individuals' lives, experiences, and perspectives. The voices of participants may be analyzed and portrayed in different forms depending upon the particular qualitative methodology, and this will be discussed in the following chapters. It is safe to say, however, that as qualitative research seeks to ground its findings in the lived experiences and subjective meaning-making of people, it is important not to lose sight of those people as we also seek to understand social interactions, events, and circumstances.

At this point, the distinctive role and value of qualitative approaches in social research is well established. Flick (2008) refers to this as the "success story" of qualitative research (p. 3). There is now broad understanding that qualitative research has different objectives, and different means of evaluation, than quantitative research. As Chenail (2010) notes, there is substantial debate even among qualitative researchers regarding the appropriateness of various assessment measures of validity, reliability, and generalizability. Some authors suggest the use of "naturalistic generalization" (Stake, 2008) or "transferability" (Lincoln & Guba, 1985), whereby readers can reflect upon how the findings associated with a given case study, for example, might relate to another similar case. Other authors use alternative terms such as "trustworthiness" and "credibility" (Marshall & Rossman, 2010) in place of validity. Patton (2002) suggests alternative criteria for judging the quality of qualitative research based on the differing claims associated with research projects. He observes, "Traditional scientific claims, constructivist claims, artistic claims, critical change claims, and evaluation claims will tend to emphasize different kinds of conclusions with varying implications" (p. 587). In light of the divergent theoretical and epistemological paradigms informing quantitative and qualitative research, as well as the different objectives and truth claims (Habermas, 1996) associated with these approaches to research, it makes sense that the appraisal of qualitative research reports would not be based on the same criteria as that of quantitative research. These issues will be discussed in the context of specific qualitative methodologies in the chapters that follow.[2]

The field of peace and conflict studies has grown tremendously in the last two decades, as has the field of peace education in K–12 schools and colleges and universities. It is our hope that this book serves as an important tool to guide the growing number of student and faculty researchers in the field, as well as the practitioners who seek to understand the causes of violence and to develop and assess peacebuilding programs. Further, there are now many nonprofits and nongovernmental organizations seeking to develop programs and to conduct process and impact evaluations that we hope can benefit from this book.

In this chapter, we highlight some of the trends in the field of peace research as well as some of the ongoing challenges. We begin by addressing some of the personal issues and challenges faced by qualitative researchers in the field, and then include discussion of more macrolevel trends. We also integrate some of the important resources that scholars, students and practitioners can consult for more information and for additional support for their work.

PERSONAL ISSUES AND CHALLENGES

Qualitative researchers have long grappled with issues of impartiality and neutrality, as the chapters in this book discuss. The argument over whether any research is truly objective will continue and is of particular importance for researchers coming from critical backgrounds in which the point is to challenge the status quo (Brantmeier, 2005). In this tradition, research is not just for the sake of knowledge production but instead for societal transformation. Peace and conflict studies researchers must continue to be attentive to reflexivity, paying attention to how our identities, histories, experiences, and perspectives shape our research (Couture, Zaidi, & Maticka-Tyndale, 2012). As Emily Welty notes in her chapter on ethnography, participant-researchers may struggle to manage insider and outsider roles. Further, Welty describes how she was both observer and the observed, which is a difficult position to manage.

Additionally, peace and conflict studies researchers must grapple with their tendency to "side with the underdogs" against perceived oppressors (Barron, 1999; Lumsden, 2013; Seal, 2012). As Lumsden (2013) notes, "we are what we research." That is, the choices we make about what to research, the questions we ask, the data we include, and the ways we analyze and report findings, all say as much about the researcher as they do about the research subject. Qualitative researchers are advised to be as transparent as possible about their processes and their perspectives, as this allow readers of their research to make their own judgments about the trustworthiness of the findings.

While decades of attention have resulted in numerous protections for human subjects, less attention has been paid to the emotional and physical health of researchers. Qualitative research about sensitive subjects can be upsetting to researchers. Sampson, Bloor, and Fincham (2008) found the emotional issues to be more frequent and difficult than the physical dangers. Those using feminist methodologies that stress the importance of connectivity and an ethic of care may be particularly vulnerable to emotional disturbance and even depression (Rager, 2005a; Sampson, Bloor & Fincham, 2008). Even reading disturbing reports, such as suicide notes from coroners, can be emotionally disruptive for researchers (Fincham, Scourfield, & Langer, 2008). Bahn and Weatherill (2013) and Rager (2005b) note the importance of self-care for researchers working in dangerous locations and/or with difficult subject matter, who are often referred to by ethnographers as "wounded in the field." Rager (2005a) calls for greater attention to these issues among those preparing to conduct qualitative studies, as well as counseling, debriefing with peers, and journal writing as strategies to address compassion fatigue that may result from studying difficult emotional subjects.

MACROLEVEL ISSUES AND CHALLENGES

As Alger (1999) notes, an important development in the field in the second half of the 20th century was the recognition, first articulated by Johan Galtung (1996), of positive peace. These developments helped propel the field to study not just peacekeeping but peacemaking and, more recently, peacebuilding. Doing so has required researchers to consider new research designs, data sources and evaluation techniques. This broader research agenda also brings unique challenges, as studying macrolevel concepts such as structural violence is daunting, to say the least. Additional research on positive peace is essential, but researchers must take great care in how they design their studies so as to ensure they use the most appropriate markers and data sources (Stave, 2011).

One trend that will continue is use of mixed research methods, in particular mixing qualitative with quantitative designs (Alger, 1999). Mixing methods helps researchers triangulate data and can be ideally suited to assessing the complexity of peacebuilding efforts. Further, as many of the chapters in this book highlight, use of mixed methods, whether it be multiple qualitative methods or a combination of qualitative with quantitative methodologies, is helpful in assessing some of the very complex subjects involved in peace and conflict studies. As Ismael Muvingi and Cheryl Duckworth point out in their chapter, case studies are ideally suited for mixed methods because anything that is relevant to the case should be included and thus ethnographic data, observations, interviews, secondary data sources and much more are typical.

One promising mixed method in regard to peace education initiatives is critical ethnographic studies (Brantmeier, 2005). This method emerges from the broader trend of critical social research. As Carspecken (1996) explains, "We are all concerned about social inequalities, and we direct our work toward positive social change.... We also share a concern with social theory and some of the basic issues ... the nature of social structure, power, culture, and human agency" (p. 3). Robertson (2005) puts it more bluntly: "Conventional ethnography tends to uphold the status quo. Critical ethnography tends to reinforce change." Carspecken offers a five-stage scheme or framework in order to conduct critical qualitative research. These five include (1) compiling the primary record through qualitative collection of data; (2) preliminary reconstructive analysis; (3) discovering dialogical data generation; (4) describing system relations; and (5) using system relationships to explain the findings.

Similarly, researchers since the mid-1990s have noted the importance of using multiple sources or tracks of data. In *Multi-Track Diplomacy: A Systems Approach to Peace* (1996), Louise Diamond and John McDonald advocate peace research using the following tracks: (1) government, diplomacy, (2) nongovernmental/professional, through conflict resolution, (3) business, peacemaking through commerce, (4) private citizens, through personal involvement, (5) research/training/education, through learning, (6) activism, through advocacy, (7) religion, through faith in action, (8) funding, through providing resources, and (9) communications and the media, through information. Bryman (2007) notes that researchers may find integrating quantitative and qualitative methods challenging, and that publishers may still reinforce the dichotomy in that specific journals are perceived to prefer one type or the other. The field must grow in its ability to produce and disseminate important mixed-method work.

Another trend that will continue to be important is to conduct longitudinal or long-term studies. For instance, Downton and Wehr (1997) studied what causes activists to stay with the peace movement. They drew on collective action theories and conducted interviews with activists to develop a "model of sustained commitment" (Downton &Wehr, 1997, pp. 152–153). Research that shows the long-term satisfaction with and effectiveness and impact of peacemaking and peacebuilding efforts will only gain in importance. Too often, research on peacebuilding has been quantitative, largely due to the monitoring tools used by organizations like the UN (Stave, 2011). As peacebuilding efforts are sustained over longer periods of time, researchers in the field will want to know what factors contribute to their continued success, what challenges were faced, and what concerns remain (Hampson, 1996; Zartman & Rasmussen, 1997).

> The United Nations alone currently spends more than $7 billion every year on international peacekeeping and peacebuilding activities, and donors are increasingly pushing for improved documentation of the effects of this work. This pressure may also be related to a growing public critique in many donor countries of whether and how well such large investments in peacebuilding (as well as in development aid) work in practic. (Stave, 2011, p. 2)

Impact assessments, known as peace and conflict impact assessments (PCIA), are particularly important but also challenging, as the nature of conflict is multifaceted and complex (Reychler, 1998). Researchers sometimes compromise data quality because of the difficulties in obtaining access (Stave, 2011). Further, as Schmelze (2005) notes, the field of conflict studies and peace research is still relatively new and is therefore still developing best practices for impact assessments.

Further, Stave (2011) notes that researchers evaluating peacebuilding efforts typically use preassumptions and peacebuilding theories that might prohibit them from developing a true understanding of what is actually happening. "The clear danger is a kind of circularity which produces only the semblance rather than the reality of knowledge, and where measurements are used to promote the construction of "virtual realities"—namely, progress against a non-existing situation rather than what is happening on the ground" (p. 3). Further, "When universal theories of change are used as a basis to measure the effects of peacebuilding, the consequence is that the selection of indicators employed in the measurement also tends to the universal—and more and more removed from any particular context" (p. 4). Yet peacebuilding absolutely must be localized and contextual. Thus researchers are advised to use preexisting indices as guides only. Local indicators should be developed in conjunction with local peoples (Stave, 2011). Additionally,

> There is a clear tendency to select indicators that suggest progress towards the achievement of objectives stated in mandates and visions, but which neglect showing setbacks or failures. This tendency might not be intentional but instead the natural result of basing the selection of indicators on particular theories of change inherent in the mandates and goals of peacebuilding initiatives. (p. 5)

Finally, Stave discusses the difficulty in linking activities with effects when studying such complex and multifaceted topics.

Qualitative research has long been used to assess the social impact of disasters, beginning with Prince's (1920) study in Halifax. Phillips (1997) explains that qualitative methods are particularly well-suited for disaster research as disasters challenge communities in unique ways and thus qualitative research methodologies that allow insight into the "backstage behavior" (Goffman, 1959) is essential. Also,

> because qualitative research is grounded in people's actual experiences, the possibility of identifying new, relevant questions becomes more likely. While disaster researchers know that we often see the same stories or 'lessons learned' in disaster after disaster, qualitative research bears the possibility of identifying new questions. Qualitative methods and naturalistic paradigms permit the researcher to follow interesting questions and to alter the research design to pursue promising areas of inquiry. In so doing, qualitative research can empower and give voice to respondents (particularly disaster managers and victims). (Phillips, 1997, p. 186)

Given the continued destruction of the planet through overconsumption, violent conflict, and resource acquisition, scholars predict that the number of man-made and natural disasters will increase. Phillips recommends researchers use participatory and observational methods, including living in a postdisaster area and assisting with recovery efforts, greater use of longitudinal studies, and cautions against the overuse of case studies.

Peace researchers must continue to grow and reflect in their capacity to conduct research in developing countries. As researchers study barriers to positive peace, and as they develop, implement and evaluate peacebuilding programs, cultural competence and rejecting the tendency to "otherize" subjects will become even more essential. As Alger (1999) notes, "those developing peace theories and strategies—most of whom are from a few developed countries ... [must] contend with peacelessness in a diversity of cultural situations" (p. 43). Likewise, peace researchers may face unique challenges when conducting research involving conflict between multiple ethnic groups. Additionally, as the chapters in this book discuss, obtaining Institutional Review Board (IRB) permission for a qualitative study in conflict or postconflict zones can be a challenge. Researchers must make great efforts to ensure they are being ethical when working with people who have been or are still dealing with trauma. Additionally, researcher safety in conflict or postconflict zones remains a challenge. Julia Chaitin notes the importance of researcher flexibility in her chapter on conflict-zones. Because the research is occurring at a time and in a place that is chaotic, researchers must be able to switch methodologies, take breaks, coordinate with other scholars, and make other necessary adjustments.

Given that many postconflict societies have engaged in reconciliation and forgiveness efforts, research on these topics has grown tremendously in the last two decades and will likely continue to be important (Alger, 1999; Lederbach, 1997; Shriver, 1995; Simpson, 1998). Observational studies of reconciliation processes, longitudinal research that assesses the impact of those processes on various stakeholders, and textual analysis of reports about forgiveness efforts are all possibilities.

One of the most important trends involves assessing prevention efforts. Scores of nonprofits and nongovernmental organizations are engaged in preventing violence, ranging from gang prevention to domestic violence prevention to the prevention of ethnic conflict, and more. In particular, impact assessments are becoming increasingly important, as nonprofits and NGOs compete for financial support from funders who want to see that the programs they support are working. Often, these organizations have little expertise in research or evaluation, nor do most organizations have the staffing or financial capacity to conduct research about their program's effectiveness. Graduate students, scholars and independent researchers can play a key role in helping nonprofits and NGOs plan and conduct assessments. Peace and conflict studies researchers often seek to incorporate the voices of silenced or marginalized groups. Given that prevention work is typically focused on young people, researchers will face challenges in accessing these populations, in utilizing methods that are fully participatory and do not "otherize" young people, and in obtaining IRB approval for their work.

One way to engage youth and to represent marginalized voices is through the arts and new technologies. Researchers today are increasingly using alternative forms of knowledge as data, that is, arts, photography (Allen, 2012; Smith, Gidlow, & Steel, 2012), and performances (Foster, 2013). Phillips (1997) predicted that visual qualitative methods would become more prevalent given the sheer number of people who have cameras, video cameras, and other technologies making obtaining visuals easier than ever. New technologies can assist researchers but must be used with care. As more scholars seek to conduct research using social media, great care must be taken to ensure that ethical standards (Eysenbach, 2001; Mann & Stewart, 2002; Shaft, 1999) and privacy are ensured (Paechter, 2013). Further, Adler and Adler (2012) caution against abandoning classical research tools like ethnography in favor of the newest, trendiest methodologies.

Scholars have noted the ongoing challenge of obtaining access to certain populations for research purposes. Given that researchers may lack the connections, time, or funding to reach the participants who would be most valuable to their study, gatekeepers are essential. Gatekeepers are those who do not have the technical expertise or financial ability to conduct the research themselves but who serve as intermediaries between researchers and participants (Clark, 2010). In return for access, researchers must demonstrate to gatekeepers how their work will be beneficial to the participants and/or to the organization (Corra & Willer, 2002). Clark's (2010) work sought to address the reasons why gatekeepers support research and the mechanisms that challenge their support. He found that gatekeepers may have both personal and organizational reasons for allowing research- ers access, and in particular, do not want to feel that they or the group/ organization they represent are dismissed or objectified. Similarly, Desch- aux-Beaume (2012) addressed the importance of research on the military, yet noted the difficulty many researchers experience in obtaining access. More studies like this are needed to help researchers navigate the process of finding gatekeepers and securing their ongoing support.

Although access can be an issue, sometimes groups are too available and become overresearched. Clark (2008) notes the importance of addressing research fatigue on the part of participants to various studies. Research that stretches over long periods of time or that involves groups that are fre- quently asked to participate is particularly likely to create fatigue (Thomson & Holland, 2003). The intensity and emotional difficulty of some types of peace and conflict studies research is another factor that might create research fatigue. As Hammersley (1995) explains,

> Research has material effects.... People's lives may be affected by being re- searched, and by being in a context that is affected by research findings. And these effects may be for good or for ill, and can run through the whole gamut of more complex combinations and possibilities that lies between those two extremes. (p. 112)

Clark (2008) found that research participants who see little to no change in their organization or on the issue of the research as a result of their partici- pation are hesitant to participate again. Similarly, the lack of change may result in gatekeepers limiting or prohibiting access to crucial participants.

TEACHING QUALITATIVE METHODS IN PEACE AND CONFLICT STUDIES

It is imperative that college programs prepare new scholars and practi- tioners in the field of peace and conflict studies to conduct qualitative research by using innovative teaching techniques and providing mentor- ing and support for young scholars. As many peace educators have noted, peace education must be both about and *for* peace. That is, the instruc- tional methods used must not only inform but should engage students in critical reflection, should provide for shared power between student and professor, and should incite passion for societal transformation (Brant- meier, 2005; Lin, 2006; Galtung, 1996; Finley, 2004, 2011; Jenkins, 2007). Yet, as Stark and Watson (1999) note,

> The teaching of qualitative research, by and large, still tends to be geared more toward a series of lectures that teach students skills such as how to conduct a semistructured interview, how to be a nonparticipant observer, and how to recognize and pull out a theme from a transcript. (p. 721)

Further,

> Technical texts often provide an orderly plan of a linear research process and "how to" methods to complete the process. Students often will demand this systematic form of teaching, which is translated into a tightly planned and structured weekly schedule highlighting the "input" and "output" expected of them and the teacher, with readable and organized texts to work from ... we would suggest that they should *supplement* an experience rather than provide a rigid structure that results in students not being able to see beyond the page to their own experience. (pp. 721–22).

Gerstl-Pepin and Patrizio (2009) describe how to use reflective journaling to help students practice the reflexivity that is essential to qualitative research. They use the metaphor of Dumbledore's Pensieve, the magical tool the Head Wizard of Hogwarts School of Witchcraft and Wizardry uses with Harry in the Harry Potter series as a way to reflect on the connections between phenomena. Similarly, Stark and Watson (1999) recommend "exercises that call for us to engage our sensual selves" (p. 721).

> Qualitative research requires desire, passion, and eros because it is fundamentally relational. Desire indicates a willingness for connection between self and "other," whether the other is the people we research, the written transcripts, or the resulting text that stirs and ignites our passion. (p. 727)

Alger (1999) argues for the increasing importance of bridging theory and action, or praxis. As Stark and Watson (1999) found, students are often taught in prescriptive ways and thus focus on preparing "a prepacked written formula, stamped with the seal of academic authority and, therefore, 'right'" (p. 724). The goal of the field is to create and sustain a more peaceful world, which requires stretching our minds and developing our creativity to make social change (Finley, 2011). Participatory methods help develop praxis that can lead to social change (Schratz & Walker, 1995).

As colleges and universities teach students how to conduct qualitative studies and to develop praxis, many are utilizing service-learning (Booker, 2009; Machtmes, Reynaud, Deggs, Matzke, Aguirre, & Johnson, 2009) and community-based research (CBR) (Strand, Marullo, Cutforth, Stoecker, & Donohue, 2003). Service-learning is a form of experiential learning that allows students to gain actual experience with the phenomena being taught in the class. Students can be involved in any or all steps of the actual research, from assisting with the literature review to crafting the study and collecting and analyzing data (Machtmes et al., 2009). Most studies of service-learning projects have involved quantitative research (Boyle-Baise, 2002), despite the fact that qualitative methodologies have much to offer in this area. Matchmes et al. (2009) noted that students who participated in service-learning involving a qualitative research project were more likely to recognize the rigor of qualitative methodologies. Further, the students began to form bonds in the community and develop as professionals—all desirable outcomes for practitioners in the field of peace and conflict studies.

Ernest Boyer's (1990) *Scholarship Reconsidered* critiqued the narrow focus of existing research, asserting that the scholarship of pedagogy and engagement were underutilized and underappreciated. CBR is a method of research that addresses Boyers' criticisms, as students and the community are involved at all levels. All parties participate in the research design, data collection, analysis and reporting. Students may be involved as part of a class assignment, service-learning, or special project. As Strand et al. (2003) note,

> the community consists of people who are oppressed, powerless, economi-
> cally deprived or disenfranchised—that is, who are disadvantaged by exist-
> ing social, political, or economic arrangements. In a broad but critical sense,
> then, CBR is about working for social and economic justice. (pp. 3–4)

One of the authors is involved in a CBR project that is helping a nonprofit assess its services to victims of domestic violence. Results of the in-depth surveys and interviews that were cocreated by the nonprofit staff and board, college students and the researchers will be used by the nonprofit to make service adjustments and to seek additional funding.

Although the value of qualitative research is well established, it can be challenging to find guidance in conducting qualitative research specifi- cally in peace and conflict studies or peace education. Currently, there are a number of texts describing qualitative research methodology and qualitative research design in general (e.g., Berg, 2007; Butler-Kisber, 2010; Creswell, 2013; Marshall & Rossman, 2010; Silverman, 2005; Stake, 2010). There is also considerable literature on conflict resolution theory, as well as books reporting on research in peace and conflict studies (e.g., Abu-Nimer, 2003; Avruch, 2004; Kemp & Fry, 2004; Kreisberg, 2007; Lederach, 2005; Lewicki, Gray, & Elliott, 2003; Schirch, 2005). However, the literature is quite limited when it comes to books describing how to apply qualitative research methods to peace and conflict studies, despite the fact that a sig- nificant portion of research in peace and conflict studies is qualitative. Even texts that reference research in the title, and which may provide examples of research studies in this field, typically do not provide information on how to conduct research in this field (e.g., Schellenberg, 1996; Wallensteen, 2011).

PURPOSE AND FOCUS OF THIS BOOK

In light of this gap in the research literature in our field, this book is designed to offer a new and valuable resource for students, teachers, researchers, and practitioners by providing a detailed exploration of how qualitative research can be applied in the field of peace and conflict studies. This book explores considerations and components of designing, conducting, and reporting qualitative research in this field, and also provides exemplars of recent original research in peace and conflict studies that employed qualitative methods. The book chapters focus on various qualitative research methodologies, and each chapter includes a discussion of how that methodology can be useful in researching peace and conflict.

The primary audience for this book is expected to be those both teaching and learning about the application of qualitative methods to peace and conflict studies, as well as those conducting research in this field. The book may also prove to be a useful tool for researchers and students in other related academic disciplines who are interested in qualitative research. Such disciplines might include sociology, criminology, gender studies, psychology, political science, and others.

As noted above, the focus of this book is quite pragmatic, and readers can expect to find practical information regarding how to design a study using one of the major traditions within qualitative research. With this applied focus, the text does not include an in-depth discussion of the theoretical and philosophical underpinnings of qualitative inquiry, although ontological and epistemological issues are touched on briefly in a number of chapters. Such information is critical to a full understanding of qualitative research, and readers are encouraged to look to other texts that address this aspect of qualitative inquiry in depth, such as those by Crotty (1998), Denzin and Lincoln (2003), and Willis (2007).

This decision to emphasize process more than philosophy in this text is based partly on the fact that no single book can address all aspects of research in depth. In addition, the choice regarding the focus of the text was informed by recent research showing that those learning qualitative research find it helpful to learn how to conduct qualitative studies early in their experience of learning qualitative research and report that such experiential learning enables them to better grasp the theoretical and epistemological foundations of this approach to research (Cooper, Chenail, & Fleming, 2012; Cooper, Fleischer, & Cotton, 2012). A qualitative meta-data-analysis of primary research reports on students' experience of learning qualitative research let to the development of a grounded theory suggesting that

> as students experience a combination of didactic and experiential learning activities, they move through a range of emotions including anxiety, frustration, excitement, and amazement as they seek to achieve their goal of learning "how to do it." Learners also seem to move through cognitive experiences such as cognitive dissonance regarding what constitutes research/science, expansive thinking, critical thinking, and consideration of ethics. They find that experiential learning is critical to understanding both the philosophical orientation and practical skills necessary to conduct qualitative research. (Cooper, Chenail, & Fleming, 2012, pp. 15–15)

A primary qualitative study employing interpretative phenomenological analysis (IPA) led to findings highlighting the value to those learning qualitative research of understanding and practicing processes associated with qualitative inquiry early in their learning experience. The essence of the learning experience was found to be that of "building connections" (Cooper, Fleischer, & Cotton, 2012, p. 11).

> Students appear to experience a range of emotions as they build connections with the qualitative research processes and become more comfortable with the theory, terminology, and methodologies of qualitative inquiry, and as they gain the skills required for collecting, transcribing, and analyzing qualitative data. Students also seem to build personal connections with those they interview through the stories shared by the interviewees. These personal connections become interwoven in the learning process, so their learning is not only a product of what they have done but what they have heard. Finally, the learning experience would seem to involve building connections between prior knowledge and perspectives and the new perspectives and discoveries gained through learning qualitative research. (Cooper, Fleischer, & Cotton, 2012, p. 11)

Based on these findings that students want to learn the "how" of conducting qualitative research and that such applied knowledge helps them understand the philosophical foundations of qualitative inquiry, we are focusing this text on this type of practical information, while at the same time recognizing the critical importance of the philosophical and theoretical foundations of qualitative inquiry. Our hope is that the experiential learning gained by conducting qualitative research in the field of peace and conflict studies will support the appreciation and understanding of the ontological and epistemological perspectives which play such a central role in qualitative inquiry applied in researching peace and conflict.

OVERVIEW OF THE BOOK'S
CONTENTS AND CONTRIBUTORS

While this opening chapter provides an introduction to the book, Chapter 2 offers an introduction to the subject of how to design a qualitative study for those conducting research on conflict or peace. In this chapter, Cooper and Rice walk the reader through the stages and steps involved in building a qualitative study, from finding inspiration for the study topic, to conceptualizing the study by clarifying the purpose statement and central research questions, and considering aspects of the operationalization of a study such as data collection, data analysis, as well as addressing ethical issues throughout the research process. This chapter on qualitative research design provides a structure that can be considered regardless of the specific qualitative methodology chosen for one's research, whereas the following chapters focus on specific approaches to qualitative inquiry.

Each of the chapters focusing on a specific methodology includes some common features. These include an overview and brief history of the methodology, a description of key approaches to that methodology, and examples of recent studies in peace and conflict studies that made use of the methodology. In addition, each methodological chapter offers a detailed description of the data collection, data analysis, and reporting conventions associated with the methodology. These methodological components are illustrated by original research studies conducted by the chapter authors.

In Chapter 3, Finley discusses grounded theory research, providing a brief overview of the history of this tradition and some of its key features, such as theoretical sampling and axial and selective coding. Based on her research on teachers' perceptions of school violence and responses to it, Finley provides a vivid example of what is involved in taking a grounded theory approach to research in this field and shows the potential of this methodology to provide findings that inform policies and processes. Chapter 4 focuses on the applications of phenomenology in studying conflict and peacebuilding experiences. This chapter highlights three models of phenomenology—transcendental, existential and interpretative phenomenological analysis—as well as referring to a study by Cooper on identity-based conflict associated with demographic changes to illustrate various stages of the phenomenological research process.

Chapters 5 and 6 feature two other major traditions within qualitative inquiry—case study research and ethnography. In Chapter 5, Muvingi and Duckworth discuss what case study research is and why one would use it in researching peace and conflict. They also draw upon their own fieldwork to illustrate the steps involved in conducting case study research in this field, describing Muvingi's comparative case study of campaigns by human rights activists related to conflict diamonds and Duckworth's case study of the Paraguayan indigenous land rights movement. In Chapter 6, Welty offers a colorful and useful explanation of organizational ethnography based on her research on an international faith-based peacebuilding and development organization in East Africa.

The two final chapters focusing on specific qualitative methodologies highlight two approaches to qualitative inquiry in which the participant plays an especially prominent role. In Chapter 7, Hiller and Chaitin present a very helpful overview of the background and various models of narrative inquiry. They then describe in detail the narrative life history approach, illustrating this discussion with examples from Hiller's research on long-term nonviolent peace activists. In Chapter 8, Morrow and Finley discuss action research and build into the chapter exercises that readers can use to get a taste of this dynamic approach to researching peace and conflict. In addition, the chapter refers to Morrow's appreciative inquiry research on the development of the National Peace Academy in the United States.

Considered collectively, these chapters not only offer practical guidance regarding selecting from these various methodologies—grounded theory, phenomenology, case study research, ethnography, narrative research, and action research—but they also provide concrete suggestions for data collection and data analysis within each of these methodologies. An additional benefit of these methodology-specific chapters is the view they present collectively of the wonderful range of topics appropriate for research in this field—school violence, identity-based conflict, human rights and land rights campaigns, faith-based peacebuilding, nonviolent peace and social justice activism, and organizational development at the national level for those committed to peace.

The final two chapters turn our thoughts to profound considerations of import to researchers in this field. Chaitin movingly discusses practical, ethical, and safety considerations related to conducting research in conflict zones. She speaks from the heart and the head about various issues related to this subject, based on her many years researching the Israeli-Palestinian conflict. Finally, Finley and Cooper discuss some of the newest developments in peace and conflict studies and peace education.

In sum, the call for qualitative research in peace and conflict studies has never been greater, nor has the challenge to the current generation of researchers to provide mentorship to the emerging group of scholars. We hope that this book can be a useful in not just teaching about qualitative research but also for inspiring new and exciting research studies that advance the field and help build a peaceful, more just world.

ACKNOWLEDGMENTS

We have many people to thank who have helped to make this book possible. All of the remarkable chapter authors have been a joy to work with, and we are so grateful for the powerful, substantive content of their work. We want to thank the book series editors, Dr. Edward J. Brantmeier and Dr. Jing Lin, for their wonderful support and helpful feedback. We also owe appreciation to Dr. Cara Meixner and Dr. Noorie Kelsey Brantmeier, for their review of the book's contents and scope. For all of the participants who contributed to the studies described in this book, we so value their role in forwarding positive social change by participating in research and sharing their voices and stories. And certainly, we are deeply grateful to the students we have had over the years who have helped us shape these ideas, and who are making their own meaningful contributions as researchers, scholars, practitioners, and educators. Finally, our deepest gratitude goes to our families, for their steadfast love, support, and encouragement.

NOTES

1. Those interested in a description and discussion of the history of qualitative research in general, and the development of qualitative research within specific disciplines, can read more about this is such texts as *The Sage Handbook of Qualitative Research* (Denzin & Lincoln, 2011).
2. See Chapter 10 in *Qualitative inquiry & research design: Choosing among the five approaches* (3rd ed.) for a useful discussion of validation and evaluation in qualitative research, including a table (pp. 244–245) outlining various perspectives and terms associated with assessing quality in qualitative research.

REFERENCES

Abu-Nimer, M. (2003). *Nonviolence and peace building in Islam.* Gainesville, FL: University Press of Florida.

Adler, P., & Adler, P. (2012). Keynote Address: Tales from the field: Reflections on four decades of ethnography. In S. Kleinknecht, A. Puddephat, & C. Sanders (Eds.), *Contemporary Issues in Qualitative Research, 8*(1) 10–33. Retrieved March 12, 2013 from http://www.qualitativesociologyreview.org/ENG/Volume21/QSR_8_1.pdf

Alger, C. (1999). The quest for peace: What are we learning? *International Journal of Peace Studies, 4*(1), 21–45.

Allen, Q. (2012). Photographs and stories: ethics, benefits and dilemmas of using participant photography with Black middle-class male youth. *Qualitative Research, 12*(4), 443–458.

Avruch, K. (2004). *Culture and conflict resolution.* Washington, DC: United States Institute of Peace Press.

Bahn, S., & Weatherill, P. (2013). Qualitative social research: A risky business when it comes to collecting "sensitive" data. *Qualitative Researcher, 13*(1), 19–35.

Barron, K. (1999). Ethics in qualitative social research on marginalized groups. *Scandinavian Journal of Disability Research, 1*(1), 38–49.

Berg, B. L. (2007). *Qualitative research methods for the social sciences.* Boston, MA: Allyn & Bacon.

Booker, K. (2009). Shifting priorities: Reflections on teaching qualitative research methods. *The Qualitative Report, 14*(3), 389.

Boyle-Baise, M. (2002). Saying more: Qualitative research issues for community service learning. *International Journal of Qualitative Studies in Education, 15*(2), 1–15.

Boyer, E. (1990). *Scholarship reconsidered: Priorities of the professoriate.* Cambridge, MA: Carnegie Foundation for the Adancement of Teaching.

Brantmeier, E. (2005). "Speak Our Language.... Abide by Our Philosophy": Language & Cultural Assimilation at a U.S. Midwestern High School. *Forum on Public Policy.* Retrieved March 27, 2013 from, http://forumonpublicpolicy.com/archivespring07/brantmeier.rev.pdf

Bryman, A. (2007). Barriers to integrating quantitative and qualitative research. *Journal of Mixed Methods Research, 1*(1), 8–22.

Butler-Kisber, L. (2010). *Qualitative inquiry: Thematic, narrative, and arts-informed perspectives.* London, England: Sage.

Carspecken, P. (1996.) *Critical ethnography in educational research: A theoretical and practical guide.* London, England: Routledge.

Chenail, R. J. (2010). Getting specific about qualitative research generalizability. *Journal of Ethnographic and Qualitative Research, 5,* 1–11.

Cheney, T. (2001). *Writing creative nonfiction: Fiction techniques for crafting great nonfiction.* Berkeley, CA: Ten Speed Press.

Clark, T. (2005). "We're over-researched here!": Exploring accounts of research fatigue within qualitative research engagements. *Sociology, 42*(5), 953–970.

Clark, T. (2008). "We're over-researched here!" Exploring accounts of research fatigue within qualitative research engagements. *Sociology, 42*(5), 953–970.

Clark, T. (2010). On being "researched": Why do people engage with qualitative research? *Qualitative Research, 104,* 399–419.

Cooper, R., Chenail, R. J., & Fleming, S. (2012). A grounded theory of inductive qualitative research education: Results of a meta-data-analysis. *The Qualitative Report, 17*(T&L Art, 8), 1–26. Retrieved from http://www.nova.edu/ssss/QR/QR17/cooper52.pdf

Cooper, R., Fleischer, A., & Cotton, F. A. (2012). Building connections: An interpretative phenomenological analysis of qualitative research: Students' learning experiences. *The Qualitative Report, 17*(T&L Art. 1), 1–16. Retrieved from http://www.nova.edu/ssss/QR/QR17/cooper.pdf

Corra, M., & Willer, D. (2002). The gatekeepers. *Sociological Theory, 20*(2), 180–207.

Couture, A., Zaidi, A., & Maticka-Tyndale, E. (2012). Reflexive Accounts: An intersectional approach to exploring the fluidity of insider/outsider status and the researcher's impact on culturally sensitive post-positivist qualitative research. In S. Kleinknecht, A. Puddephat, & C. Sanders (Eds.), *Contemporary Issues in Qualitative Research, 8*(1) 86–105. Retrieved March 12, 2013 from http://www.qualitativesociologyreview.org/ENG/Volume21/QSR_8_1.pdf

Creswell, J. W. (2013). *Qualitative inquiry and research design: Choosing among the five approaches* (3rd ed.). Thousand Oaks, CA: Sage.

Crotty, M. (1998). *The foundations of social research: Meaning and perspective in the research process.* London, England: Sage.

Denzin, N. K., & Lincoln, Y. S. (Eds.). (2003). *The landscape of qualitative research: Theories and issues* (2nd ed.). Thousand Oaks, CA: Sage.

Denzin, N. K. & Lincoln, Y. S. (Eds.). (2011). *The Sage handbook of qualitative research* (4th ed.). Thousand Oaks, CA: Sage.

Deschaux-Beaume, D. (2012). Investigating the military field: Qualitative research strategy and interviewing in the defence networks. *Current Sociology, 60*(1), 101–117.

Diamond, L., & McDonald, D. (1996). *Multi-track diplomacy: A systems approach to peace* (3rd ed.). West Hartford, CN: Kumarian Press

Downton, J., & Wehr, P. (1997). *The persistent activist: How peace commitment develops and survives.* Boulder, CO: Westview.

Eysenbach, G. (2001). Ethical issues in qualitative research on internet communities. *BMJ.* Retrieved March 12, 2013 from, http://www.bmj.com/content/323/7321/1103

Fincher, B., Scourfield, J., & Langer, S. (2008). The impact of working with disturbing secondary data: Reading suicide files in a coroner's office. *Qualitative Health Research, 18*(6), 853–862.

Finley, L. (2004). Teaching peace in higher education: overcoming the challenges to addressing structure and methods. *Online journal of peace and conflict resolution, 5*(2).

Finley, L. (2011). *Building a more peaceful world: Creative integration of peace education.* Charlotte, NC: Information Age.

Flick, U. (2008). *Designing qualitative research.* London, England: Sage.

Foster, V. (2013). Pantomime and politics: The story of a performance ethnography. *Qualitative Researcher, 13*(1), 36–52.

Galtung, J. (1996). *Peace by peaceful means: Peace and conflict, development and civilization.* Thousand Oaks, CA: Sage.

Gerstl-Pepin, C., & Patrizio, K. (2009). Learning from Dumbledore's Pensieve: Metaphor as an aid in teaching reflexivity in qualitative research. *Qualitative Research, 9*(3), 299–308.

Goffman, E. (1959). *The presentation of self in everyday life.* New York, NY: Anchor.

Habermas, J. (1996). *Between facts and norms: Contributions to a discourse theory of law and democracy.* Cambridge, England: Polity.

Hammersley, M. (1995). *The politics of social research.* London, England: Sage.

Hampson, F. (1996). *Nurturing peace: Why peace settlements succeed or fail.* Washington, DC: United States Institute of Peace Press.

Jenkins, T. 2007. *Community-based institutes on peace education (CIPE) Organizer's Manual*. New York, NY: IIPE.

Kemp, G., & Fry, D. P. (2004). *Keeping the peace: Conflict resolution and peaceful societies around the world*. New York, NY: Routledge.

Kreisberg, L. (2007). *Constructive conflicts: From escalation to resolution* (3rd ed.). Lanham, MD: Rowman & Littlefield.

Lederach, J. P. (2005). *The moral imagination: The art and soul of building peace*. New York, NY: Oxford University Press.

Lederbach, J. (1997). *Building peace: Sustainable reconciliation in divided societies*. Washington, DC: United States Institute of Peace Press.

Lewicki, R. J., Gray, B., & Elliott, M. (2003). *Making sense of intractable environmental conflicts: Frames and cases*. Washington, DC: Island Press.

Lin, J. (2006). *Love, peace, and wisdom in education*. Lanham, MD: Rowman & Littlefield.

Lincoln, Y. S., & Guba, E. G. (1985). *Naturalistic inquiry*. Beverly Hills, CA: Sage.

Lumsden, K. (2013). "You are what you research": Researcher partisanship and the sociology of "the underdog." *Qualitative Research, 13*(1), 3–18.

Machtmes, K., Reynaud, A., Deggs, D., Matzke, B., Aguirre, R., & Johnson, E. (2009). Teaching qualitative research methods through service learning. *The Qualitative Report, 14*(1), 155–164.

Mann, C., & Stewart, F. (2002). Internet interviewing. In J. F. Gubrium & J. A.Holstein, (Eds.).*Handbook of interview research: Context and method* (pp. 603–627). Thousand Oaks, CA: Sage.

Marshall, C., & Rossman, G. B. (2010). *Designing qualitative research* (5th ed.). Thousand Oaks, CA: Sage.

Paechter, C. (2013). Researching sensitive issues online: Implications of a hybrid insider/outsider position in a restrospective ethnographic study. *Qualitative Research, 13*(1), 71–86.

Patton, M. Q. (2002). *Qualitative research and evaluation methods* (3rd ed.). Thousand Oaks, CA: Sage.

Phillips, B. (1997). Qualitative methods and disaster research. *International Journal of Mass Emergencies and Disasters, 15*(1), 179–195.

Prince, S. (1920). *Catastrophe and social change*. New York, NY: Columbia University.

Rager, K. (2005a). Compassion stress and the qualitative researcher. *Qualitative Health Research, 15*(3), 423–430.

Rager, K. (2005b). Self-care and the qualitative researcher: When collecting data can break your heart. *Educational Researcher, 4*(4), 323–327.

Reychler, L. (1998). Proactive conflict prevention: Impact assessment. *International Journal of Peace Studies, 3*(2), 87–98.

Robertson, T. (2005). Class issues: A critical ethnography of corporate domination within the classroom. *JECPS, 3*(2).

Sampson, H., Bloor, M., & Fincham, B. (2008). A price worth playing? Considering the "cost" of reflexive research methods and the influence of feminist ways of "doing." *Sociology, 42*(5), 919–933.

Schellenberg, J. A. (1996). *Conflict resolution: Theory, research, and practice*. Albany, NY: State University of New York Press.

Schirch, L. (2005). *Ritual and symbol in peacebuilding*. Bloomfield, CT: Kumarian Press.

Schratz, M., & Walker, R. (1995). *Research as social change: New opportunities for qualitative research*. London, England: Routledge.

Schmelze, B. (2005). New trends in peace and conflict impact assessment (PCIA). Berghof Research Center for Constructive Conflict Management. Retrieved April 18, 2014 from, http://www.berghof-handbook.net/documents/publications/dialogue4_pcianew_intro.pdf

Seal, L. (2012). Emotion and allegiance in researching four mid- 20th-century cases of women accused of murder. *Qualitative Research December, 12*(6), 686–701.

Shaft, B. (1999). The ethics of doing naturalistic discourse research on the Internet. In S. G. Jones (Ed.), *Doing Internet research* (pp. 243–257). Thousand Oaks, CA: Sage.

Shriver, D. (1995). *An ethic for enemies: Forgiveness in politics*. New York, NY: Oxford University Press.

Silverman, D. (2005). *Doing qualitative research* (2nd ed.). London, England: Sage.

Simpson, G. (1998). *A brief evaluation of South Africa's Truth and Reconciliation Commission: Some lessons for societies in transition*. Johannesburg, South Africa: Center for Study of Violence and Reconciliation.

Smith, E., Gidlow, B., & Steel, G. (2012). Engaging academic participants in academic research: The use of photo-elicitation interviews to evaluate school-based outdoor education programmes. *Qualitative Research, 12*(4), 367–387.

Stake, R. E. (2008). "Qualitative case studies." In (N. K. Denzin & Y. S. Lincoln, eds.), *Strategies of qualitative inquiry* (3rd ed., pp. 119–149. Thousand Oaks, CA: Sage.

Stark, S., & Watson, K. (1999). Passionate pleas for "passion please": Teaching for qualitative research. *Qualitative Health Research, 9*(6), 719–730.

Stake, R. E. (2010). *Qualitative research: Studying how things work*. New York, NY: The Guilford Press.

Stave, S. (2011, May). Measuring peacebuilding: Challenges, tools, actions. *NOREF Policy Brief No. 2*.

Strand,K., Marullo, S., Cutforth, N., Stoecker, R., & Donohue, P. (2003). *Community-based research and higher education: Principles and practices*. San Francisco, CA: Jossey-Bass.

Thomson, R., & Holland, J. (2003). Hindsight, foresight and insight: The challenges of longitudinal qualitative research. *International Journal of Social Research Methodology, 6*(3), 233–244.

Vidich, A. J., & Lyman, S. M. (2003). Qualitative methods: Their history in sociology and anthropology. In N. K. Denzin & Y. S. Lincoln (Eds.), *The landscape of qualitative research: Theories and issues* (2nd ed., pp. 55–129). Thousand Oaks, CA: Sage.

Wallensteen, P. (2011). *Peace research: Theory and practice*. New York, NY: Routledge.

Willis, J. W. (2007). *Foundations of qualitative research: Interpretive and critical approaches*. London, England: Sage.

Zartman, I., & Rasmussen, J. (Eds.). (1997). *Peacemaking in international conflict: Methods and techniques*. Washington, DC: United States Institute of Peace Press.

CHAPTER 2

QUALITATIVE RESEARCH DESIGN

Preparing to Study Conflict and Peace

Robin Cooper and Claire Michèle Rice

Qualitative research design is both an intellectual and creative adventure. In this chapter, we will discuss why you might choose a qualitative approach for your research study, as well as review stages of the research design process, elements of a qualitative research proposal, and special considerations for designing a qualitative study in the field of peace and conflict studies. The following chapters will address specific qualitative research traditions and methodologies in more depth. In each of those chapters, the authors will discuss unique aspects of data collection, data analysis, and reporting that pertain to particular qualitative methodologies. This chapter offers a broader overview of general issues related to designing a qualitative research study.

Peace and Conflict Studies Research: A Qualitative Perspective, pp. 23–48
Copyright © 2014 by Information Age Publishing

WHY CHOOSE A QUALITATIVE APPROACH FOR
YOUR STUDY?

Research Objectives: Exploration, Discovery, Deeper Understanding

Attaching meaning to interactions with others, reflecting upon lived experiences and critical events, or appreciating the impact of context and environment on the lives of individuals are important elements of human inquiry that can be satisfied through qualitative research. Within the field of peace and conflict studies, these elements of exploration play a crucial role in understanding how people perceive conflict and envisage peaceful solutions. Qualitative methods can bring these elements to life for readers through vivid description, in-depth analysis, and interpretation. Berg (2009) remarks, "Clearly, certain experiences cannot be meaningfully expressed by numbers. Furthermore, such things as smells can trigger memories long obscured by the continuing demands of life" (p. 3). The following excerpt comes from a field observation in an ethnographic study conducted by one of the authors. Note that the description of the setting involves sight, sound, smell—the essence of which can only be captured qualitatively:

> Upon entering the home, I could smell the aroma of traditional Haitian cooking with a medley of herbs and spices. Today, I was certain that they were cooking some type of meat product. My hostess's name was Mary. Mary's mother walked past me as we neared the kitchen and briefly greeted me with a nod and some words in Haitian Creole. She looked like a woman in her late 60's with dark brown skin, and a slightly wrinkled face. Gray hair adorned the rim of her forehead and temples, and black hair, parted into little plots of hair, was braided into little plats on the rest of her head. She was carrying a mop as she walked past me and moved in the direction of the kitchen. (Michele Rice, Ethnographic field notes, 1999)

The description of this setting offers the reader a mental picture of the site and of the culture under study in this ethnographic piece. The image itself cannot be quantified. This is what qualitative research does best: it provides imagery, context and a depth of insight through rich, "thick description" (Geertz, 1973) of interactions and of the space within which activity is taking place. In the natural sciences, one studies how certain environmental factors such as temperature may influence a metal, for example. However, the social sciences recognize that in addition to responding to the influences of their environment, humans use their minds to negotiate the realities of the environment in which they find themselves. Human beings are thus affected by how they perceive the context in which they live their lives and their interactions with others. These processes are subjective and can be unearthed through in-depth observation and interviewing. This approach is called interpretivism, which is in essence the manner in which social scientists ascribe meaning to lived experiences. Wilhelm Dilthey advanced this notion of interpreting subjective realities by positing that *verstehen*, the empathic understanding of other human beings, should be the purpose of social science inquiry—a theme later reflected in Max Weber's work (Willis, 2007).

Seeking deeper understanding of a subject from a qualitative approach typically entails delving into the field, interviewing participants and sometimes involves gathering multiple forms of data such as written records, field observations, physical artifacts and more. Thus, qualitative research involves time commitment—time in the field, time to sort through a lot of information and make sense of it all. While it may often require more time than quantitative research, qualitative research affords the researcher a certain degree of flexibility in collecting and analyzing data that survey research may not. Qualitative methods allow researchers to delve more deeply and gain more insight into the meanings and understandings of social phenomena beyond what is provided by quantitative descriptive or inferential statistics (Willis, 2007). In her chapter on ethnography in this text, Welty borrows the phrase of Clifford Geertz (1998) "deep hanging out" to capture this aspect of qualitative inquiry.

Some research questions are not answered by such methods as the comparison of mean scores of two groups (i.e., *t* tests), for instance. In addition, sometimes the number of participants who are available better lends itself to a qualitative approach. What if a researcher wanted to understand the lived experiences of eight survivors of a hostage crisis? Obviously, a quantitative study of eight individuals could not be generalizable to the experiences of all hostages who have survived such an ordeal. Another reason to look to qualitative methods is when a researcher does not find any readily available theory to explain a particular social phenomenon. Therefore, the researcher may seek to explain the process and capture in a model the pattern of behavior she has observed. This is the basis for grounded theory research, wherein the researcher develops a theory from the data collected from participants who have experienced a particular phenomenon (Berg, 2009; Creswell, 2013; Willis, 2007).

While quantitative research is a deductive process in which hypothesis testing is the basis for survey research or experimentation, qualitative research is primarily an inductive process. Qualitative researchers propose questions for study based on the research problems they have identified, and set out to answer those questions, sometimes with a few theories to support their analyses. However, the inductive process carries a great deal of flexibility in that researchers are open to finding new variables that may add insight to the inquiry, such that they may amend their questions as they interview more participants or uncover new data. Thus, the qualitative process is dynamic. The description of the research process may make it seem a bit linear: beginning with selecting the research topic and exploring relevant theoretical concepts, then moving to designing a study to answer the research question; collecting data, analyzing and interpreting them; then presenting the findings (Babbie, 2007; Berg, 2009). However, qualitative inquiry is all but linear. It is a reflective and reflexive process. Sometimes it is not until a researcher has spent time in the field, interviewing and observing her study participants that she may have a clearer picture regarding the true nature of the research problem. Thus, it is not uncommon in qualitative inquiry for researchers to adjust their study design in some way during the course of the research.

Researcher Perspectives and Preferences: Theory, Epistemology, and Ontology

Qualitative and quantitative methods are informed by certain world views. Willis (2007) cites three theoretical frameworks—postpositivism, interpretivism, and critical theory—that greatly influence the way research is done. Interpretivism and critical theory most often inform qualitative methods. Interpretivism suggests that we construct our own social realities by interpreting the actions and events that take place. This is essentially a subjective process, and this theoretical perspective bucks against the traditional empirical and positivist approaches which purport that reality is "out there"; and that as social scientists, we are charged to be value neutral in our observation of this reality to render analyses from a distance. Critical theory is "ideologically oriented theory" (Willis, 2007, p. 44) which finds its roots in neo-Marxism. In the 19th century the work of neo-Marxist scholars contested the social and economic oppression of the masses in favor of giving voice to marginalized people. However, their critique went further than classical Marxist ideology whose main focus was power relations between the rich and the poor. In seeking to expose patterns of domination and the inequities of power, critical theorists challenge established ideology, societal structures, norms, and taken-for-granted assumptions in societies, whose end result is the oppression of minority and racial groups, women, the poor and other marginalized segments of society. The postpositivist (or positivist) framework, with its emphasis on following set rules to achieve empirical results, has its limits. Positivists or postempiricists, according to Willis (2007), "take very specific, very strong positions on everything from the acceptable reasons for doing research to the proper methods for collecting and analyzing data" (p. 17).

While classical research methods based on the scientific method may work well for many research objectives, qualitative inquiry provides a depth and insight very relevant to research involving human subjects in the field of peace studies and conflict resolution.

The question of epistemology is critically important as distinctions are drawn between qualitative and quantitative methods. Epistemology is concerned with the knowledge we have about social reality and how we gain that knowledge. In quantitative methods, survey research or experimentation are ways of gathering knowledge about social phenomenon. Following the script from natural sciences where natural processes are governed by a set of laws that are observable, quantitative methodology and the positivist approach to social inquiry also operate by a set of rules (Willis, 2007); and thus, social phenomena must be empirically tested, observed and analyzed. Such inquiry is meant to be free of bias, values and subjectivity (all of which relate to issues of reflexivity); though it is often not. The human element cannot entirely be extricated from any human enterprise no matter how much researchers theorize and try to be purely objective or how well survey instruments are constructed to account for bias or to avoid errors. In his discussion on "Emancipatory Knowledge," Jürgen Habermas addresses the question of objectivism by stating, "objectivism is eliminated not through the power of renewed theoria but through demonstrating what it conceals: the connection of knowledge and interest" (Habermas, 1968, as cited in Lemert, 1999, p. 381). The random sampling of subjects is done to ensure the results from the surveys are generalizable to the population of individuals who have experienced a certain phenomenon for the purpose of prediction. In qualitative methods, observation, in-depth interviewing, and document analysis are some of the ways social scientists explore social phenomena. These forms of data collection ground research and theory-making in the experiences of individuals within a social context, and thus guard against what Habermas calls "sterilized knowledge" propagated by "the illusion of pure theory" (Lemert, 1999, pp. 380–381). This manner of "knowing" takes place within a subjective space. Recognizing this, researchers do what they can to bracket their biases, values and possible errors in judgment due to their own perceptions and experiences.

Ontology, the study of what is the nature of reality or of truth, also plays a central role in research design in the field of peace studies and conflict resolution. Often, conflicts are generated based upon what people perceive to be their reality: they may believe that they have been slighted and such an affront merits action. In addition, according to Berger and Luckman (1966), the process of creating reality in society takes place before one even comes into the world. If one is born into a Mayan world, it is a reality different than one born in the Haitian world. All groups will pass their traditions and customs, perceptions of reality and what life is, from one generation to another. These explanations as to life and reality have subjective origins, but to people born within those societies, these concepts are taken for granted. Ultimately, every object or phenomenon that is incorporated into a culture is ultimately taken for granted. As you provide explanation for social phenomena and the conflicts that arise from them based on your own observations and the depth of insights you have gained from engaging people who have experienced those multiple realities, you are marrying the emic (subjective, insider's point of view) and the etic (objective, analytical, outsider's point of view). Ultimately, qualitative researchers studying conflicts or peace processes alike can couple their own observations with their study participants' perceptions of their social reality. This is what provides much depth to qualitative inquiry. We now turn to some of the steps involved in a systematic approach to designing qualitative studies.

SELECTING YOUR RESEARCH TOPIC

Qualitative research design can be thought of as encompassing three major stages: inspiration, conceptualization, and operationalization. In the inspiration stage, you find your research topic and focus. In the conceptualization stage, you clarify your research objectives and identify such central elements of the study as the research questions, study site, and population. In the operationalization stage, you select the methodology and describe the steps that would be required to actually conduct the study. As this chapter is focused on the planning and design of a qualitative study, we do not address here the implementation of the research; however, the following chapters will speak to conducting qualitative research using specific methodologies. In this section, we discuss how you might go about selecting the topic and focus for your study.

Where can you draw inspiration in finding the topic for your qualitative study? Saldaña (2011) notes, "Generally, a researcher develops a specific topic or selects a particular problem for inquiry based on *disciplinary or social needs, pragmatic* parameters, and *personal passion*" (p. 66, emphasis in original). You might approach this in several different ways. There may be circumstances or situations from your personal experience, or challenges encountered in your professional life, which you have puzzled over or about which you have found little information. Perhaps you've observed or experienced a certain form of interpersonal or organizational conflict that has raised questions for you. Or there may be issues related to social, national, or international conflict that you want to understand more fully and that inspire you to make a contribution through research. It is often such personal and professional inspiration that motivated those of us in peace and conflict studies to enter this field. These personal or professional

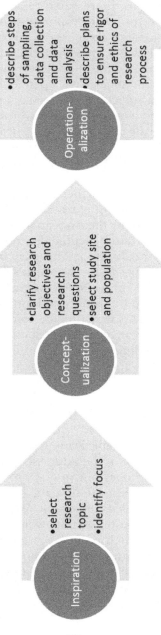

Figure 2.1. Stages of the research design process.

interests may provide motivation for your research and inspire your topic selection. It is not unusual for qualitative researchers to conduct studies on topics they care about on a personal or professional level. In fact, the researcher's relationship to the research topic is addressed openly and explicitly in qualitative research proposals and reports. If, however, a researcher feels so passionately about an issue that his or her bias cannot be managed effectively, this will negatively impact the trustworthiness of the research findings. It is a good idea to reflect on your motivations for your research and to assess your ability to be open to discovering new findings.

If you do not have a subject that interests you based on personal or professional experience, you might look to the research literature for inspiration. Typically at the end of research articles, authors will offer suggestions for future research. If you are not sure what you want to study, you could turn to articles published recently on topics related to conflict or peace studies that interest you and look for the suggestions of other researchers regarding areas for further research. These recommendations may be made based on gaps in the research literature that these authors identify, or questions raised by their research that call for further study. In addition to gaps in the literature identified by other scholars, your reading may result in your own identification of gaps in the research literature. As you read through a number of recent articles published on a subject of interest, such as those cited in the following chapters, you may notice that there is a certain aspect to this topic that hasn't been addressed by other qualitative researchers. This may provide some inspiration for you and help you to see where you can make a contribution. In the end, the inspiration stage is all about finding something within the field of peace studies or conflict analysis and resolution that instills a passion for deeper inquiry.

WRITING THE PROBLEM STATEMENT

The selection of the research topic leads to writing the problem statement, which summarizes the issue to be addressed in your study. To develop a research problem it is important to build towards its description. For instance, provide a brief exposition of the context and background on your topic and why the topic is important. While coupled with your own observations, this exposition must come from existing literature. Having reviewed a number of research proposals, we have noted a mistake often made by novice researchers it to state the problem in what appears to be entirely subjective language. That is, they make a number of assertions about the problem under study and why it is important to study it without providing enough supporting evidence from existing research to buttress their remarks. Thus, in the exposition of the nature of the problem under study, you will also provide a description of who is concerned with the issue; the context in which the conflict or issue under study occurs; and a discussion of how pervasive the issue is. Showing how the problem has or has not been addressed in the existing body of literature will be critical in making the case for the significance of your research. Once the background and context of the issue have been established in your introduction through supporting literature, a concise problem statement is provided that addresses the issue under study. In a few sentences, your problem statement should reveal (1) the social problem you have identified (2) the gap in the existing literature that you seek to fill and (3) the need for your study. Consider the problem statement the equivalent of a one-minute elevator speech, which succinctly summarizes the topic of your study. In the following excerpt from Cooper's (2010) phenomenological study of a county in Florida's transition to a majority-minority community, we provide an example of how one researcher introduced a research problem:

> In 2006, Broward County, Florida, passed a significant demographic milestone when it became a so-called majority-minority county (Collie, 2007). This designation signifies that the number of residents with minority ethnic or racial status surpasses the number of non-Hispanic white residents. This is a shift that is taking place in an increasing number of communities across the United States. Broward is now one of 22 counties in the country that are majority-minority (Daniel, 2006), and this number is growing. In fact, it is expected that the nation as a whole will be majority-minority by the year 2050. Currently, "non-Hispanic whites are a minority in four states—Hawaii, New Mexico, California and Texas—and the District of Columbia" (Ohlemacher, 2006). Such social change raises important questions related to the sense of national belonging within communities, perceptions of collective identity, and the need to prevent identity-based conflict.... Scholars are conducting important research examining the sense of belonging and collective identity for key immigrant populations in the region (e.g., Chaitin, Linstroth, & Hiller, 2009; Cooper, Edsall, Riviera, Chaitin, & Linstroth, 2009). There is also a considerable amount of literature on the social phenomenon of transnationalism and how it impacts the construction of identity for transnationals (e.g., Fouron & Glick-Schiller, 2002; Levitt & Waters, 2002; Rumbault, 2002). [This study] contributes a different perspective to this body of literature by exploring how the changing demographics in Broward County are experienced and understood by non-Hispanic white Americans. This research will contribute to a more fully-developed understanding of the social impact of immigration and changing demographics in the United States. (pp. 1–2)

The original problem statement may evolve depending on the specific type of qualitative research being conducted. For instance, in an ethnographic study, a researcher may start with a specific problem statement, which evolves during the study to a degree that it becomes reconstituted by the time the study is completed. Also, researchers may go into communities with a specific problem for study, but must then negotiate with community leaders and gatekeepers what dimensions they are allowed to explore. Not all areas may be open to observation within the communities they wish to study. Thus, the problem statement must encompass the resulting understanding between the researchers, gatekeepers, community leaders and participants (LeCompte & Schensul, 1999). This is particularly important in community-based, participatory research.

Once you have selected a topic you are interested in and articulated the problem statement for your study, you then are ready for the conceptualization phase of the research design process. Conceptualization is perhaps the most challenging and yet most important and stimulating stage of qualitative research design. If a study is not well conceived initially it is going to lead to problems throughout the design and conducting of the study. This stage involves defining key terms, clarifying your specific research objectives related to this topic, choosing your study site and population, and developing your research questions. These elements of the conceptualization of your study are interrelated, and the selection of one element is influenced by and in turn influences the other design choices. For the sake of clarity, however, we will address each in turn.

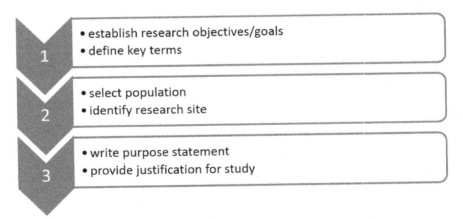

Figure 2.1.   Initial steps of the conceptualization process in qualitative research design.

DEFINING KEY TERMS

An issue related to selecting your topic is that of defining the key terms pertaining to your study. It is very important to define the phenomenon in question because you cannot assume that everyone shares the same understanding of various terms, and because terms hold different meanings and connotations based upon contextual factors. Researchers sometimes overlook this step because they already have a strong interest in the study topic and a solid understanding of the central terms associated with the topic. To make things clear for readers of a research proposal or a research report, however, it is important to explain what you mean by key terms related to the study topic and how such terms will be used in the research proposal. (see Berg, 2009, pp. 38–41, for a helpful discussion of defining key terms in your research proposal.)

It is a good idea to cite scholarly sources in support of your definitions. This is important for at least two reasons. By using a definition grounded in the theoretical literature relevant to your topic, you provide a justification for the definition you are choosing, and have a greater likelihood of shared understanding. Second, by using and citing a definition from the research literature, you are in a stronger position to compare your research findings with earlier research findings on this topic, because the phenomenon was conceptualized the same way across research studies. This does not require extensive references to the research literature, but rather the select use of those citations that are most relevant.

CLARIFYING YOUR RESEARCH OBJECTIVES AND PURPOSE

An initial consideration in the conceptualization stage is to consider what you hope to achieve as a result of conducting your study. What are your goals for the study? What are your research objectives? These will be tied to your research questions, but are distinct. The research questions are the questions you seek to answer through your study, whereas the research goals or objectives reflect what you hope will be accomplished as a result of your study. Marshall and Rossman (2011) refer to the do-ability, should-do-ability, and want-to-do-ability of a study. Munhall and Chenail (2008) also discuss the importance of do-ability in qualitative research design. The research objectives are linked to both the do-ability and want-to-do-ability of the study. Are your research objectives realistic? If you plan to design a study to find out how to achieve world peace, you are to be commended for your goals, but your objectives exceed what is "do-able" in a single study. Are you enthusiastic about your research goals? If not, you may lack the want-to-do-ability that will help you see the study through to completion.

There are a number of purposes to research: description, exploration, explanation, evaluation and emancipation. Exploration entails investigating a particular phenomenon to discover hidden factors, new insights and understanding of a subject matter or to generate new hypotheses for future research. In descriptive studies, the researcher observes events or settings and interviews people to provide an in-depth description of what is occurring. Explanatory studies take this process a step further as researchers try to explain the causes for these events, behaviors, or phenomena. Studies may incorporate all three research goals—exploration, description and explanation (Babbie, 2007), for example to evaluate the efficacy of a program or project. Marshall and Rossman (2011) note, "These traditional discussions of purpose, however, are silent about critique, action, advocacy, empowerment, or emancipation—the purposes often found in studies grounded in critical, feminist, or postmodern assumptions" (p. 69). Particularly salient for the field of conflict resolution and peace studies, is the "emancipatory" purpose for research. Emancipatory research in the field of peace studies and conflict resolution can involve participatory action research, in which participants are engaged in the research process in finding ways to resolve conflict and to engage in problem-solving relative to contentious issues in their communities.

To frame your research purpose, identify at least two research goals, making sure they align with qualitative inquiry. Clarifying your research goals leads to writing your purpose statement for your study. The purpose statement goes beyond the problem statement in that it is a window into how you will conduct your study to answer your research questions, relating to the problem under study. The purpose statement provides the "who, what, where, when, and how" of your research. The "what" of your study relates to the core of your research problem: what do you want to study? As we have discussed, there are a myriad of social issues and problems that lend themselves to conflict resolution and peace studies. The "who" relates to the people you will interview or observe. The "where" and "when" provides the context and timeframe for the research. Finally, the "how" speaks to the qualitative approach you will use. Building upon the example of the problem statement provided above, we offer an example of how Cooper (2010) described the purpose, goals, and research approach in her study of social change in Broward County, Florida:

> This study is focused on understanding the lived experiences of white Americans in Broward County experiencing social change tied to demographic shifts, and exploring the meaning this social change holds for them as it relates to their sense of collective identity and national belonging. This focus on meaning constructed by informants regarding a particular social phenomenon grounds this study in the phenomenological tradition of social science research (Creswell, 1998)....There were several goals undergirding this research project. The first goal was to explore how the transition to a majority-minority community is experienced by members of the national ethnic majority.... The second goal of the study was to learn how the social changes brought about by demographic change impact the perception of

national belonging among these residents....The third goal was to understand how the transition to majority-minority status affects the experience of
social conflict for members of the national ethnic majority. (pp. 3–4)

Once you have articulated the purpose of your study through your
purpose statement, you still need to provide a justification for the value
of such a study. The justification relates to the "should-do-ability" of your
study (Marshall & Rossman, 2011). A way of thinking about this is that
you need to answer the "so what" question. You need to make the case for
why a study on this topic or a study that takes this particular approach to
looking at the topic is important. What justifies the study? You can find that
justification in current social problems that are unresolved and for which
additional information and understanding is needed. Be clear about who
will benefit from this research and how. You can also find that justification
in academic literature that has been published in which other scholars and
researchers are pointing out the need for further research in this area.

There is some debate among qualitative researchers over whether the
researcher should review the research literature prior to designing and conducting their studies (e.g., Creswell, 2003; Lichtman, 2010; Patton, 2002).
The argument for not doing so is the concern that it might bias researchers if they look at how other researchers design their studies and also what
the findings were of those prior studies. The concern would be that being
exposed to that information might influence a researcher and prevent him
or her from designing the study in the way that they otherwise might if they
just were approaching the topic with a completely open-minded position
(e.g., Corbin & Strauss, 2008). The other concern would be that if you are
aware of the findings of previous studies in this area as you are analyzing
your own data you might not take note of findings that differ or are unrelated to previous findings. The concern is that this exposure to published
literature might limit the open stance you take to conducting your study.

On the other hand, there are advantages to familiarizing yourself with
the research literature prior to conducting your study. As other authors
have noted (e.g., Marshall & Rossman, 2011; Moustakas, 1994), one advantage is that you are able to situate the study in the literature. In other words,
if you are aware of what has been published in this area you are better able
to justify a study that contributes to that literature based on recommendations of other scholars who point to the need of further research or because
you are able to identify a gap in the literature that you seek to address by
conducting your study. Another advantage is to have some familiarity with
the topic under study, while still retaining an open-minded stance (e.g.,
Fetterman, 1989; Haverkamp & Young, 2007). We endorse the strategic
approach advocated by Chenail, Cooper, and Desir (2010), who suggest
that it is useful to review the research literature to fulfill several functional

objectives, including identifying the gap in the literature. You do not have to include in your proposal every relevant published article or book on your topic. However, you can make judicious use of sources in the literature that are most relevant to supporting your study's research objectives.

Having established what you will study and why it is important, you will need to identify specific elements of the study design such as unit of analysis, site and population. Are you focused on individuals who have experienced a particular form of conflict or peacebuilding? Is your focus on an entire organization or social group? You also want to identify the population that you are interested in studying. You are not yet determining your specific sample (the participants in your study), which we will address below in the section on sampling; but in the conceptualization phase it is important to be clear about the group or population that you intend to focus on in your study. In addition, you will want to select the location where you plan to conduct your study. Each of these elements of the con-ceptualization process will have an impact on your research design. All of the elements discussed so far would be included in the opening section of a qualitative research proposal.

DEVELOPING YOUR RESEARCH QUESTIONS

An essential element of the conceptualization phase in designing a qualita-tive research study is the development of your research questions. Having clear, focused research questions is critical to the success of your study. Sometimes people are a bit confused between research questions and interview questions, and they will present as their research questions the questions they might use in interviews. Research questions are typically written in the third person; while interview questions are written in the second person ("you"). Keep in mind that interview questions are the ques-tions you will pose to your study participants in seeking to generate the data that will help you to answer your research questions. Research ques-tions are the questions you seek to answer by conducting your study. They are the heart and soul of your study, because so many choices will be deter-mined by your research questions.

Research questions in qualitative inquiry are exploratory and discovery-oriented in nature. Munhall and Chenail (2008) observe that

> your research is designed to explore the phenomenon of interest without preconceived notions or hypotheses about presenting problems or predicted variables. This is critical to understand. Questions that include relationships between variables or comparisons between or among groups are usually not qualitatively oriented. (p. 24)

Sometimes in seeking to be very open ended and exploratory, a researcher may be overly broad in their research questions. On the contrary it's important to be very specific and focused. An image that many researchers find helpful in thinking about developing research questions in a qualitative study is that of a funnel (Marshall & Rossman, 2011) or an inverted triangle (Creswell, 2003). Any topic could be approached in an unlimited number of ways. So it can be helpful to picture pouring the topic into that funnel, and then considering the following questions as the topic swirls around and down the funnel: What is it that you most want to know about this topic? If you had to look at just one angle, issue, or aspect of that topic, what would you focus on? If you were to focus on just one group or population in relation to this topic, who would it be? What site or context is of most interest to you or is most do-able for you at this time? These are the kinds of considerations that assist you in narrowing your topic until it can come out the bottom of the funnel as one or two very specific research questions. You are trying to achieve a balance in this process. You want to maintain the discovery-oriented purpose of qualitative inquiry, but the scope of the study needs to be sufficiently narrow and the study's research questions need to be sufficiently focused so that the study is doable, practical, and something you can achieve in a single study.

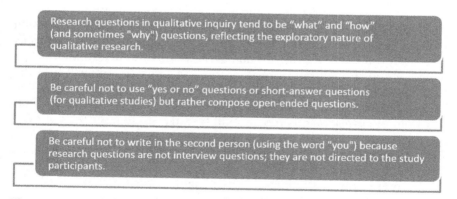

Figure 2.3. Tips on developing qualitative research questions.

Research questions in qualitative inquiry begin with the words "What," "How" or "Why." These words reflect the exploratory nature of qualitative research. A research question in a qualitative study would not be one that you could answer with "yes" or "no" or even with a short answer. Rather, because you are seeking to understand subjective experience and meaning in qualitative inquiry, your research questions will be open ended.

Your research questions may be theoretical questions, questions focused on a particular population, or site specific questions (Marshall & Rossman, 2011). The role of methodology is also important in the development of research questions. Ordinarily, you would develop your research questions first, and then, based upon your research questions, you would select the qualitative methodology that would be most appropriate and most useful in helping you to answer those research questions. There can be times, however, when you are seeking to expand your knowledge and experience regarding a particular methodology. In such cases, if one of your goals is to gain experience in conducting a particular type of research, this would influence the development of your research questions, as you would need to have questions that align with that methodology. You will find examples of research questions that align with specific approaches to qualitative inquiry in the chapters that follow.

SELECTING YOUR METHODOLOGY

Once the conceptualization phase is well underway, you can begin thinking about the methodology that is most appropriate for your study. How are you going to actually carry out the study that you have now conceived? How are you going to set about answering those research questions that you have developed? There are several steps to this phase of research design. You select the type of qualitative design that is appropriate for your study, and then you select your methodology. After this you determine the specific methods to be used in carrying out the research. You will find that sometimes the terms *method* and *methodology* are used interchangeably in texts on qualitative research. We use these terms making the following distinction: the *methodology* is your overall research strategy, or the approach you are using to find out the information that you seek in your study. Your *methods* are the actual procedures that you follow in conducting your study. You would describe both your selection of methodology and your planned procedures in the methods section of a qualitative research proposal.

There are a number of types of qualitative research design that one can consider, including primary qualitative research design, secondary qualitative data analysis, qualitative program evaluation, metastudy, and mixed methodology designs. In secondary qualitative data analysis, your conduct research on data collected previously for another study, but you now bring to that data a new research question and approach to analysis. In program evaluation the researcher examines the processes, outcomes and impressions of a program's mission, objectives, and activities. Qualitative metastudies, such as metaethnography, grounded formal theory, and qualitative metasynthesis, are systematic reviews of primary qualitative research studies in which the researcher's data set is comprised of published reports of multiple primary studies on a particular topic. Mixed-methods research combines quantitative and qualitative approaches within a single study. All of these research designs are useful in different circumstances, and you can find more information about these designs in other texts. In this chapter, we will address the most widely practiced form of qualitative inquiry, primary research, such as that typically conducted for dissertation research.

Matching Your Methodology With Your Research Objectives and Research Questions

Within qualitative research, there are several major traditions. These include but are not limited to grounded theory, phenomenology, case study, ethnography, narrative research, and action research. Each of these methodologies is described in some depth in the following chapters. What is most important in selecting the methodology for your study is to have a clear rationale for that choice. Ultimately the intent is to select the methodology that is best suited to help you achieve the research objectives outlined in your purpose statement. For example, if one of your research objectives is theory development, you would want to take a good look at grounded theory. In some of the other qualitative methodologies you may develop a theory, but in grounded theory you approach the study with that as a central goal. If your objective, however, is to explore the experience and meaning of a particular phenomenon, you would likely select phenomenology. While describing experience and exploring meaning may be included in other qualitative methodologies, these are the primary objectives of phenomenology. If your objective is to describe and interpret a conflict situation within a particular culture or social group, ethnography might be a good choice for you; whereas, if your objective is to provide detailed analysis of a specific case or multiple cases, you could consider case study research. The following chapters will provide more insight into the objectives of these and other approaches to qualitative research.

We recommend that, before you settle on the methodology for your study, you consider more than one. You may already have in mind one methodological approach that you are leaning towards, but we would encourage you to consider a second one before making a final decision. What would be an alternative methodology you might consider? What would make each of those that you consider an appropriate choice for your study? How would you argue in favor of each of those methodologies? What will be the factors that help you make a final decision? Reflecting on these questions can give you confidence that you have considered several options and are making an informed choice. In making your final selection, it is important to revisit your research questions, as well. As we noted earlier, although we are presenting these elements of research design in a rather linear fashion, when you are designing a qualitative study each choice may impact previous and later choices. Thus, if you determine a particular methodology is appropriate for achieving your research objectives, you may need to go back and revise your research questions to be sure that they are consistent with the methodology you have selected. When explaining your choice of methodology, you can cite relevant research literature to support your choices. For example, if you are explaining why you would choose ethnography in a particular study, you could cite literature that highlights the objectives and goals of ethnography. Then you could show how those methodological objectives are in line with the research objectives that you have in your study. If you have indicated that your research objective is to identify the essence of a particular experience, and you have chosen phenomenology for your study, then you can cite sources on phenomenology indicating this is a goal of phenomenology.

In this way, you use research literature to provide a rationale for your selection of a methodology for your study.

Table 2.1.   Matching Research Objective and Methodology

Research Objective	Methodology
to provide detailed description and explore meaning of a particular phenomenon	Phenomenology
to describe and interpret a particular cultural or social group	Ethnography
to explore the life of an individual(s) and how that life reflects social context	Narrative Research
to develop a theory grounded in data from the field	Grounded Theory
to provide detailed analysis of a specific case or multiple cases	Case Study Research
to bring about change through the research process in collaboration with participants	Action Research

Another way in which you can draw upon the research literature is to highlight how researching your subject using a particular methodology will offer new insights by offering findings that can be compared with previous related studies. For example, it could be that scholars have used grounded theory to investigate your subject in other settings but not in the setting you're interested in. So you might want to see whether using the same methodology in a different context sheds new light on that subject. On the other hand, you might see that a number of studies have been conducted on the subject using various qualitative methodologies, but none has employed biographical narrative research. So you might want to design a study that employs this methodology in order to contribute to the body of knowledge in this area by offering findings resulting from a different methodology. These are just a few of the things to consider as you select your methodology. The bottom line is to be sure that the methodology fits with your research objectives and research questions. Of course there are distinctions and various approaches within the traditional methodologies as well. There are various forms of phenomenology, several approaches to grounded theory, different types of case study, and so on. The following chapters will describe some of these differences.

DESCRIBING YOUR PROCEDURES

As mentioned above, we make a distinction between methodology and methods. We have discussed briefly the methodology as the overarching research strategy you take in your study. Now we turn to a brief discussion of the methods you may employ in conducting your study. The specific techniques you use will vary depending upon the methodology guiding your study. However, there are several procedures that are consistent across qualitative studies, and we will address these here. In designing a qualitative research study, you develop a plan for these procedures, which is what you would present in a qualitative research proposal. Thus, in the design stage, you refer to these procedures in the future tense. We also recommend that you describe each step conceptually and operationally, explaining both what the step is and how you will conduct that step in your study, and citing sources as appropriate to support your design choices.

Choosing Your Sample

Sampling in qualitative research usually involves nonprobabilistic sampling processes. Sampling is nonprobabilistic because it is not randomized. Participants are often selected either through purposive or snowball sampling. Purposive sampling involves the selection of individuals who fit the criteria for the qualitative research being undertaken. Snowball sampling involves gaining access to a particular field of study by forming relationships with individuals who know and understand the people and the environment in which a particular conflict is taking place. The gatekeepers signal whom may serve as informants and these individuals, in turn, may point the researcher to others who can be interviewed for more insight into a given topic.

There are special challenges related to sampling for those seeking to conduct research in conflict areas, as is discussed more fully by Julia Chaitin in Chapter 9. Gaining the trust of individuals living under the stress of conflict and finding individuals who might safely share potentially dangerous information about the conflicts or issues they face within their environment, relate to issues of both access and sampling. In light of such challenges, some researchers may choose for their samples members of the diaspora of warring nations in order to avoid such dangers for themselves and their participants. However, the concern is that the researcher is not truly getting first-hand accounts and insight into the conflicts under study. While for some research purposes, gaining insights from diasporic groups is certainly valid and useful, the question becomes, would diasporic groups have first-hand understanding of what is actually happening in the country from which they are taking refuge or are exiled? Such people may have left their countries of origin due to fear, persecution or economic depression. Depending on the research objectives, the viewpoints shared by some in the diasporic groups may negatively influence the validity of findings unless the researcher specifically wanted to understand the unique experiences and perceptions of these individuals.

Each qualitative approach carries slightly different expectations and criteria for the selection of participants for study. For example, in a phenomenological study, the participants must all have experienced the phenomenon under study. In ethnography, participants are members of a culture-sharing group. Similarly, in a case study, which involves researching a bounded system, an activity or program; participants who are engaged in activities in the setting, or who have experienced the phenomenon under study in the case are selected for any insight they may bring to understanding elements of the case (Creswell, 2013). The number of participants varies depending on the purpose and methodology of the study. In a narrative approach known as biographical research, for instance, a single individual may be studied (though biographical narrative research may also include larger sample sizes). The individual for the study may be selected due to convenience, political importance, or how critical the individual's experience is for research. Additionally, family members, friends, coworkers and other colleagues of the individual under study are often asked to be interviewed to glean more insight into the life story of the subject. Though in a research proposal for a grounded theory, a researcher might stipulate that she will interview 30 or even 50 subjects; in reality, the final number of participants will be determined by achieving theoretical saturation, when she is no longer able to uncover any new information. Specific sampling approaches associated with the various qualitative traditions will be discussed in the following chapters.

Data Collection

Once you have determined how you will go about identifying and recruiting your study sample, you then need to consider how you are going to go about generating and collecting the data for your study. Your research questions help you to decide what data to collect, what is less important, and what can be left out of the study all together. There is a lot of data that can be collected relevant to your topic, but what you want to generate and collect are data that will help you to answer your research questions. Your selection of a methodology can also provide guidance regarding your data collection strategy. Different methodologies have a tradition of using different data collection methods based upon the methodological objectives. For example, in an ethnographic study you would plan to spend an extended period of time in your research site in order to conduct observations regarding social structures and communication dynamics in that cultural context. In a phenomenological study, you would be expected to conduct phenomenological interviews to collect relevant data. In the following chapters, specific information about data collection techniques used in various methodologies is presented in more detail.

Data Analysis

Once you have collected your data, how are you going to analyze that data? As with data collection, your research questions and methodology influence the approach you will use in your data analysis. For any qualitative study, the research questions indicate what you seek to learn through your analysis. Keeping your research questions before you as you conduct your analysis can provide clarity regarding what is important in the data and where to keep your focus in the analysis process. Many qualitative studies employ at least two stages of analysis, sometimes called first and second cycle coding (Saldaña, 2009). In first cycle coding, the researcher comes to an interview transcript or other data set with an open mind, identifies relevant text based upon the study's research questions, and labels those excerpts of text according to the procedures associated with the chosen methodology. In second cycle coding, the researcher identifies broader categories or patterns, which leads to the development of themes. The following chapters describe specific data analysis procedures associated with each of the major qualitative methodologies covered in this book.

LIMITATIONS

As you plan your study or as you write a qualitative research proposal, keep in mind that each design choice has associated limitations. By choosing to take a qualitative approach, you recognize that your study will not lead to statistical generalizability. By choosing phenomenology, you can generally assume that your study will not result in development of new theory. Each choice pertaining to population and sample, site and length of time in the field, methods of data collection and data analysis, is likewise associated with various limitations. Do not be discouraged by this, or think that you need to feel defensive on this account. Every study has limitations, and limitations are not necessarily weaknesses. To the degree that you can explain each design choice, provide your rationale for that choice supported by research literature, and demonstrate how that choice serves your research objectives, even limitations can be seen as tied to strengths in your overall study design.

ETHICAL CONSIDERATIONS

Since social scientists delve into the private lives of their participants, they are not only accountable to them but also to their colleagues and to their communities as well. Berg (2009) categorizes the areas of concern related to research ethics as follows: "ethics revolve around various issues of harm, consent, privacy, and the confidentiality of data" (p. 60). While accountability takes on many forms in social science research, one of the most important issues of accountability has to do with ethical conduct on the part of the researcher: research participants have a right to privacy and anonymity; researchers must not do physical or emotional harm to their subjects; they must not force or coerce their subjects into participating in the research endeavor; and they must not be deceptive in conducting studies and reporting findings. Additionally, due to technological innovations that afford researchers the ability to collect data in a variety of ways, there is also an ethical concern to protect confidentiality.

Research related to conflict and peace studies can especially benefit from a feminist perspective on research ethics, which emphasizes giving voice to marginalized populations with respect to their human rights in the research process (Mauthner, Birch, Jessop, & Miller, 2002). Accountability and ethical responsibility are key considerations in ethical research. For instance, when does establishing a friendly rapport to gain access to research subjects become coercive, or at the very least, disingenuous? What of the role of gate-keepers? They are those who open the door for researchers to gain access to certain populations. If gate-keepers occupy a position of authority within a community, are they infringing upon the rights of less authoritative members of that community? Also, how much of an influence do professional demands have on the research process itself? Are there ethical lines being drawn when relationship building gets in the way of ethical professionalism? What does it really mean to get informed consent from the participants? Is this completely viable?

Ethical violations may take on many forms; for instance, undercover research resulting in the invasion of privacy for study participants, or studies in which participants undergo emotional duress or psychological stress. There were well-published cases of researchers whose practices pushed the bounds of ethical conduct: The Tuskegee Syphilis Study from 1932 to 1972 on African American males who were led to believe that they were being treated for the disease, but were in effect being experimented upon while a cure was withheld from them well after it was discovered in the 1940s (Brandt, 1978, cited in Berg, 2009); Laud Humphreys's study of casual sexual encounters among men, published in *The Tearoom Trade* (1970), in which several of his research practices were seen as a violation of these men's privacy; Stanley Milgram's experimentation (1963) on students in which he had one group of subjects playing the roles of teachers or learners, in which the teachers would administer electric shock to learners in another room (albeit, the apparent recipients were actors) when they made mistakes, in attempt to see how far they would go in following orders, as had Nazi sympathizers when obeying their superiors' commands while dealing with the Jews; and in 1972, Phillip Zimbardo's experiment, which involved a simulated prison environment where students were asked to serve either as inmate or as prison guards escalated into altercations, fights and prison break out attempts so that the researcher soon realized the adverse affect of the experiment (Zimbardo, 1972).

Ethical violations in research with human subjects in the past have prompted a national review of policies pertaining to research practices. This has resulted in the establishment of Institutional Review Boards (IRB) in universities through the passage of the National Research Act by Congress in 1974 and the National Commission on Protection of Human Subjects of Biomedical and Behavioral Research (Title II of that law). The IRB's job is to ensure that the rights of human subjects are protected. To do this, they review research proposals and examine whether the proper protocols are followed relative to gaining informed consent from subjects. Additionally, some IRBs try to ascertain whether research methods used in the studies will yield beneficial scientific findings or results (Berg, 2009).

This brings us to important practical considerations. Research participants must understand their rights and must not feel coerced into engaging in research. This is why it is important to develop and have participants sign an informed consent forms before you start their interviews—no matter how informal the process might seem. Institutional Review Boards (IRB) often rely on written consent forms as proof that researchers have done due diligence in informing participants concerning the research process and objectives. However, in cases wherein researchers deal with illiterate populations, having participants sign an "X" on informed consent forms does not guarantee that they truly understand what they are getting into. For instance, in ethnographic research where interviews are more informal and unstructured; researchers must ensure to the IRB that they have taken every possible precaution to alert the participants of the fact that the information they provide will be used as part of a study and that they have secured at least verbal consent from the participants. Additionally, let us suppose you are interviewing someone by telephone, it might be possible to have the subject give a recorded informed consent over the telephone, but it may still be necessary to obtain written consent forms as well. Another ethical consideration relates to the safety of the researchers as they undertake studies in conflict-prone or dangerous areas. Researchers and their institutions are now grappling with what to do about thesis students, dissertation students or researchers who wish to conduct research in potentially dangerous locations. Due to the threats to the researcher's safety, as well as considerations of liability for universities, it may be difficult to justify allowing researchers to put themselves in harm's way in order to bring to light the experiences of individuals in war zones, in civil conflicts or in simply dangerous situations, such as in gang or drug warfare. In some instances, researchers may sign a disclaimer form excusing a university from any responsibility for the safety of the researcher when they venture into areas deemed dangerous. Does the institution have an ethical obligation to avoid sending their employees to conflict areas? Or do university officials have an ethical obligation to provide resources to ensure that their faculty and students are protected while in the field? It is often up to the researcher to make provisions for himself as he embarks upon this kind of qualitative study. Some strategies might include the following: (1) making sure he has a trusted gatekeeper who can help him navigate difficult situations in case of emergency; (2) avoiding putting others in harm's way should he choose to undertake the research despite state department and institutional warnings about the region; (3) making plans for a quick exit strategy from the conflict prone area should he need to evacuate upon the eruption of sporadic civil unrest; (4) making sure that he is accompanied by trusted bodyguards or helpful people who know how to navigate the terrain in particularly dangerous places; and (5) registering with embassies in host countries to ensure that officials know that they are in-country in case of emergency. In the field of peace studies and conflict resolution, these concerns are still a relatively new phenomenon and must be considered carefully. They have not been fully covered by Institutional Review Board protocols.

FINAL CONSIDERATIONS

Finally, in designing your study and considering how you will actually conduct the research, it's important to think through the logistics involved. Do you need special training or other preparation? Do you need a research assistant? What kind of time is going to be required? What kind of supplies are you going to need? What will they cost? Do you need to create a budget (a necessity if you are planning to apply for research funding)? Considering these issues is part of assuring that your study is realistic and doable. What is your plan for reporting your findings? Do you intend to make presentations to stakeholders affected by your study? For example, if you're doing a study that relates to conflict over environmental resources in a particular community, are you planning to hold a community meeting where the findings of your study are shared? Are you going to present your findings to government officials, policymakers, scholars, and other researchers via conference presentations or journal articles? Knowing your intended audiences can serve as a good reminder to include elements in the research design that will lead to findings of interest to these stakeholders and ensure that you design your study in such a way as to have significant impact and make a meaningful contribution to resolving social problems related to conflict, conflict resolution, and peacebuilding.

REFERENCES

Babbie, E. (2007). *The practice of social research*. Belmont, CA: Wadsworth.

Berg, B. L. (2009). *Qualitative research methods for the social sciences* (7th ed.). Boston, MA: Allyn & Bacon.

Berger, P. L., & Luckman, T. (1966). *The social construction of reality*. New York, NY: Anchor Books Doubleday.

Chenail, R. J., Cooper, R., & Desir, C. (2010). Strategically reviewing the research literature in qualitative research. *Journal of Ethnographic and Qualitative Research, 4*, 88–94.

Cooper, R. (2010). *Shades of acceptance: A phenomenological study of the transition to a majority-minority community*. Fort Lauderdale, FL: Nova Southeastern University.

Corbin, J., & Strauss, A. (2008). *Basics of qualitative research: Techniques and procedures for developing grounded theory* (3rd ed.). Thousand Oaks, CA: Sage.

Creswell, J. W. (2003). *Research design: Qualitative, quantitative, and mixed methods approaches* (2nd ed.). Thousand Oaks, CA: Sage.

Creswell, J. W. (2013). *Qualitative inquiry and research design: Choosing among five traditions*. Thousand Oaks, CA: Sage.
Fetterman, D. (1989). *Ethnography: Step by step*. Newbury Park, CA: Sage.
Geertz, C. (1973). *The interpretation of cultures*. New York, NY: Basic Books.
Geertz, C. (1998). Deep Hanging Out (Review of the book *Routes: Travel and Translation in the Late Twentieth Century*, by James Clifford). *New York Review of Books 46*(16), 69–72.
Haverkamp, B., & Young, R. (2007). Paradigms, purpose, and the role of the literature formulating a rationale for qualitative investigations. *The Counseling Psychologist, 35*, 265–294.
Humphreys, L. (1970). *Tearoom trade: Impersonal sex in public places*. Chicago, IL: Aldine.
LeCompte, M. D., & Schensul, J. J. (1999). *Designing & conducting ethnographic research*. New York, NY: Altamira Press.
Lichtman, M. (2010). *Qualitative research in education: A user's guide*. Thousand Oaks, CA: Sage.
Mauthner, M., Birch M., Jessop, J., & Miller, T. (Eds.). (2002). *Ethics in qualitative research*. London, England: Sage.
Marshall, C., & Rossman, G. B. (2011). *Designing qualitative research* (5th ed.). Thousand Oaks, CA: Sage.
Milgram, S. (1963). Behavioral study of obedience. *Journal of Abnormal and Social Psychology, 67*(37), 1-378.
Moustakas, C. (1994). *Phenomenological research methods*. Thousand Oaks, CA: Sage.
Munhall, P. L., & Chenail, R. (2008). *Qualitative research proposals and reports: A guide* (3rd ed.). Sudbury, MA: Jones and Bartlett.
Patton, M. Q. (2002). *Qualitative research and evaluation methods* (3rd ed.). Thousand Oaks, CA: Sage.
Saldaña, J. (2009). *The coding manual for qualitative researchers*. London, England: Sage.
Saldaña, J. (2011). *Fundamentals of qualitative research*. New York, NY: Oxford University Press.
Willis, J. W. (2007). *Foundations of qualitative research: Interpretive and critical approaches*. London, England: Sage.
Zimbardo, P. G. (1972). Pathology of imprisonment. *Society, 9*, 4-6.

CHAPTER 3

GIVING VOICE

Using Grounded Theory to Examine Teachers' Perceptions of School Violence and Responses to It

Laura Finley

OVERVIEW OF GROUNDED THEORY

Grounded theory is a method of data collection and analysis used to identify common meanings and themes as they emerge. It can be used with interview, focus group, or open-ended survey research and is particularly well-suited in conjunction with action research (AR) or participatory action research (PAR). Developed by sociologists Glaser and Strauss (1967), it was originally intended to offer a methodology for obtaining qualitative data and to help develop theory. Grounded theory is used in a variety of disciplines, although it is perhaps most frequently used in communications as a means of analyzing media discourse (Altheide, 1996;) and in feminist research (Plummer & Young, 2010; Stapleton, 2001).

Peace and Conflict Studies Research: A Qualitative Perspective, pp. 49–68
Copyright © 2014 by Information Age Publishing

Rather than focusing on the number of items analyzed—be it media texts or other—grounded theory emphasizes the depth of the analysis (Tucker-McLaughlin & Campbell, 2012). Glaser and Straus (1967) were critical of the overemphasis on hypothesis testing and verification of results in traditional research and sought to develop a more fluid and responsive tool. They, and others, criticized other forms of qualitative research as "impressionistic, anecdotal, unsystematic and biased" (Charmaz, 2006, p. 5). Asserting that traditional methods were divorced from theory, Glaser and Strauss saw grounded theory as a more honest and holistic method of analysis.

In introducing grounded theory, Glaser and Strauss (1967) sought to provide a method of data collection and analysis that could be used as a tool for social change. It has been used for social changes purposes in a variety of institutions, including education (Lopez, Eng, Randall-Davie, & Robinson, 2005; Plummer & Young, 2010). Because research involving educators has often viewed them as subjects it has denied them the agency and voice so critical to school reform. Gitlin (1994) recommends that educators' voices be heard through what he calls educative research. Educative research involves restructuring the typical relationship between subject and researcher to one that is less hierarchical and more dialogical. Voices that have historically been silenced, such as those of classroom teachers, can emerge through the dialogue with the researcher as well as with colleagues. The hope is that educative research can prompt educators to engage in meaningful dialogue that betters their classroom practice and informs the structuring of the school. Grounded theory is ideally suited for educative research as it recognizes that each teacher, student, or administrator will have a different lived experience with schooling. Grounded theory has been used to examine postsecondary social justice educators' use of storytelling to create social change (Byron, 2011), to assess the impact of a course on conflict resolution, to evaluate a sport-related peace education program, to assess the roles of popular educators working with NGOs to promote peace and social justice (Ty, 2011) and how principles of restorative justice can be integrated into K–12 urban school district reform (Carson, Chandler, Collins, & Snow, 2009).

KEY CHARACTERISTIC OF GROUNDED THEORY

Key characteristics of grounded theory include that data collection and analysis occur simultaneously and that, through constant comparison and induction, core themes emerge from data (Birks & Mills, 2011; Charmaz, 2006; Corbin & Strauss, 2008; Glaser, 1978; Glaser & Strauss, 1967; Mills, Bonner, & Francis, 2006). According to Charmaz (2008), "The comparative and interactive nature of grounded theory at every stage of analysis distinguishes grounded theory from other approaches and makes it an explicitly emergent method" (p. 163).

Originally, the idea was that researchers would focus on the data, with no presumptions about what they might find. Thus grounded theory was intended to be an entirely inductive method (Glaser & Straus, 1967) and, according to Clarke (2005), was a reaction to the positivist movement that dominated research from the 1950s on. Grounded theory has been heavily influenced by the symbolic interactionism of sociologist George Herbert Mead in that it sees humans as deriving meaning from social interaction and from the interpretation of symbols (Charmaz, 2008; Plummer & Young, 2010; Strauss & Corbin, 1998). As Glaser and Strauss (1967) explained, in *Grounded Theory*, "categories and properties emerge, develop in abstraction, and become related, their accumulating interrelations form an integrated central theoretical framework—the core of the emerging theory" (Glaser & Strauss, 1967, p. 40).

In the 1990s, however, Strauss and a group of followers changed their positions, asserting that even the researcher's choice of items or ideas to analyze and the codes used to analyze them were somewhat deductive. Glaser remained convinced that the original methodology was best. Others believe that even the original version of grounded theory contained positivist elements and advocate a "constructivist" version of grounded theory (Charmaz, 2008). In contrast to classical versions of grounded theory, constructivist grounded theory is described as "epistemologically subjective" and "ontologically relativist" (Mills, 2006, p. 6). That is, meaning is coconstructed through interaction with participants (Charmaz, 2000; Hesse-Biber & Leavy, 2008). New theory is not discovered but rather emerges from the data that reflects participants lived experiences (Charmaz, 2009; Fassinger, 2005). As such, grounded theory is well-suited for peace and conflict studies inquiry, in that it allows all participants equal power and voice in the process (Hesse-Biber, & Leavy, 2008).

Initially Glaser and Strauss (1967) felt that researchers should not conduct a review of existing literature before engaging in a grounded theory inquiry. The idea was that researchers would be too influenced by previous work and would thus not develop their own interpretations of the themes that emerge. McCallin (2003) maintained that "the researcher may be sidetracked by received knowledge and interpretations that support taken-for-granted assumptions, which are not relevant in the new area of study" (p. 63). Glaser (1998) thought that reviewing scholarly literature would result in excessive jargon. Further, Glaser argued that "exposure to established theoretical ideas could leave the researcher 'awed out' by the work of others, thus undermining their sense of self-worth and competence in the realm of theory development" (p. 68). Further, Glaser (1998), Dick

(2007) and Locke (2001) have maintained that conducting an extensive literature review might be a waste of time in that the literature most relevant to the study may yet to be published.

However, most scholars today agree that the literature review is an important component of a study but disagree about when, precisely, it should occur during a grounded theory inquiry and precisely how extensive the review should be (Cutcliffe, 2000; McGhee, Marland, & Atkinson, 2007). As Dunne (2011) noted, most scholars, in particular doctoral students, are simply unable to postpone conducting a literature review, as it is required to receive project approval, funding, and support. Further, as Coffey and Atkinson (1996) explained,

> The open-mindedness of the researcher should not be mistaken for the empty mindedness of the researcher who is not adequately steeped in the research traditions of a discipline. It is after all, not very clever to rediscover the wheel, and the student or researcher who is ignorant of the relevant literature is always in danger of doing the equivalent. (p. 157)

One of the key debates about grounded theory is, as with much qualitative research, the degree to which researchers can be objective. Strauss and Corbin (1990) explained that "the researcher is shaped by the data, just as the data are shaped by the researcher," and "a state of complete objectivity is impossible and that in every piece of research—quantitative or qualitative—there is an element of subjectivity" (pp. 42–43). Corbin and Strauss (2007) argued that complete objectivity is not possible, as analysts are always interpreting data based on their impressions. For grounded theorists, reflexivity is key. That is, researchers must be upfront about their own thinking and their perceptions and must make this clear to those who read their work.

Some scholars have criticized grounded theory. Burawoy (2009) refers to it as "antitheoretical microempiricism, brilliantly mislabeled as grounded theory" (p. 8). Others note that because samples are generally small, results may not be generalizeable and the theories developed from grounded theory may not have robust explanatory power. Thomas (2002) maintained that wanting to interpret data and develop theory simultaneously was akin to wanting to "have one's cake and eat it" too (p. 421). Yet, as Merriam (1988) maintains, the traditional notion of validity does not apply to most qualitative research in general. Instead, researchers should instead be concerned with other qualities, like reader generalizability rather than generalizability to the broader society. Glaser and Strauss (1967) recommended that grounded theory studies be judged on fit, relevance, workability and modifiability. Fit refers to how closely the concepts or codes developed in the study represent what they are supposed to. The method of constant comparison is intended to ensure that the fit is good. Relevance addresses whether the study generates more than simply academic interest. That is, it is relevant if it captures the attention of the participants. Workability is achieved if the theory generated can explain the problem. Modifiability is essential, as theory must be alterable when new data is identified that challenges it.

Gitlin (1994) explains that reliability, too, should not be the goal of this kind of research, as it is intended to identify what needs to be addressed and to prompt change. Therefore further research would not and should not identify the same issues. Instead, Gitlin asserts that this form of qualitative research is about satisfying a voice, not about replicability.

CONDUCTING GROUNDED THEORY STUDIES

The first step in grounded theory study is to initiate the study. This involves selecting a research topic, devising a specific research question or set of questions, identifying the type of data that would be necessary for the study, and finding the research site.

The second step is data selection and collection. Here researchers may utilize a variety of sampling methods. In fact, Glaser and Straus (1967) assert than anything that is observed or encountered during the study can be considered data, as all can be helpful in developing theory. Thus interviews, focus groups, and direct observations may be included as well as meeting notes, lectures, Internet listserv exchanges and more. Differing from other methods, sampling in grounded theory may be ongoing throughout the study, as emerging themes point the researcher to new sources of data. Glaser and Strauss (1967) called this theoretical sampling. As Egan (2002) explains,

> rather than delimiting populations under study or attempting to control variables, sites and participants may be considered based on their potential capacities to offer intriguing and important variation in comparisons associated with the phenomenon under investigation. Following initiation of the research process, the data collection and analysis begin to strongly influence the modes, locations, and persons engaged by the researcher. (p. 283)

The third step, data analysis, occurs simultaneously with data collection in a grounded theory study. That is, researchers are constantly collecting and comparing data to identify themes. Throughout the grounded theory data collection and analysis, researchers often use a process called memoing, or short notes written to oneself about the research and the process. These memos are used to help develop codes. Coding refers to the process of developing categories and concepts. Researchers use some form of coding to record their ongoing analysis. In open coding, researchers review field notes or transcripts line by line to develop categories and conceptualizations. Essentially, concepts are identified, named, and described (Strauss & Corbin, 1990). Axial coding involves comparing codes to one another to identify relationships. Codes are then fit into frames that describe the general relationships. Alternatively, researchers may use selective coding, which involves choosing one category as the core and building from that, with the idea that there is always one central component or idea to any set of data (Strauss & Corbin, 1990). As the researcher begins to identify what might be the theory emerging from the data, he or she might write what is referred to as a theoretical memo, which can be anything from a few words on the side of the page to a post-it to a separate field note that begins to explain the phenomena being studied. These are then compiled into the final theory and reporting of the study.

Thematic analysis involves, according to Morse and Field (1995), searching for and identifying commonalities that occur throughout a research project. Themes may not always be obvious and thus researchers utilize a variety of tools to identify them. Some are grounded by what sociologist Charmaz (2003) has called "sensitizing concepts," or "those background ideas that inform the overall research problem." Sensitizing concepts help "provide starting points for building analysis, not ending points for evading it. We may use sensitizing concepts *only* as points of departure from which to study the data (p. 259, emphasis in original). According to Bowen (2006). "Sensitizing concepts give the researcher a sense of how observed instances of a phenomenon might fit within conceptual categories" (pp. 7–8). Sensitizing concepts can replace hypotheses in qualitative work (Blaikie, 2000).

The following list provides some of the more common methods of theme identification used by grounded theorists.

1. Word analysis. Researchers can informally identify words used frequently in a text, or can more formally list all unique words and then identify those used most often.
2. Indigenous categories. Researchers identify words that are unfamiliar or that are used in unique or different ways.
3. Key Words in Context. Researchers first identify key words and, for each time a specific word is used, record its immediate context. Additional analysis can then identify themes in how words are being used.
4. Compare and contrast, or what Glazer and Strauss (1967) call the "constant comparison method." Similarly, Cragan and Shields (1995) recommend analyzing focus group data by identifying and describing emergent themes coming from redundancy, intensity, and individuation. Redundancy refers to the frequency that a

particular concept or idea is described by participants. Intensity refers to the degree to which participants are particularly emphatic or emotional about a response. Individuation involves information that was not solicited by that was brought up by more than one participant.

5. Searching for missing information. This might involve paying attention to issues or items that literature would suggest should come up in a research study but that do not.

6. Searching for metaphors, similes and analogies.

7. Identifying transitions. In written texts, authors often use new paragraphs to shift to important new topics. Pauses or changes in tone may help identify speakers' shift to new themes.

> ## Conducting a Grounded Theory Study
>
> 1. Initiate the study by selecting a topic, specifying a research question(s), identifying a research site and articulating the type of data that should be collected.
> 2. Data collection.
> 3. Data analysis (an ongoing process occurring simultaneously with collection).
> 4. Conclusion of research-data yields no new contributions and/or development of new theory.

Finally, the grounded theory research is concluded "when the researcher has observed a point of data saturation and a sufficient theory has emerged from the data. Data saturation is evident when data collection no longer contributes to elaboration of the phenomenon being investigated" (Egan, 2002, p. 286).

A CASE STUDY OF TEACHERS' PERCEPTIONS OF SCHOOL VIOLENCE AND RESPONSES TO IT

This remainder of this chapter focuses on the use of grounded theory in a case study involving teachers' perceptions of school violence and reactions to it. The research utilized applied grounded theory to analyze and make meaning of teacher's unique perspectives, which are so often silenced. Data was collected through a series of focus groups.

In Spring 2002, I conducted focus group research with teachers at a small high school in Midwest Michigan. The population of the school is generally lower-middle-class and overwhelmingly Caucasian. At the time of the research, there were 22 teachers on staff. Ten had been with the district for more than ten years, and the principal at the time had been in that position for three years (and was a middle school teacher in the district before).

I chose to conduct this research because, at the time, I was teaching high school at a district approximately one hour away while simultaneously completing my doctoral degree. I had become concerned about the changes I saw being made in my school out of fear of school violence. I noticed a particularly punitive and technological streak of changes implemented the fall after the April 1999 Columbine shooting. My district hired a school resource officer, installed locks on additional doors, barred students from entering and exiting most locations, and required students to bring only see-through bags to school. These changes were not necessitated by any particular incident or specific threat at school but rather were instituted based on a perceived need to react to what was happening elsewhere. The result of these changes at my school was not that the campus was noticeably safer. Instead, students felt stifled. The impact on the school climate was palpable. Both students and staff (to a large degree, at least) felt they had no voice in making any of the changes. Many students expressed that they actually felt less safe, as they wondered if perhaps there was something that had happened that triggered such an extreme response and began to question the administration's motives and transparency. I became curious whether other schools had responded in the same way to this moral panic about school violence and if other educators felt so disempowered by the process. I wondered whether others had experienced the same negative impact on school climate as well.

I chose to uses focus groups because I wanted to help the teachers begin a dialogue about these issues. Given my experience that teachers had not been consulted and had virtually no voice in the process of making important changes at the school, I felt it critical that other educators be given a chance to talk through how they saw the issue of school violence and the responses to it. This school was also unique, as it was one of the few remaining high schools to have an "open" physical structure. No walls divided the classrooms. Instead, pseudo-walls, made of book cases, generally, had been erected.

I coordinated four focus groups at the selected school in March 2002. Two or three teachers were involved in each session for a total of eleven participants, or half the staff. Participants included six males and five females with teaching experience ranging from one and a half years to 19 years. Each focus group was 90 minutes long, thus allowing teachers to participate during their planning periods (due to the schools' block schedule). During the first hour, the conversation focused on their general perception of violence at the school, the types of changes they had noticed related to violence-prevention, their overall perception of safety on campus, and their perception of changes in school climate. In addition, teachers were asked to share any other thoughts they had on these matters as well as to complete a survey assessing school climate. The actual focus group questions are included as Appendix A.

Like many researchers who use grounded theory, I chose to triangulate my findings, or to "circulate my data," as Featherston and Kelly (2007) describe it, through other forms of data collection and analysis. Using my review of the literature as well as modeling from other existing tools, I created a survey to further assess teachers' perceptions of school violence and the responses to it. The survey is included as Appendix B.

The following section highlights several themes that emerged from the focus groups.

Teachers' Roles

In general, participants felt they had both a preventative and responsive role in reference to school violence. Three of the respondents indicated a lack of faith in administration to handle any potential violence problems, asserting that they would try to handle things themselves, work with colleagues, or deal with parents rather than ask the administration for assistance. Most felt that the school did not stress cooperation among staff.

Changes Identified

Participants identified a host of safety-related changes the school had recently initiated. These included additions to portable walls, doors locked that previously were not, limited distribution of keys to staff members, changes in procedures around the gym and shop area, enforcement of rules that were previously not enforced, increased staff concern about liability, installation of a key pad on the main staff entrance, a ban on bags and jackets in classes, stricter enforcement of the school dress code, limited guest passes for school dances, and police presence during lunch periods. Interestingly, no curricular, pedagogical, or extracurricular efforts were noted, nor were any specific training initiatives for staff described. No one mentioned conflict resolution or student-led initiatives either. In fact, participants pointed out that most of the changes were administratively-driven and concern was noted about the way these changes were communicated. For instance, "Eric" noted that "We did receive some written information, but we never did actually practice it or talk about what to do in those situations," while Howard concurred, stating "We've received absolutely no emergency training whatsoever." "John" explained that "we sort of do our own thing" in regard to curricula.

Perceptions of Safety-Related Changes

The staff response to the changes listed above varied. Some participants described them as a joke. Howard specifically noted the key pad on the staff door, saying teachers all thought it was "ridiculous." Others said that staff members were apathetic about the changes, as they do not generally see the need for enhanced vigilance about school safety. Some, however, responded negatively, and were not cooperative with the changes. "David" referred to the locked doors and the key pad, explaining "I still think there's a perception that they're able to handle it and be responsible. Having keys to certain locks and stuff. There's not a willingness to accept that you're just an employee. I think it boils down to a perception that you're a professional and you deserve these things." "Eric" explained that he felt demeaned by administration some times, saying, "treat us like professionals or I'll go elsewhere." "Jack" thought the administration did not make the most well-informed, cost effective changes in regard to safety. Joan reiterated that point, noting "I think that some of the decisions have not been necessarily sound, have just been more arbitrarily done." Some pointed the finger higher than the building principal, noting the "weak and ineffectual" Superintendent.

"Roland" expressed that he and others felt comfortable with the changes, offering an "anything goes as long as we feel safe" perspective. He liken the responses to those made after the 9/11 attack and asserted, "if you want to take a little longer than usual, take the time to make sure I'm safe, I'm all for it."

Similar to the staff, student reactions to the changes cited were mixed as well. Some participants mentioned students who grumbled or became rebellious. "Howard" explained, "We think it's ridiculous, our students think it's completely unreasonable. They absolutely don't think we need to be even as security conscious as we are, so a lot of them are pissed off." Some said they thought the students simply accepted the changes. None noted that students were thankful for or reacted positively to the changes.

Overall Perceptions of Safety

Participants expressed that they generally felt safe at work. When discussing what made them feel unsafe, a few participants noted specific students they felt would be capable of severe violence. "John" and "Eric" noted that students are allowed to get away with disrespectful attitudes towards teachers and their peers, and "John" said "the maturity level of kids, of some kids here, as very, very, low." "Howard" said he felt safe largely due to his personal training and preparations. All agreed that the openness of the facility made them feel less safe, in particular in the event of a gunman on campus. "David" called the school "the perfect spot" for a gunman. "Tammy" noted that while the construction of the school would make it easy for a violent attack, it's placement in valley with hills surrounding it was dangerous as well. "So the idea that if an intruder were in the building there's nowhere to go within the building that's safe, then to leave the building, to walk out, you don't know who is out there and what their plan is, that makes it scarier." "Tammy" brought up the concern about sexual violence, citing several incidents and even one in which a student used "very abusive sexual language towards me in another teacher's class." She expressed concern that when teachers complete disciplinary referrals, they have to worry "is this going to come back to haunt me? Is this, am I just causing a personal safety issue for myself?" "Carol" shared her concern about the way announcements were made, citing the occasional canine search for drugs. The principal announced that teachers are not to let anyone out of their classrooms, and she said "it's like, you're wondering what's going on." Several participants brought up the concern about living in the same, small community as the students. "Eric" explained, "As far as living in the community, say I discipline a kid or kick a kid off a team—there's always that possibility, they all know where you live."

When asked if they perceived that students felt safe at school, most responded that they don't think students spend much time considering safety. "Carol" explained, "I think our kids feel safe here. I think our kids are very naïve about what the rest of the world is like." When they did note that some intimidation or harassment occurs, participants were quick to follow it with the qualifier that those things happen everywhere. Several participants noted that students and staff were quick to label those who look or act different as the potential threats. Yet two other participants noted that this was profiling based on a stereotype of "Gothic" looking students. Participants generally agreed that the school was lacking a strong counseling presence and that students might not feel comfortable sharing any safety concerns with teachers. "David" noted that he had observed some race-related intimidation as the school as well.

School Culture

Participants generally assessed staff pride in the school as being very low. "Carol" said "I guess I don't really sense a lot of pride by staff or students," noting that pride had been decreasing over her tenure there. "Howard" specifically noted a lack of camaraderie in the school. He also expressed that the school was too harsh on students, resulting in their lack of pride. He explained "You can't color your hair, you can't pierce your eyebrows, you can't wear shorts, you can't , you can't, you can't. All we do is say the thou shant's, we don't talk about the thou shalt's." Interestingly, several participants pointed to the poor showing from the football team in the previous few years as the reason for the lack of student pride in the school. "Joan" explained "I do feel there's an inferiority complex our kids have so far as their perception of themselves and other schools." "Howard" stated that many of the students use methamphetamines, which affects their mental outlook. "Carol" cited the fact that there isn't a lot of student-driven activity at the school.

In the event that a violent incident occurred at the school, participants were generally unsure of what the response would be, again citing that they had not explicitly discussed protocol. Consequently, each staff member had generally developed their own unique crisis plan, especially in the event of a gunman on campus. "Eric" mentioned he had noted the exit routes and would be "looking out for myself." "Howard" had an elaborate plan for a gunman on campus: "we're gonna circle the wagons if that happens. I already know what I'm gonna do. We'll pull all of the cabinets in, and start throwing computer parts at them." "Joan" expressed "I think it would be chaos, because we don't have a plan, we have nothing. And the facility causes some problems that most schools wouldn't have, so I think it would be disastrous."

Key Themes

Some overall themes emerged from this grounded theory. One theme was that participants felt concerned about the climate of the school and noted that little had been done to address it. Another theme was that the physical structure contributed to feelings of vulnerability. Further, participants brought up September 11 numerous times, noting that in general they felt less safe than before the attack. Most expressed that more should be done to train and equip staff to deal with violent events and that the things the administration had done were not the most effective. These teachers admitted that they should play a larger role in keeping the place safe, but generally also admitted they were doing very little in that regard.

While many complained about the lack of student or staff input, none mentioned anything they had proposed or initiated. Female participants were more negative toward administration and felt less safe than did male participants. Younger staff members tended to feel less safe but more supportive of the administration..

CONCLUSION

Although this study did not generate a new, unique theory, as grounded theory research often does, it did suggest that school climate is a key factor in regards to school safety. That is, when educators and students have pride in the school and feel that their input is solicited and their voices are heard, extreme violence is much less likely. Additionally, this study confirmed that school violence takes many forms and that technological and punitive responses may not only be inadequate to address some of those forms, they may also exacerbate the violence in some cases. Further, this case study helped educators at the selected school think critically about their personal and collective responses to concerns about school violence. Several participants expressed the importance of having these discussions and seemed thankful for the opportunity. Results of the focus groups and survey data were shared with the Principal, who then used the next staff meeting to further engage in dialogue about these issues. Additionally, the concerns brought up through this research played a pivotal role in helping the district convince the community to pass a bond to build a new high school building.

Grounded theory can and is a useful tool for qualitative inquiry. As in this case study, it helps allow important voices to emerge and can be the starting point for dialogue that promotes peace and social justice. Grounded theory can be particularly useful to asses peace-related initiatives in an educational setting, as it can allow individual educators, whose voices are often marginalized, to emerge. It can also help develop theories of social change in various institutions that can then be tested and implemented by scholars and activists. In addition to many books describing how to conduct grounded theory research, there is now an online journal called *The Grounded Theory Review: An International Journal* to present research and to address issues in the use of grounded theory.

Many scholars and activists in the field of peace and conflict studies have utilized grounded theory. For instance, Women's International League for Peace and Freedom (WILPF) coordinated a study to assess the level of women's involvement in informal and formal peacemaking practices (Hermoso, 2010). In addition, peace educators have made use of grounded theory to improve their classroom. These studies have shown how storytelling can be used in the K–12 classroom to develop praxis (Byron, 2011), the types of conflict and conflict resolution strategies used in elementary school classrooms, and the impact of a shift to critical pedagogy in a college classroom (Fetherston & Kelly, 2007).

Grounded theory researchers must, however, take care not to abuse their insider knowledge. That is, while it is useful for the results of the study to be shared with participants and organizations for their continued improvement, researchers must take caution not to be overly critical and to present themselves in ways that reek of power and privilege. While this is true of many qualitative methods, because of the fluid nature of grounded theory the balance can be even trickier. Further, as I experienced with one of the participants in this study, participants in grounded theory research may misrepresent the truth and thus manipulate the study. Because the research is based on encouraging and including each participant's input, grounded theory studies may be more susceptible to this issue than are other types of research. In research investigating issues related to people's particular experiences with violence and peace, for instance, participants may be prone to exaggeration of misrepresentation (Rennie, Phillips & Quartaro, 1988).

APPENDIX A

FOCUS GROUP QUESTIONS

Background Information:

Gender of each participant.
Teaching experience at the school (described in categories of under 10 years and 10 years plus).

1. What do you see as your role in addressing school problems?
2. Is cooperation stressed in the school? In what ways? How about the individual classroom?
3. What safety-related changes do you recall the school making in recent years?
4. What was the staff response to those changes? The student response?
5. Do you generally feel safe at work?
6. Did you feel safe prior to the safety changes you indicated earlier?

7. How do you perceive that students feel at school regarding safety? Have you noticed a difference in how students feel about school safety in recent years? Please provide examples.
8. Do you feel that staff is more positive or negative towards the school and/or administration as a result of these safety-related changes? Please provide examples.
9. Are students more positive or negative towards the administration and/or teachers as a result of the safety measures? Please provide examples.
10. Have the changes had any impact on what is taught or how it is taught? On the educational goals of the school? Please provide examples.
11. Do you sense a chance in student or staff pride in the school? Explain any difference you have noticed by providing examples.
12. How would a violent incident be handled at your school?
13. What do you feel is the best way to respond to school violence? To prevent it?

APPENDIX B

SCHOOL CLIMATE SURVEY

Please respond to the following statements by circling the most appropriate response. Use the scale provided below.

1=Strongly Disagree   2=Disagree   3=Neutral   4=Agree
5=Strongly Agree

1. The principal at my school seeks and values teachers' ideas.

    5   4   3   2   1

2. Teachers at my school are not involved in the decision-making process.

    5   4   3   2   1

3. Teachers at my school are kept informed about current school-related issues.

    5   4   3   2   1

4. The principal at my school is friendly and supportive most of the time.

    5   4   3   2   1

5. The principal at my school seeks and values students' ideas.

    5   4   3   2   1

6. Teachers who do a good job at my school are rarely praised for their work.

    5   4   3   2   1

7. Teachers at my school are encouraged to be innovative in the classroom.

    5   4   3   2   1

8. The mission of my school provides a clear sense of direction for teachers.

    5   4   3   2   1

9. Teachers at my school generally support the school mission.

    5   4   3   2   1

10. Students at my school help one another to accomplish things at the school.

    5   4   3   2   1

11. Teachers at my school are rarely supportive of one another.

    5   4   3   2   1

12. Teachers at my school are willing to help out when something needs to be done.

    5   4   3   2   1

13. Teachers at my school do not generally trust one another.

    5   4   3   2   1

14. Teachers and parents at my school have common expectations for student performance.

    5   4   3   2   1

15. Parents at my school trust teachers' judgment.

    5   4   3   2   1

16. My school has adequate equipment and supplies.

    5   4   3   2   1

17. I seek and value students' ideas in the classroom.

    5   4   3   2   1

18. My behavior is viewed by students at my school as friendly and supportive most of the time.

5   4   3   2   1

19. Students at the school generally feel pride in their school.

5   4   3   2   1

20. Students at the school generally dislike coming to school.

5   4   3   2   1

21. I generally enjoy my job at the school.

5   4   3   2   1

22. I feel loyalty to my school district.

5   4   3   2   1

23. Teachers at my school are role models for students.

5   4   3   2   1

24. Teachers at my school emphasize empathy, tolerance, and compassion in the classroom.

5   4   3   2   1

25. Teachers at my school value school improvement.

5   4   3   2   1

26. In general, my school has high expectations for students.

5   4   3   2   1

27. Teachers at my school have few opportunities for collaboration and dialogue.

5   4   3   2   1

28. Different departments at my school collaborate on school and classroom projects.

5   4   3   2   1

29. Students at my school are frequently asked to work together in the classroom.

5   4   3   2   1

30. Competition, rather than cooperation, is stressed at my school.

5   4   3   2   1

REFERENCES

Altheide, D. (1996). Qualitative media analysis. Thousand Oaks, CA: Sage.

Barnett, D., (2012). Constructing new theory for identifying students with emotional disturbance: A constructivist approach to grounded theory. *The Grounded Theory Review, 11*(1), 47–58.

Birks, M., & Mills, J. (2011). *Grounded theory: A practical guide.* Thousand Oaks, CA: Sage.

Bowen, G. (2006). Grounded theory and sensitizing concepts. *International Journal of Qualitative Methods, 5*(3). Retrieved March 8, 2013 from http://www.ualberta.ca/~iiqm/backissues/5_3/HTML/bowen.html

Burawoy, M, (2009). *The extended case method: Four countries, four decades, four great transformations and one theoretical tradition.* Berkeley, CA: University of California Press.

Bryon, A. (2011). *Storytelling as loving praxis in critical peace education: A grounded theory study of postsecondary social justice educators.* Dissertation submitted to Portland State University. Retrived from http://dr.archives.pdx.edu/xmlui/bitstream/handle/psu/7053/Byron_psu_0180D_10334.pd f?sequence=1

Carson, S., Chandler, S., Collins, E., & Snow, D. (2009). Education higher education and school leaders in matters of peace. *International Journal of Education, 1*(1), 1–17.

Charmaz, K. (2000). Grounded theory: Objectivist and constructivist methods. In N. Denzin & Y. Lincoln (Eds.), *Handbook of qualitative research* (2nd ed., pp. 509–535). Thousand Oaks, CA: Sage.

Charmaz, K. (2003). Grounded theory: Objectivist and constructivist methods. In N. K. Denzin & Y. S. Lincoln (Eds.), *Strategies for qualitative inquiry* (2nd ed., pp. 249–291). Thousand Oaks, CA: Sage.

Charmaz, K. (2006). *Constructing grounded theory: A practical guide through qualitative analysis.* Thousand Oaks, CA: Sage.

Charmaz, K. (2008). Grounded theory in the 21st century. In: Denizin, N., & Lincoln, Y. (Eds.), *Strategies of qualitative inquiry* (3rd ed., pp. 203–241). London, England: Sage.

Charmaz, K. (2009). Shifting the grounds: Constructivist grounded theory methods. In J. M. Morse, P. N. Stern, J. M. Corbin, B. Bowers, & A. E. Clarke, (Eds.). *Developing grounded theory: The second generation* (pp. 127–154). Walnut Creek, CA: University of Arizona Press.

Clarke, A. (2005). *Situational analysis: Grounded theory after the postmodern turn.* London, England: Sage.

Corbin, J. A., & Strauss, A. (2008). *Basics of qualitative research* (3rd ed.). Thousand Oaks, CA: Sage.

Coffey, A., & Atkinson, P. (1996). *Making sense of qualitative data: Complementary research strategies.* Thousand Oaks, CA: Sage.

Cragan, J., & Shields, D. (1995). *Symbolic theories in applied communication research: Bormann, Burke and Fischer.* Cresskill, NJ: Hampton Press.

Cutcliffe, J. (2000). Methodological issues in grounded theory. *Journal of Advanced Nursing, 31*(6), 1476–1484.

Dick, B. (2007). What can Grounded Theorists and Action Researchers Learn from Each Other? In A. Bryant & K. Charmaz (Eds.), *The Sage handbook of grounded theory* (pp. 370–388). Thousand Oaks, CA: Sage.

Dunne, C. (2011). The place of the literature review in grounded theory research. *International Review of Social Research Methodology, 14*(2), 111–124.

Egan, T. (2002). Grounded theory research and theory building. *Advances in Developing Human Resources, 4*(3), 277–295.

Fassinger, R. (2005). Paradigms, praxis, problems, and promise: Grounded theory in counseling psychology research. *Journal of Counseling Psychology, 52*(2), 156–166.

Fetherston, B., & Kelly, R. (2007). Conflict resolution and transformative pedagogy: A grounded theory research project on learning in higher education. *Journal of Transformative Education, 5*(3), 262–285.

Gitlin, A. (Ed.). (1994). *Power and method: Political activism and educational research.* New York, NY: Routledge.

Glaser, B. (1963). Retreading research materials: the use of secondary data analysis by the independent researcher. *American Behavioural Science, 6*(10), 11–14.

Glaser, B. (1978). *Theoretical sensitivity: Advances in the methodology of grounded theory.* Mill Valley, CA: Sociology Press.

Glaser, B. (1998). *Doing grounded theory: Issues and discussions,* Mill Valley CA: Sociology Press.

Glaser, B. (2001). *The grounded theory perspective: Conceptualization contrasted with description.* Mill Valley, CA : Sociology Press.

Glaser, B. (2005). *The grounded theory perspective III: Theoretical coding,* Mill Valley, CA: Sociology Press.

Glaser, B., & Strauss, A. (1967). *The discovery of Grounded Theory: Strategies for qualitative research.* Chicago, IL: Aldine.

Heaton, J. (2004) *Reworking qualitative data,* London: Sage Publications Limited.

Hermoso, J. (2010). Weaving the threads of peace: Creating a gender evaluation methodology for women's participation in peacemaking. Retrieved June 30, 2013 from www.peacewomen.org/.../partunimp_genderevaluationmethodologyparticipationpeacemaking_hermoso_aug2010

Hesse-Biber, S., & Leavy, P. (2008). (Eds.). *Handbook of emergent methods.* New York, NY: Guilford Press.

Locke, K. (2001). *Grounded theory in management research.* Thousand Oaks, CA: Sage.

Lopez, E., Eng, E., Randall-David, E., & Robinson, N. (2005). Within rural North Carolina: Blending the techniques of photovoice and grounded theory. *Qualitative Health Research, 15*, 99–115.

McCallin, A. (2003). Designing a grounded theory study: Some practicalities. *Nursing in Critical Care, 8*(5), 203–208.

McGhee, G., Marland, G., & Atkinson, J. (2007). Grounded theory research: Literature reviewing and reflexivity. *Journal of Advanced Nursing, 60*(3), 334–342.

Merriam, S. B. (1988). *Case study research in education: A qualitative approach.* San Francisco, CA: Jossey-Bass.

Mills, J., Bonner, A., & Francis, K. (2006). The development of constructivist grounded theory. *International Journal of Qualitative Methods, 5*(1), 1–10.

Morse, J. & Field, P. (1995). *Qualitative research methods for health professionals* (2nd ed.). London, England: Chapman & Hall.

Plummer, M., & Young, L. (2010). Grounded theory and feminist inquiry: Revitalizing links to the past. *Western Journal of Nursing Research, 32*(3), 305–321.

Rennie, D., Phillips, J., & Quartaro, G. (1988). Grounded theory: A promising approach to conceptualization in psychology? *Canadian Psychology, 29*(2), 149–52.

Simmons, O. (2010). Is that a real theory or did you just make it up? Teaching classic Grounded Theory. *The Grounded Theory Review, 9*(2).

Stapleton, K. (2001). Constructing a feminist identity: Discourse and the community of practice. *Feminism & Psychology, 11*, 459–491.

Strauss, A., & Corbin, J. (1990). *Basics of qualitative research: Grounded Theory procedures and techniques.* London: Sage.

Strauss, A., & Corbin, J. (1998). *Basics of qualitative research: Techniques and procedures for developing grounded theory* (2nd ed.). Thousand Oaks, CA: Sage.

Thomas, G. (2002). Theory's spell on qualitative inquiry and educational research. *British Educational Research Journal, 28*(3), 419–434.

Tucker-McLaughlin, M., & Campbell, K. (2012). A grounded theory analysis: Hillary Clinton represented as innovator and voiceless in TV news. *Electronic news, 6*(3), 3–19.

Ty, R. (2011). Human rights, conflict transformation and peacebuilding. Retrieved March 8, 2012, from http://www.academia.edu/721522/Rey_Ty._2011_._Human_Rights_Conflict_Transformation_and_Peace_Building_The_Role_of_the_State_NGOs_Social_Movements_and_Civil_Society_in_the_Struggle_for_Power_Social_Justice_and_Social_Change

CHAPTER 4

PHENOMENOLOGY IN PEACE AND CONFLICT STUDIES RESEARCH

Getting to the Essence of an Experience

Robin Cooper

This chapter provides an introduction to phenomenology and how it applies to peace and conflict studies research. Following a brief description of phenomenology and overview of why it can be a useful methodology for research in this field, the chapter presents a brief description of characteristics associated with three major approaches to phenomenology, as well as the steps involved in conducting a phenomenological study. Sample studies are referenced throughout the chapter to illustrate the application of this methodology in researching conflict, conflict resolution, and peacebuilding. This chapter does not attempt to provide a complete discussion of the philosophical perspectives associated with phenomenology, nor does it describe all of the various methodological approaches associated with phenomenological research in qualitative inquiry. Rather, this chapter is merely an introduction to the rich, varied world of phenomenology. Readers are encouraged to look to primary texts on phenomenology for a

Peace and Conflict Studies Research: A Qualitative Perspective, pp. 69–90
Copyright © 2014 by Information Age Publishing

more in-depth review of the philosophy and methodology of phenomenology. Several authors of such texts are cited throughout the chapter.

WHAT IS PHENOMENOLOGY?

Phenomenology is both a philosophy and a methodology. Phenomenology was introduced by Edmund Husserl in 1900 as a new development in the field of philosophy that was designed to move away from "abstract metaphysical speculation wrapped up in pseudo-problems, in order to come into contact with the matters themselves, with concrete living experience" (Moran, 2000, p. xiii). Phenomenology as a philosophy is rooted in the notion that in order to gain knowledge of an object, it must be understood through the consciousness of the one who experiences it. Thus, phenomenology as a philosophy can be referred to as "knowledge as it appears to consciousness, the science of describing what one perceives, senses, and knows in one's immediate awareness and experience" (Moustakas, 1994, p. 26). The focus is not on an object or phenomenon, per se, but on how that phenomenon is experienced, from the perspective of the one who experiences it. "The reason for this is that nothing can be known or spoken about that does not come through consciousness" (Giorgi, 2009, p. 4).

In keeping with these philosophical origins, phenomenology as a research methodology is focused on exploring the lived experience of a phenomenon and the meaning that experience holds for the one having the experience. In its original, philosophical form, phenomenology was primarily conceptual and focused on individuals seeking to understand their own experience (Smith, Flowers, & Larkin, 2009). As a research tradition within qualitative inquiry, however, phenomenology is primarily methodological and focused on seeking to understand the experiences of others. The objective of phenomenology as a research methodology is to obtain detailed descriptions of the lived experience of a particular phenomenon in order to identify the essence of that experience. "The aim is to determine what an experience means for the persons who have had the experience and are able to provide a comprehensive description of it. From the individual description general or universal meanings are derived, in other words the essences or structures of the experience" (Moustakas, 1994, p. 13).

There is not just one theoretical perspective among those who subscribe to phenomenology as a philosophy. Nor is there a single approach to practicing phenomenology as a methodology, as will be discussed in more detail below. However, a unifying thread among qualitative researchers who practice phenomenology is the focus on individual lived experience and meaning-making—what happened and what it means to those who had the experience. Another central characteristic is the emphasis on taking an open-minded stance—seeking to gain understanding by learning from firsthand experience and reflection (Munhall, 2012).

WHY CHOOSE PHENOMENOLOGY?

While phenomenology has its origins in philosophy, and has often been employed as a methodology in psychology, nursing, and education among other fields, this qualitative research approach holds great promise for peace and conflict studies research. There have been calls for wider application of phenomenology in the social sciences (e.g., Pollio, Henley, & Thompson, 1997), and it is easy to see why phenomenology holds benefits for those conducting research in conflict, conflict resolution, and peace-building. Phenomenology is an appropriate methodology to choose for topics where little research has been done and a deeper understanding is required. As a relatively young field, there remains so much to understand about various conflict experiences, about the experiences of those seeking to resolve conflict, and about peacebuilding efforts. In addition, experiences related to conflict and conflict resolution are particularly impactful and meaningful for those involved in them. Phenomenology is an ideal methodology for gaining knowledge about those experiences and what meaning they hold. It has been described as "a method sensitive enough to articulate the nuances of human experience and reflection" (Pollio, Henley, & Thompson, 1997, p. vii).

Phenomenology can also be beneficial when certain information has been determined through quantitative research methods, yet there is a lack of understanding of the meaning of those statistical findings. Speaking of his field of psychology, but making a point that applies more broadly to other fields as well, Giorgi (2009) noted,

> Most psychological researchers know how to use statistical procedures to determine the differences in results that are statistically significant. But such procedures do not determine the psychological meaning of the differences—only that what happened was most probably not due to chance. Phenomenologists, when they use the phenomenological reduction or the method of free imaginative variation, are using strategies that help precisely in clarifying the meaning of the results. (p. 65)

How do you know if phenomenology is the right methodology for your study? There are a few factors you can consider in deciding whether this is the right approach for your study. The focus on the lived experience of a particular phenomenon is the key factor. The names of qualitative methodologies often suggest their primary focus: case study is primarily focused on describing and explaining factors related to a particular case or set of cases; narrative research is primarily focused on exploring individuals' narratives; grounded theory research is primarily focused on development of theory; and so forth. Phenomenology, as the name suggests, is primarily focused on a particular phenomenon, or experience. If the primary focus of your study is on a particular case or social group, you might be better served to employ case study or ethnographic research. If you seek to develop theory or to conduct close analysis of individuals' narratives of their lives, grounded theory or narrative research might be the better way to go. But if you really want to gain a better understanding of what it is like to have a particular experience, then phenomenology is likely the best choice for your study. The range of potential experience is limitless in our field; for example, what is the experience of workplace bullying, or the experience of designing a community forum to address a local conflict related to an environmental issue, or the experience of participating in a war protest?

Another factor to consider is your research objective. Phenomenology is primarily descriptive, rather than explanatory. A phenomenological study is not designed to result in the development of theory, though there may be theoretical implications. Nor is it designed to develop a model or evaluate a program, though the results of a phenomenological study may inform the development of a model or revision of a program. What phenomenology can provide perhaps better than any other methodology, however, is a detailed, comprehensive description of experience. Moustakas (1994) notes that phenomenology is ideal for arriving at a description of experience which is "vivid," "accurate," "complete," and which illuminates and accentuates the meaning that experience holds. Phenomenology "provides a portrayal of the phenomenon that is vital, rich, and layered in its textures and meanings" (p. 59). Such rich description is not only valuable in terms of providing deeper understanding, but it also "awaken[s] further interest and concern" (p. 59), which is of vital importance to those conducting research in peace and conflict studies. For those seeking to bring greater awareness and understanding of particular conflict experiences that are missing from the research literature, phenomenology can provide the comprehensive description of those experiences from the perspective of participants that can be so valuable in laying the groundwork for further research or policy efforts. By recording the insider's account of a particular experience, and exploring the meaning people find in that experience, we can better understand the emic perspective on a phenomenon that can sometimes be lost in large-scale quantitative studies.

Finally, phenomenology may be the right fit for you if you have an interest in a reflexive approach to research. The nature of phenomenology as a methodology is that it relies upon the reflections of the participants and the reflections of the researcher in arriving at the research findings. The data collection and data analysis procedures employ a reflexive approach, and even the process of preparing for research known as bracketing, which is discussed below, requires reflexivity on the part of the researcher. This holds great appeal to some and is not appealing at all to others. If you enjoy and appreciate reflexivity and reflective practice, phenomenology may be a good fit for you.

Phenomenology has been used in conflict studies research to explore a wide range of issues and experiences related to different types of conflict. With its roots in philosophy and psychology, phenomenology is a highly effective methodology for researching intrapersonal conflict. For example, Davis (2002) explored the experience of gender role conflict for college men and how it impacted their identity construction. A study by Rubin and Wooten (2007) addressed the conflict experienced by highly educated stay-at-home mothers. Phenomenology also provides valuable knowledge regarding interpersonal and intergroup conflict. Examples of phenomenological research related to interpersonal conflict have included Kane's (2006) phenomenology of meditation for female survivors of intimate partner violence, and a study of the lived experience and meaning of filial therapy for victims of family violence (Kinsworthy & Garza, 2010). In terms of intergroup conflict, this methodology has been used to study the lived experience of Rwandan women who witnessed genocide and served as witnesses in the Gacaca courts (Funkeson, Shroder, Nzabonimpa, & Holmqvist 2011) and the lived experience of juvenile insurgents in Kashmir who experienced torture and incarceration (Rashid, 2012). Phenomenology is appropriate for researching various forms of social conflict, as well. For example, phenomenological studies have been conducted on the lived experience of racism within the LGBTQ community in Toronto (Giwa & Greensmith, 2012) and discrimination experienced by Asian women in Christian academia (Kim, Anderson, Hall, & Willingham, 2010). Studies such as that of Wisler (2010) on the lived experience of gaining "peace knowledge" in a higher education peace studies program, and Buldu's (2009) study of the perceptions of war of 5- to 8-year-olds and their teachers in the United Arab Emirates, also highlight the value of this methodology in peace education research. The potential for further phenomenological research in peace and conflict studies is vast.

THREE APPROACHES TO PHENOMENOLOGY

This section provides a brief discussion of three major approaches to phenomenology in qualitative inquiry, as well as some of the characteristics of each of those approaches. The approaches presented include transcendental phenomenology, existential phenomenology, and interpretative phenomenological analysis (IPA). This intent of this section is to provide merely an introduction to these approaches to phenomenology, and the section certainly does not offer a complete representation of all the various approaches to phenomenology that are available to researchers. Other approaches, such as empirical phenomenology and hermeneutic phenomenology, are not addressed specifically below. The decision not to discuss these additional approaches to phenomenology is based not only on space limitations, but also on the assessment that transcendental phenomenology incorporates aspects of the empirical approach while also expanding beyond it to provide a more comprehensive analysis, and that both existential phenomenology and IPA incorporate aspects of the hermeneutic model of phenomenology, thus providing some exposure to the hermeneutic approach. Some researchers may disagree with this assessment and selection; readers are encouraged to review the various models of phenomenology through primary sources and arrive at their own determinations regarding the distinctions and various applications of these differing models of phenomenology.

Transcendental Phenomenology

One of the most well-established and widely-employed approaches to phenomenology is transcendental phenomenology as described by Clark Moustakas, whom sadly we lost in 2012. In keeping with the focus of this research tradition, transcendental phenomenology is concerned with the lived experience of a particular phenomenon and with how that experience is understood in its meanings through essential insights. Thus, its focus is on the phenomenon and the perception, knowledge and meaning, or what Moustakas referred to as facts and essences. Transcendental phenomenology includes an emphasis on both textural and structural descriptions of an experience or phenomenon—which can be thought of as the "what" and the "how" of an experience. The textural description describes in rich detail the qualities of the experience, while the structural description describes "the underlying and precipitating factors that account for what is being experienced" (Moustakas, 1994, p. 98). The findings of a transcendental phenomenological study should answer the questions: What is the nature of the phenomenon or the experience of the phenomenon? And, "How did the experience of the phenomenon come to be what it is?" (p. 98).

The language of transcendental phenomenology is often unfamiliar to novice researchers and can be challenging at first. As an example of the unique jargon of transcendental phenomenology, preparation for the research process includes a process known as *bracketing*, which is meant to achieve *epoché*. Bracketing involves setting aside the biases and preconceived ideas of the researcher regarding the phenomenon under study through a reflective or even meditative process. Complete bracketing is associated with the achievement of "epoché," an attitude in which "no position whatever is taken" (Moustakas, 1994, p. 87). The process that results in the textural description is referred to as *phenomenological reduction*, which includes *horizonalization*. The process that results in the structural description is referred to as *imaginative variation*. The final process involved in transcendental phenomenological analysis is the *synthesis* of textural and structural descriptions "into a unified statement of the essences of the experience of the phenomenon as a whole" (p. 100). This terminology definitely takes some getting used to! But as with any professional jargon, once you understand what these terms mean, you will become more comfortable with how to practice the methodology, which is actually quite straightforward. These steps will be discussed in more detail below in the section on "Conducting Phenomenology."

Existential Phenomenology

Existential phenomenology combines the philosophical perspective of existentialism with the methodology of phenomenology. In keeping with its existential orientation, this approach to phenomenology focuses on human experiences in everyday life. Describing this focus of existential phenomenology, Pollio, Henley, and Thompson (1997) state,

> This interest does not view experience (or consciousness, in more technical terms) as a consequence of some internal set of events such as mind or brain but as a relationship between people and their world, whether the world at that moment consists of other people, nature, time, one's own body, personal or philosophical ideals, or whatever. What is sought by both existentialism and phenomenology is a rigorous description of human life as it is lived and reflected upon in all of its first-person concreteness, urgency, and ambiguity. For existential-phenomenology, the world is to be lived and described, not explained. (pp. 4–5)

This approach to phenomenology relies upon bracketing, as was true of transcendental phenomenology, but with some differences that are worth noting. This model emphasizes the importance of viewing bracketing not merely as an early, isolated step in the research process, but as an ongoing endeavor throughout the analysis process of attempting to note and correct misinterpretations of the data based on researcher preconceptions. In addition, this approach does not set a goal of achieving epoché. (Bracketing and epoché will be discussed further below.) Existential phenomenology as described in this model also draws upon hermeneutics in a purposeful way in the analysis process by employing the hermeneutic circle. This term refers to an analytic approach in which the researcher does not consider any portion of text in isolation but in relation to earlier and later portions of text within the same transcript, and in relation to the text of other transcripts.

The Pollio, Henley, and Thompson (1997) model moves through five overarching stages of the research process. In the first stage, the researcher is the focus. In this stage, the researcher selects her research topic and performs a bracketing interview or writes a personal statement on the research topic. In the second stage, the participants are the focus. The researcher chooses the sample and conducts phenomenological interviews. The text is the focus in the third stage, in which the interviews are transcribed and analyzed. This model also recommends using group analysis in this stage. The focus returns to the participants in the fourth stage, when the researcher shares her analysis with them as a means of strengthening the validity of her findings. In the final stage, the research community is the focus, as the researcher prepares her final report.

Interpretative Phenomenological Analysis

A more recent approach to phenomenology is known as interpretative phenomenological analysis, or IPA. Developed in the mid-1990s in Great Britain, IPA has gained widespread use throughout English-speaking regions over the past decade. This approach has its roots in psychology, as does transcendental phenomenology, but it has come to be seen as having broad applicability across the social, health, and human sciences. In keeping with phenomenology as a methodology, IPA focuses on lived experience and meaning. Whereas existential phenomenology emphasizes human experience in everyday life, IPA is especially focused on experiences perceived as having

> major significance to the person, who will then engage in a considerable amount of reflecting, thinking and feeling as they work through what it means.... When people are engaged with "an experience" of something major in their lives, they begin to reflect on the significance of what is happening and IPA research aims to engage with these reflections. (Smith, Flowers, & Larkin, 2009, p. 3)

Exploring students' experiences and understandings of their first course in peace studies, for example, would be a fitting topic for an IPA study.

IPA draws upon and links phenomenology, hermeneutics, and idiography. As the name indicates, IPA places special emphasis on the interpretative nature of the research process. This emphasis relates to the hermeneutic dimension of the method. Smith, Flowers, and Larkin (2009) note, "It can be said that the IPA researcher is engaged in a double hermeneutic because the researcher is trying to make sense of the participant trying to make sense of what is happening to them" (p. 3). The idea is that the thorough analysis undertaken by the researcher according to the systematic approach outlined in IPA may provide interpretation that the person who had the experience may not achieve on their own. The IPA approach to analysis differs from other forms of phenomenology in terms of process, though the overarching focus on lived experience and meaning is consistent with the methodology. These differences in analysis will be described briefly below.

As was true of existential phenomenology as described by Pollio, Henley, and Thompson (1997), IPA makes use of the hermeneutic circle, reflecting an iterative, nonlinear approach to the research process and data analysis. Regarding the idiographic thread of IPA, this approach to phenomenology places a stronger focus on individual experience than do some other approaches to phenomenology, which emphasize the shared experience of a particular phenomenon. In fact, IPA advocates for the "importance of the single case study" even within a phenomenological approach. This appreciation of the individual experience and idiographic approach is reflected in the fact that IPA studies generally include a smaller sample size than do other phenomenological models.

Summary of Approaches to Phenomenology

As the brief descriptions above of these three approaches to phenomenology indicate, there are various philosophical and procedural differences associated with different models of phenomenology in qualitative research. How you choose which model to use in your study may be determined by one or a combination of several factors. Perhaps the philosophical orientation of one approach or another resonates with your own theoretical perspective. Perhaps you like the procedural steps of one method more than another. Perhaps you find one text easier to understand and follow than another. If your research objective is to identify the structures and essences of a particular shared conflict experience, you would choose transcendental phenomenology. If your focus is on conflict experiences that are interwoven in everyday life, you might choose existential phenomenology. If you wish to focus on just a few individuals and take a more idiographic approach, without seeking to identify the essence of a phenomenon, IPA might be an appropriate choice for your study.

In spite of their differences, the common thread that runs through all true phenomenological methods is a focus on generating in-depth description of experience for the purpose of arriving at deeper understanding of what it is like to have particular experiences and what those experiences mean for the people who have them. Another shared attribute of these approaches is a clear structure to the method. This aspect of phenomenology can be quite helpful to novice researchers. The overall research process, and the data analysis procedures in particular, are clearly outlined in these approaches to phenomenology, which provides support to the researcher. The next section will explore these procedures in a bit more detail.

CONDUCTING PHENOMENOLOGICAL RESEARCH

Having reviewed what phenomenology is and when you might choose this methodology for your research in peace and conflict studies, and having briefly considered a few approaches to phenomenology, the chapter now turns to a closer look at the steps involved in conducting phenomenological research, from the selection of research questions and study sample, to data collection, data analysis, and reporting of findings. Each of these elements of a qualitative research study will be considered from the perspective of phenomenology. To illustrate each of these steps of the research process, I will refer to a phenomenological study I conducted in 2009 of the experience of non-Hispanic White community members in Broward County, Florida, who experienced the county's transition to majority-minority status. In light of the focus on everyday life, as well as my own theoretical orientation, I selected existential phenomenology as the approach I followed in this study, though I also drew upon elements of transcendental phenomenology.

Research Questions

Research questions in a phenomenological study highlight the research objectives of phenomenology—namely, to understand the lived experience of a particular phenomenon and what meaning that experience holds. As a result, you will generally see these key terms—*lived experience* and *meaning*—embedded in a phenomenological study's overarching research questions. You may also see the term *essence* in a phenomenological study's research questions, particularly if the researcher is following transcendental phenomenology. For example, in my research related to ethnic change in Broward County, Florida, the study's three guiding research questions were: How is the transition to a "majority-minority" community experienced by non-Hispanic White Americans? What impact, if any, does social change related to demographic shifts have on the meaning of national belonging for these community members? How does the transition to majority-minority status affect the experience of social conflict for non-Hispanic White community members?

Sample

Sometimes the participants in a phenomenological study are referred to as *co-researchers*. This reflects the central role that each interviewee plays in reflecting upon their experience and actively sharing in the exploration of a particular phenomenon. In this chapter, I use the term *participant*, a term which also acknowledges the active role of those in the study sample in the research process. The sample size in a phenomenological study tends to be relatively small. Creswell (2013) describes it as ranging from 3–15 people, though it can be more depending upon the specific research objectives of a study. Regardless of the specific number of participants, the relatively small sample size is related to the inclusion criteria in phenomenology, which stipulates that every participant must have experienced the phenomenon under study. As a result, all participants are able to generate relevant data, contributing to the researcher reaching data saturation following a smaller number of interviews than might be true in other types of qualitative studies. In selecting participants who have had a particular experience, the researcher conducts purposive sampling.

As the focus in phenomenology is on the common experience all study participants have had, apart from that unifying characteristic, the sample may be quite heterogeneous. One caution is to be thoughtful about your ability as a researcher to understand and interpret the meanings experiences hold for people quite culturally different from yourself. Derrida, father of deconstruction, argued "that phenomenological imagination is never rich enough to reconstruct the intellectual lives of people of radically different cultures" (Moran, 2000, p. 446).

In order to be sure that participants would be able to describe their experience of the social change I was exploring in this study, I chose participants who had lived in Broward County for 10 years or longer. Participants ranged in age from 20–89. In order to be able to compare and contrast the experiences and perspectives of people of different ages, I selected participants who fell into three general age categories: Young Adults, made up of individuals in their 20s and 30s; Middle Aged, including people in their 40s or 50s; and Senior Citizens, made up of individuals aged 60 and older. The sample for the study included eight participants in the Young Adult category, eight participants in the Middle Age category, and seven Senior Citizens. In terms of gender, the sample included 13 women and 10 men, which also allowed for gender analysis of the data. Participants resided in seventeen different cities within the county.

Bracketing and Epoche

Bracketing is conceived of in the phenomenological tradition as setting aside the biases and preconceived ideas of the researcher regarding the phenomenon under study through a reflective or even meditative process. As mentioned above, complete bracketing is associated with the achievement of "epoché." "Epoché is a Greek word meaning to refrain from judgment, to abstain from or stay away from the everyday, ordinary way of perceiving things" (Moustakas, 1994, p. 33). Epoché is sometimes considered a separate step; in this view it may take place prior to data analysis or as part of phenomenological reduction (Giorgi, 2009). Many researchers feel that epoché is not a realistic goal. Even Moustakas, who emphasized the importance of this aspect of phenomenological research, acknowledged that epoché is elusive. At the same time, he suggested,

> approached with dedication and determination, the process can make a difference in what and how we see, hear, and/or view things. Practiced wisely, realistically, and with determination to let go of our prejudices, I believe that the actual nature and essence of things will be disclosed more fully, will reveal themselves to us and enable us to find a clearing and light to knowledge and truth. (p. 90)

Recognizing the challenges and limits of bracketing, Pollio, Henley and Thompson (1997) suggest that the researcher either write a personal statement (which I refer to as a bracketing statement) or take part in a bracketing interview. The former approach involves writing a reflexive statement about the researcher's experience related to the phenomenon under study, as well as his attitudes and beliefs about the phenomenon. (Over the past few years, I have introduced the use of collage in conjunction with the personal statement as a technique to aid bracketing.) With the latter approach, the researcher actually becomes the first person to be interviewed for the study.

> In both cases, the intention is not to have interviewers become objective— only to have them become more attuned to their presuppositions about the nature and meaning of the present phenomenon and thereby sensitize them to any potential demands they may impose on their co-participants either during the interview or in its subsequent interpretation. (Pollio, Henley, & Thompson, 1997, p. 49)

In my study of identity-based conflict in Broward County, I conducted bracketing by writing a bracketing statement prior to conducting the phenomenological interviews with my participants and felt this was an important phase of the research process because it raised my awareness of my own perceptions and emotions related to the research topic.

Data Collection

Data collection in phenomenology typically takes place by means of individual phenomenological interviews with the participants. Some studies include other sources of data, such as various art forms pertaining to the phenomenon, but the primary source of data is the phenomenological interview. As Pollio et al. (1997) note, "What we experience is also never separate from the culture or language in which we live, talk, and act. Our actions—linguistic, conceptual, and otherwise—take on meaning only within some sociolinguistic framework" (p. 8). As a result, the discourse used in interviews provides critical information about lived experiences and meaning-making. The questions participants are asked in a phenomenological interview explore the meaning of the phenomenon they are experiencing; participants are also asked to describe their everyday lived experiences related to that phenomenon. The opening question in a phenomenological interview is designed to be open-ended but related to the experience under investigation. Alternatively, interviews may begin with a statement, in which the researcher requests that participants describe a particular type of situation they have experienced (e.g., Graves, 2006). In keeping with the qualitative research tradition, the researcher's questions and statements have the purpose of eliciting descriptions rather than seeking to confirm a preexisting hypothesis. Pollio et al. recommend that researchers avoid "why" questions in phenomenological interviewing because they "often shift the dialogue away from describing an experience to a more abstract, theoretical discussion" (p. 30).

In the study in Broward County, I began each interview with a few questions designed to establish a degree of comfort between myself and the participant. For example, I began by asking the person how long he or she has lived in Broward County and what city he or she lives in. I then asked the participant what changes he or she had seen take place in Broward County during the time he or she had lived in the county. I then moved on to questions linked to my research questions. For example, "How would you characterize the ethnic make-up of your neighborhood?" And "Have you experienced any conflicts related to the changes taking place in the county? If so, would you describe an experience you have had along these lines?"

Follow-up questions in a phenomenological interview flow from the participants' responses. Moustakas (1994) suggested a few general follow-up questions that can elicit descriptive replies. These include the following questions: "How did the experience affect you? What changes do you associate with the experience?" "What feelings were generated by the experience?" and "Have you shared all that is significant with reference to the experience?" (p. 116).

DATA ANALYSIS

Data analysis in phenomenology requires becoming "intimate" with the data (Marshall & Rossman, 2011, p. 210). As Pollio et al. (1997) observe,

> The transformation that leads from protocols to themes ... involves an insight-like process that comes from a complete immersion with both the original interview in the form of dialogue and in its subsequent written form as protocol. (p. 52)

This means listening to recorded interviews and reading interview transcripts repeatedly. IPA data analysis includes the following characteristics: (a) movement from what is unique to a participant to what is shared among the participants, (b) description of the experience which moves to an interpretation of the experience, (c) commitment to understanding the participant's point of view, and (d) psychological focus on personal meaning-making within a particular context (Smith et al., 2009). This description can be applied to phenomenological data analysis more generally, as well. The specific steps of data analysis differ among the three models reviewed in this chapter; an outline of the data analysis procedures for each approach is presented below, but readers are urged to refer to primary sources for fuller descriptions of these procedures. A few phases of the phenomenological data analysis process can be described in general terms.

The initial stage of data analysis, first cycle coding as practiced in phenomenology, is reading the transcript for relevant data—words and phrases that say something about the nature of the experience under study. Moustakas (1994) called these *horizons*, and so this process is also referred to as *horizonalization*. These excerpts of text, meaning units, can be coded to capture the lived experience and meaning of the phenomenon. In IPA, this phase is referred to as *initial noting*, in which the researcher notes descriptive comments, linguistic comments, and conceptual comments regarding relevant data in the transcripts (Smith et al., 2009).

In the study of social change and ethnic conflict in Broward County, following horizonalization, I coded the horizons as an aid to analysis. I selected two coding methods to capture the lived experience and two methods to capture the meaning participants found in that experience. To identify the lived experience of the social change under study, I used descriptive coding and versus coding. Versus coding highlighted how participants' everyday life compared under the current demographics of the county versus the time period before it became a majority-minority county. To grasp participants' understanding of this social change and the meaning they find in it, I applied emotion coding and culture/values coding. This latter coding method is an adaptation of values coding as described by Saldaña (2009). This adaptation better suited the horizons, or meaning units, included in the interview protocols because comments related to values typically pertained to cultural issues in this study.

The next step of data analysis in phenomenology is moving from the initial round of horizonalization or noting toward the development of broader themes and fuller descriptions of experience. In any phenomenological study, the researcher would be expected to arrive at a detailed, rich description of the experience under study for each participant and across the sample collectively. In transcendental phenomenology, this is referred to as organizing horizons into thematic clusters, leading to the writing of a textural description. In existential phenomenology as outlined by Pollio et al. (1997) this is discussed as identifying thematic and descriptive patterns. According to this model, the researcher is aided in the analysis process by conducting at least some of the analysis in a group setting, so that the group can serve to raise questions and highlight alternate perspectives (Pollio et al., 1997). In IPA, this stage of analysis involves the development of emergent themes and identification of recurrent themes. The identification of these themes takes place through use of the hermeneutic circle.

In traditional phenomenology, the research process continues beyond the textural description to the development of a structural description. In transcendental phenomenology, the structural description depicts how the phenomenon is experienced, "the underlying and precipitating factors that account for what is being experienced" (Moustakas, 1994, p. 98). The structural description is developed through imaginative variation, a reflective and interpretive process. Pollio et al. (1997) refer to developing a "specific thematic structure, describing experiential patterns and interrelationships among themes" (p. 52). This stage relies upon an interpretive process that incorporates both insight and staying close to the words of the participants.

In transcendental phenomenology, the final stage of analysis involves the researcher integrating the textural and structural descriptions to arrive at a synthesis of description and meaning—"a unified statement of the essences of the experience of the phenomenon as a whole" (Moustakas, 1994, p. 100). Pollio et al. (1997) differ from Moustakas in that they do not attempt to identify a single essence to an experience. Their focus is on identifying a thematic structure that is both "plausible" and "illuminating" (p. 55). The structural description or thematic structure can be presented in both narrative and graphic formats. IPA does not lead to a structural description or statement of the essential aspects of a phenomenon.

Outline of Phenomenological Data Analysis Procedures

Transcendental Phenomenology

- Bracketing
- Horizonalization
- Clustering Horizons into Themes
- Individual and Composite Textural Description
- Imaginative Variation
- Individual and Composite Structural Description
- Synthesis of meanings and essences of phenomenon or experience

Existential Phenomenology

- Bracketing statement or interview
- Reading for meaning units
- Employing hermeneutic circle
- Individual and group analysis leading to identifying descriptive and thematic patterns
- Development of thematic structure, describing experiential patterns and thematic interrelationships

Interpretative Phenomenological Analysis

- Reading and Re-reading
- Initial Noting, including Descriptive, Linguistic, and Conceptual Comments
- Developing Emerging Themes
- Searching for Connections Across Emergent Themes
- Moving to the Next Case
- Looking for Patterns Across Cases

REPORTING PHENOMENOLOGICAL RESEARCH FINDINGS

In keeping with the emphasis on description in phenomenology, a research report presenting the findings a phenomenological study would be expected to provide a detailed and comprehensive description of the experience under study. In addition, this description would be expected to include verbatim quotes from participants as a support to the trustworthiness of the description. While individual participants will be quoted, the focus in reporting on a phenomenological study is not on the individual per se but on the common elements making up the experience of a particular phenomenon. As a result, the report can be organized thematically by essential aspects of the experience rather than organized by participant. The objective of phenomenology is to describe the shared aspects of an experience so the description can be presented collectively, or as Moustakas would say, as a "composite." If using transcendental phenomenology, be sure to highlight the essence(s) of the phenomenon. And if following a model that includes a structural description or thematic structure, this may be depicted in the form of a graphic to illustrate the factors contributing to the structure of the experience. As an example, I provide below the graphic (Figure 4.1) developed to portray findings of my phenomenological study of the transition to a majority-minority community in Broward County, Florida.

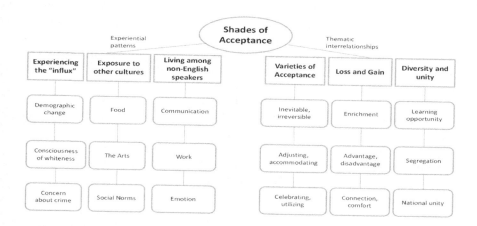

Figure 4.1.   Thematic structure of transition to majority-minority community.

In the study referenced in this chapter, the overarching theme I identified is what I termed "shades of acceptance." This phrase indicated that all of the participants expressed a sense of acceptance about the transition to a majority-minority county; however, within that sense of acceptance there was significant variability. Participants conveyed different degrees of acceptance, and even, within individuals, different levels of acceptance depending on the issue, such as exposure to cultural events (which was viewed very positively) or communicating with non-English speakers (which evoked negative emotions). The word "shades" suggests variation, a range from darker to lighter, which in this case corresponded to the range of attitudes from less to more positive response toward the social change underway in Broward County.

Participants in the study repeatedly referred to the demographic change in the county as "the influx" and experienced this social change in their everyday lives in terms of more diverse neighborhoods and workplaces, increasing cross-cultural encounters involving foods and arts from various nations and cultures, a growing number of interactions with non-English speakers, and a raised consciousness of Whiteness. While these aspects of lived experience were consistent across the study sample, there were some differences that could be noted among the three age groups. The young adults appeared to be the most comfortable with the increasing ethnic diversity of the community and explicitly stated that they miss the diversity of South Florida when they are in other parts of the country. All of the young adult participants spoke of having a diverse group of friends. At the same time, while the young adults all indicated that they supported other ethnic groups' identity claims, some of them were concerned that they were perceived as lacking ethnicity or felt some resentment about being stereotyped based on their Whiteness. This age group also felt the most directly threatened by this social change in terms of their employment prospects. This concern was related less to ethnic difference than to the growing demand for bilingual employees in South Florida.

While the participants of all ages had seen the ethnic makeup of their neighborhoods change around them, the middle aged participants experienced the greatest change in their work environments. This change was experienced by the women as a loss of personal connections with their co-workers; the men perceived themselves to be at a disadvantage as compared to their Hispanic colleagues. Both men and women had found it challenging to adjust to a multilingual working environment, but the middle aged participants expressed an appreciation for the cultural enrichment that they perceived as coming with a more diverse community. They spoke of enjoying new cultural experiences and of willingly adjusting to the new social realities of a majority-minority county.

The senior citizens had seen the greatest social change over the course of their lifetimes, but they were the least directly affected by the transition to a majority-minority county. Even for the participants in this age group, however, everyday experiences at the grocery store or in their apartment buildings included exposure to other cultures' foods and interactions with people who didn't speak English. These participants seemed to feel the most negatively about the growing presence of non-English speakers in the county. While the senior citizens in this study may not have desired a more diverse community, they accepted this demographic change as inevitable and irreversible both locally and nationally.

Participants indicated they were struggling to reconcile respect for diversity with a desire for a unifying national culture. The men tended to express a greater concern regarding cultural change; they seemed to feel more strongly about wanting immigrants to assimilate so that their sense of national culture did not undergo a significant or rapid change. The women tended to be more concerned about separation between ethnic groups and expressed a desire for social cohesion. Participants of all age groups indicated some internal conflict regarding the impact of increasing diversity on their sense of national identity, though the women were more apt to express angst regarding prejudiced thoughts or feelings they sometimes had.

As this brief summary of key themes indicates, results in a phenomenological study are presented collectively, rather than participant by participant. This is due to the methodological objective of identifying the common experiences and shared meanings found in a particular social phenomenon. In this case, the report of findings included comparative analysis by age and gender, as that was an objective of the study from the outset. In a full research report, quotes from participants would be included to serve as exemplars of the various findings; such quotes are not included here due to space limitations.

ISSUES OF CREDIBILITY IN PHENOMENOLOGICAL RESEARCH

In support of the credibility of phenomenological research findings, it is a good idea to maintain a clear audit trail of the data analysis process throughout the course of the study (Lincoln & Guba, 1985). This audit trail may consist of the researcher's bracketing statement, the recorded interviews, the interview transcripts in which horizons were initially identified, the documents in which the horizons were coded according to type of horizon and grouped into thematic clusters, any analytic memos, and the textural descriptions written for each participant. All of these elements of the audit trail shed light on the path leading to the thematic structural description, which conveys the essential aspects of the lived experience and meaning of the phenomenon under study.

Another technique often utilized to strengthen the credibility of qualitative reports is that of triangulation. Flick (2007) points out that there are different types of triangulation. In phenomenology, one may not employ triangulation of methods of data collection, but there are other types of triangulation that can be considered. For example, triangulation of data sources; while all participants will necessarily have experienced the phenomenon being investigated, they may reflect diversity in terms of age, gender, and location. In addition, a phenomenologist can employ triangulation of analytical lenses by using different coding methods to highlight relevant information pertaining to lived experience and meaning. This form of triangulation is built into IPA through the use of descriptive, linguistic, and conceptual comments, but other approaches of phenomenology can likewise utilize descriptive, emotion, and values coding, among other methods.

Member checking is another technique that enhances the credibility of a researcher's findings in a phenomenological study. The researcher may review the research findings with study participants to assess the accuracy of the interpretation of the data. Researchers can also conduct peer debriefing. The model of existential phenomenology presented in the chapter builds this technique into the analysis process by employing at least some group analysis. If the researcher does not follow this approach, he or she may ask colleagues to review the study audit trail and read the report to see if they find the methodology to be sound and the findings to be supported by the data.

LIMITATIONS AND CONCLUSIONS

Researcher bias plays a role in any study; in phenomenology, where the researcher is the primary research instrument, the unique personal history and circumstances of the researcher inevitably influence his analysis of the data. However, the built-in process within phenomenology of bracketing does support researchers in becoming sensitized to their preconceptions. Researchers conducting phenomenology may want to employ member checking and peer debriefing as a check against this limitation. Another limitation in phenomenological studies pertains to the study sample. The sample is typically small in number; as a result, the findings are not broadly generalizable. The sample is also generally selected through a purposive, snowballing sampling strategy, and thus the experiences and understandings of the study participants cannot be assumed to represent all people who have had the experience under study.

Phenomenological studies are not designed with an explanatory purpose and typically do not result in the development of new theory.

In spite of these limitations, phenomenology is a valuable methodology for those seeking to provide a detailed, comprehensive description of a particular experience. For those seeking to understand how a particular experience related to conflict, peacebuilding, or peace education is experienced, and what meaning that experience holds for those affected by it, phenomenology provides the tools to conduct a deep exploration of such perceptions and experiences.

REFERENCES

Buldu, M. (2009). Five- to 8-year-old Emirati children's and their teachers' perceptions of war. *Journal of Research in Childhood Education, 23*(4), 461–474.

Creswell, J. W. (2013). *Qualitative inquiry and research design: Choosing among the five approaches*. Thousand Oaks, CA: Sage.

Davis, T. L. (2002). Voices of gender role conflict: The social construction of college men's identity. *Journal of College Student Development, 43*(4), 508–521.

Flick, U. (2007). *Designing qualitative research*. London, England: Sage.

Funkeson, U., Shroder, E., Nzabonimpa, J., & Holmqvist, R. (2011). Witnesses to genocide: Experiences of witnessing in the Rwandan Gacaca Courts. *Peace and Conflict, 17*, 367–388.

Giorgi, A. (2009). *The descriptive phenomenological method in psychology: A modified Husserlian approach*. Pittsburgh, PA: Duquesne University Press.

Giwa, S. & Greensmith, C. (2012). Race relations and racism in the LGBTQ community of Toronto: Perceptions of Gay and Queer social service providers of color. *Journal of Homosexuality, 59*(2), 149–185.

Graves, T. R. (2006). The thematic meaning of face-to-face conflict experiences: A hermeneutic phenomenological investigation (Doctoral dissertation). University of Tennessee, Knoxville.

Kane, K. E. (2006). The phenomenology of meditation for female survivors of intimate partner violence. *Violence Against Women, 12*(5), 501–518.

Kim, C. L., Anderson, T. L., Hall, E. L., & Willingham, M. M. (2010). Asian and female in the white God's world: A qualitative exploration of discrimination in Christian academia. *Mental Health, Religion & Culture, 13*(5), 453–465.

Kinsworthy, S. & Garza, Y. (2010). Filial therapy with victims of family violence: A phenomenological study. *Journal of Family Violence, 25*, 423–429.

Lincoln, Y., & Guba, E. (1985). *Naturalistic inquiry*. Newbury Park, CA: Sage.

Marshall, C., & Rossman, G. B. (Eds.). (2011). *Designing qualitative research* (5th ed.). Thousand Oaks, CA: Sage.

Moran, D. (2000). *Introduction to phenomenology*. New York, NY: Routledge.

Moustakas, C. (1994). *Phenomenological research methods*. Thousand Oaks, CA: Sage.

Munhall, P. L. (2012). A phenomenological method. In P. L. Munhall (Ed.), *Nursing research: A qualitative perspective* (5th ed., pp. 113–175). Boston, MA: Jones and Bartlett Press.

Pollio, H. R., Henley, T. B., & Thompson, C.J. (1997). *The phenomenology of everyday life*. Cambridge: Cambridge University Press.

Rashid, J. (2012). An analysis of self-accounts of children-in-conflict-with-law in Kashmir concerning the impact of torture and detention on their lives. *International Social Work, 55*(5), 629–644.

Rubin, S. E., & Wooten, H. R. (2007). Highly educated stay-at-home mothers: A study of commitment and conflict. *Family Journal, 15*(4), 336–345.

Saldaña, J. (2009). *The coding manual for qualitative researchers.* London, England: Sage.

Smith, J. A., Flowers, P., & Larkin, M. (2009). *Interpretative phenomenological analysis: Theory, method, and research.* London, England: Sage.

Wisler, A. K. (2010). Portraits of peace knowledge in post-Yugoslav higher education. *Journal of Peace Education, 7*(1), 15–31.

CHAPTER 5

PAINTING THE WHOLE PICTURE

Qualitative Case Study in Conflict Resolution

Ismael Muvingi and Cheryl Lynn Duckworth

INTRODUCTION

This chapter introduces the reader to the case study methodology in qualitative research in the field of conflict resolution. A definition of case study and of "case" is presented, followed by a discussion of why and when it would be desirable to use case study methodology when researching conflicts. The designing of case studies is then introduced as is the doing of case study with examples of conflict resolution case studies in order to help guide the reader. The chapter is not and cannot be a comprehensive treatment of the case study methodology and thus the reader is referred to more detailed guide texts on each aspect of case study with the chapter acting as an introduction to the broad view of the methodology as it pertains to conflict analysis and resolution.

Peace and Conflict Studies Research: A Qualitative Perspective, pp. 91–110
Copyright © 2014 by Information Age Publishing
All rights of reproduction in any form reserved.

WHAT IS CASE STUDY METHODOLOGY?

Case studies are widely used in social science studies, and Stake (2000) suggests that case studies have become "one of the most common ways to do qualitative inquiry" (p. 435). Yet "case" is not that well defined (Ragin, 1992). Loose usage of the term has led sometimes to case study being applied to everything that is qualitative research, leading to much confusion. Part of the confusion stems from the overlap in term usage with other methods and methodologies such as fieldwork, ethnography, participant observation, grounded theory, qualitative research and life history. When loosely stated, every study can qualify as a case because we do bound our studies of phenomenon both in space and time so as to make them manageable. The confusion is worsened by the use of cases illustrative of other methodologies also being referred to as "case studies." There is need therefore to explore, what is meant by case study research.

In quantitative study, the parameters of "case" are defined quite clearly prior to beginning data collection and those parameters guide the research. In qualitative study on the other hand, the nature and definition of "the case" cannot be closed prior to the research and tends to continue emerging through the research. This is especially so with methods that emphasize participant involvement in which the meanings of the subjects are elicited and may include the setting of case boundaries. The incorporation of the subjects' understanding of their own belonging, participation, categories and norms may thus shift the definition of the case. This elective, participatory nature of research design, data collection and analysis is of course central to the ontology and epistemology of qualitative research (Creswell, 2013). Because of the need to seek participant (conflict party) narratives and perspectives in order to understand and intervene in a conflict, this flexibility makes case study an especially useful tool for conflict research. Ragin (1992) posits in fact that the question "what is a case?" remains open and maybe should remain open because the qualitative methodological approach implies tentative conclusions, meaning that even at the conclusion of a particular research project, the "case" definition may still remain open. For Ragin the question in any research should rather be "What is this a case of?" (Ragin, 1992). This however, may be conflating methodology with substance. Other case study scholars have set out fairly clear guidelines on the definition and process of case study.

As with Creswell (2013) and Yin (2009), we approach case study as both a methodology or a research strategy and a product of inquiry, that is, choice of what is to be studied. We adopt Creswell's definition of case study as an approach through which " the investigator explores a real-life, contemporary bounded system (a case) or multiple bounded systems (cases) over time, through detailed, in-depth data collection involving multiple sources of information (e.g. observations, interviews, audiovisual material, and documents and reports), and reports a case description and case themes" (Cresswell, 2013, p. 97). Yin approaches a case study as a methodology (type of design) and not simply a choice of what is to be studied and sets out fairly clear guidelines on how to define a case and conduct a case study so we reference his work to a substantial degree.

Conflict resolution research can be conducted using either quantitative or qualitative research methodologies and cases can be either or both. Yin (2009) includes both quantitative and qualitative approaches under case study, while Stake (1995) stays within the qualitative arena. The distinction is significant because in quantitative analysis we are concerned with comparison and repetition and thus the greater the number of "cases," the more reliable the results and conclusions. In qualitative research the approach is primarily constructivist in epistemology. While there is acknowledgment of the existence of an objective, real world, truth is perceived as more fluid and based on the creation of meaning by humans that have agency. Because reality is perceived as socially constructed, there is greater recognition of the subject and the researcher as cocontributors to knowledge creation. The search thus becomes primarily one of understanding and there is an acceptance of a plurality of truth perceptions. If, then, the subject is a participant in knowledge creation, the definition of the case remains more fluid than in a more positivist or objectivist approach. Again, this is one feature of especially qualitative (or mix-methods) case studies that enable them to allow the research process itself to be a form of intervention into the conflict. Through exploration and analysis of the conflict in which parties find themselves, with the partnership and methodological expertise of the researcher, parties can come to better understand themselves, their opponents, their context and hence possibly find resolutions to their conflict which had not previously been obvious or seen as possible.

Because of this fluid and interpretivist understanding of truth, qualitative methods are messier for being open-ended but as Baxter and Jack (2008), as well as Creswell (2013) assert, case study research is a rigorous qualitative methodology that enables the researcher to explore phenomenon in context through the use of a multiplicity of data sources. Case is viewed in two senses, as unit of analysis and as study focus. The study of conflicts over access to water on the island of Bali is an illustrative example (Cole, 2012). In the study Bali was the geographical and socially bounded case of study as well as was the issue of competition for water between tourism and local populations which led to the social and economic conflicts in Bali (Cole, 2012). A proposition guiding the research was that water distribution in Bali was inequitable and unsustainable. Using a case study approach, the researcher explored the whole range of factors including social and political dynamics, tourism's ability to outcompete local needs for water and the resultant social conflicts and environmental problems. The case study approach allowed the researcher to include investigation of the whole panoply of factors that related to water issues in Bali including the context in which the case took place.

Case study research shares many characteristics with other research methods, but it has its own distinctive features. It is able to cope with the multiplicity of factors relating to the distinctive phenomenon that constitutes the case in large measure because the case is the focus and all factors that impinge on the case can and should be included. As such, case study relies on many sources of data and can incorporate both quantitative and qualitative data. For example, in the Paraguay land conflicts between indigenous peoples, government and the agricultural industry actors, the qualitative inquiry would explore and reveal the factors that give rise to the conflicts (Duckworth, 2011). Such factors may include the different conceptualizations or meanings of land and the resources that attach to it, the issues of language, conceptualizations of exploitation of resources and the power dynamics that relate to the positions of each of the parties to the conflict. This requires in depth study that can reveal the meanings and understandings of the parties, which qualitative methods are best suited to. However, there are also quantitative elements to the conflicts such as population densities and distributions, availability or possibilities of alternative income, and the earnings and distribution of earnings from resource extraction, to name a few. All the factors are relevant to the conflicts and their possible resolution and the factors need to be analyzed in convergence for effective resolution options. Thus case study can utilize mixed methods, making for richer explanation, understanding and interventions.

It is not unusual for both ethnography and case study to be used in unison. A researcher may choose a topic and identify a target population of study, but thereafter, the boundaries and characteristics of the study group emerge and/or get refined inductively through joint production by the researcher and the subjects. Harper's (1992) illustration of the fluidity and varying definitions of the "homeless" is a good example. Contrary to prevailing signification of the subjects as "homeless" Harper found that the homeless defined themselves differently as "tramps," and had their own categories of internal identity, norms and values which defied the external homogenization of "homeless." Initial perceptions of homeless as defined by bounded spatial location gave way to the homeless as a physically, mentally and socially mobile community with varying social norms applicable at different points and locations. From the tramps perspective therefore, "case" assumed very different connotations than the external world imposed on the tramps. Parameters of dress, work habits, movement, and etiquette all contributed to a much more nuanced definition of boundedness which redefined the researcher's original notion that the "boundaries" of the case would be geographical. Instead, they were cultural and based in shared identity. What emerged then was a layered experience of case(s). Thus within ethnography, cases can be defined by spatial location, through imagined social ties based on moral, political, cultural integration or combinations thereof, by topic of research, institutions or structures such as occupation or work places, and now increasingly virtual communities. Notably, the participants themselves in this study reshaped how the case itself was defined. This again exemplifies one of the great utilities of case study for conflict research, which is the ability for the research to be driven and shaped by the perspectives of the research participants (conflict parties) themselves. Once again, research here can be a form of intervention/resolution.

The most distinctive feature of case study, which sets it apart from ethnography and grounded theory, is its requirement for prior development of theoretical propositions (Yin, 2009). The structuredness of the propositions varies from case to case, but it is the propositions that help guide data collection and analysis. We will return to the role of propositions below.

WHY QUALITATIVE CASE STUDY?

Qualitative research is the generic term for methodologies that emphasize investigation of phenomenon in the natural setting in which they are found. Qualitative research entails detailed data gathering and inquiry that seeks to allow and incorporate the views of the subjects. The researcher is not removed from the research and becomes a cocreator of knowledge in collaboration with the subjects (Jacob, 1988). This differs from quantitative research which attempts to gather data by objective methods and insists on detaching the investigator from the creation of the knowledge. Qualitative case study falls within this ambit.

According to Yin (2009), one should consider using case study when (a) the focus of the study is to answer "how" and "why" questions; (b) when the data or subjects cannot be manipulated or controlled; (c) when context is important; and (d) when the boundaries between phenomenon and context are not clear. Case study research is therefore suitable for investigating complex social phenomena such as conflicts and the efforts to resolve them. Conflicts take place in the real world in which the researcher has little to no control over the behaviors of parties to the conflict, and where invariably numerable and contested factors are involved. The field of conflict analysis and resolution is concerned with understanding the causes of conflicts and their processes so as to find appropriate ways of resolving them. Why and how are thus questions that are core to the field, but to these two would have to be added a search as well for the disputed narratives regarding "what" happened in a particular conflict. Case studies can therefore be used to describe, interpret or evaluate. Focusing the study on a specific conflict or aspects of conflict, the researcher can investigate a conflict experience, an individual actor, a community, a decision making process or an institution. The researcher can discover interactions between numerous and different but significant factors, which other types of research neglect or may be incapable of incorporating.

CASE STUDY TYPES

The nature of the case study varies. Yin (2009) has three categories of cases: descriptive, exploratory and explanatory, while Stake's (1995, 2000) categories are intrinsic, instrumental and collective. In addition, Yin also argues that case studies have a special place in evaluative research. Baxter and Jack (2008) provide very succinct synopses of each case type. Examples of each of Yin's categories are given below.

Descriptive case studies provide detailed accounts of phenomenon. They are useful in presenting basic information and often form a database for future comparison and theory building. Kim's case study of the United States covert war in Chile was aimed at presenting information that revealed contradictions between the thesis of democratic peace and the reality of US covert actions against democracy in Chile (Kim, 2005). Using multiple sources of data such as documents, reports, archives and interviews and focusing on the issue of U.S. involvement in Chile, the researcher revealed a sustained and concerted effort by U.S. policymakers to subvert the democratic process in Chile by funding groups opposed to socialist candidates and eventually orchestrating the assassination of Chilean president Salvador Allende. The case also challenged the theory of democratic peace (that democracies do not go to war against each other) by revealing that violent conflicts can be prosecuted through other means than open warfare. In this sense, the case study was revelatory but also explanatory. Description can be followed by interpretation wherein the thick and rich descriptions can be used to develop typologies or to illustrate, support or challenge preexisting theoretical assumptions. The level of abstraction and conceptualization in such case studies will vary but the preference is for inductive analysis.

The exploratory case study is one where an intervention or a number of interventions have no clear or single set of outcomes. This overlaps considerably with the descriptive case study and evaluative studies and is exemplified again by the Kim (2005) study. Another recent exploratory case study focused on peacebuilding in Rwanda (Sentama, 2009). Sentama focused on the role that local cooperatives played in the restoration of interpersonal relationships postgenocide. Noting that, "there is little knowledge with regard to the bottom-up approach to peacebuilding, notably when it comes to the mechanisms or methods to be used in order to overcome the painful past between conflicting parties" (p. 3), Sentama's dissertation was an exploration via case study of who these local cooperative organizations were and what role they seemed to be able to play in the arduous process of reweaving the social fabric after one of history's worst genocides. He considered the two following research questions: "1. What is the impact of a cooperative on conflicting parties' relationships, and how does it have that impact? 2. Which factors explain the impact of a cooperative on conflicting parties' relationships, and how do those factors explain that impact?" Because much more remains known about "grass-tops" peace building, as opposed to "grassroots" peacebuilding, the researcher chose to address this gap in the field's knowledge based by exploring the role of cooperatives in building peace after the Rwandan genocide as a means of building our knowledge based on this under-studied aspect of peace building.

An explanatory case study is useful when one is seeking to induce new understanding as to how and why things happened the way they did at a deeper level than simply the correlations or generalizations one can get from surveys. Because of its in-depth and detailed analysis, a case study is able to reveal and explain causal links in real-life interventions that would be too complex for survey or experimental strategies (Yin, 2009). The correlations between scarcity and conflict for example have long been known, but the causal links have been harder to get at and statistical methods are not capable of yielding such explanation. Thus Adano and others turned to a qualitative research study to investigate and draw the linkages between scarcity and ethnic violence in Kenya's drylands, drawing in all the possible impinging factors such as livelihoods, cultural practices, decision making, geographical and climatic parameters and institutional arrangements (Adano, Dietz, Witsenburg, & Zaal, 2012). The context, both physical and social, was a key part of the inquiry and data sources included long-term historical data, archival information and fieldwork sources. Causal links are the staple of conflict analysis and resolution with its insistence on understanding the causes in order to work out solutions that are relevant to and address the fundamental causes of conflicts, making case study especially attractive as the research methodology.

Explanation can also be of process. Muvingi's (2008) comparative case study of two U.S. based campaigns by human rights activists seeking to ameliorate the violence that was accompanying extractive industries in Africa, focused on the processes utilized by the campaigns to try and bring human rights into the market place. The guiding question was how activists seek to translate human rights norm violations into credible threats of material loss in a market dominated economic world. The two cases were the Conflict Diamonds campaign and the Capital Markets Sanctions campaign. In the case of conflict diamonds, the activists mobilized selective purchasing of diamonds in consumer societies in tandem with legislative regulation. In the capital market sanctions, activists sought to deny access to money markets by offending corporations and the activists backed that up with divestment efforts and legal suit. The two cases had similarities and differences, but both proved that in the very markets that enabled the funding of violence lay the means and opportunities for realization of human rights. Data for the research comprised in documentary research, legislative process records, correspondence between U.S. legislators and the executive, media coverage of the campaigns, interviews with activists and corporate executives as well as participant observation.

Evaluative case studies involve description, explanation and judgment for example on intervention models or initiatives. Evaluations of interventions where the objective is to provide more effective methodologies would fall into this category. Case study research would enable the effective exploration of the relationships between structures, agents, processes and outcomes. An example of evaluation is Lynn S. Urban *et al*'s evaluation of victim-offender dialogue which is a core strategy in the restorative justice paradigm (Urban, Markway, & Crockett, 2011). The evaluation of the chosen program was on its adherence to leading scholar/practitioner Umbreit's recommendations for practice as well as the recommended best practices themselves. The imperative for evaluation was multifaceted. Victim – offender encounters raise numerous concerns about motives, emotions, psychological harm, victim acquiescence, vulnerabilities and power differentials. While restorative justice has been gaining in popularity and is accompanied by anecdotal claims of advantage over traditional retributive processes, evidence of the benefits, advantages and operationalization is sorely needed. Through Urban et al's (2011) evaluation, implementation problems and useful strategies were identified for avoidance or adoption by practitioners in other cases. The case study was therefore a contribution to the development of evidence-based restorative justice practices.

Case studies can be single, single embedded or multisite, single longitudinal, collective and/or comparative. Single cases can be chosen because of seeming intrinsic importance or currency such as the Iraq war, 9/11 attacks on the United States, the Arab Spring, and so on. Events that deeply influence or change the course of history attract interest in an effort to describe and interpret them. The embedded or multisite case study is suitable when a unitary phenomenon has subunits or multiple sites of occurrence. In an embedded design, attention is given to the subunits within the case. The difference from a simple single case design is that a single case has a holistic design that examines the global nature of the phenomenon; in other words it treats the phenomenon as unitary. Multisite cases are really one case with several sites when the numerous sites can serve as confirmation of propositions. A longitudinal study involves the tracking over time of a designated phenomenon. Collectivities arise when cases that are closely similar can be identified and studied simultaneously. Comparative case studies contrast cases either on the basis of their similarities or differences. A collective case study is inherently comparative, looking at two or more cases either because of their perceived similarities or differences and what we can learn from them. Yin (2009) calls this a multiple case study and Muvingi's (2008) comparative study of two social movement campaigns would fall into this category.

Whether a case is single or multiple depends on the formulation of the study question or issue. A study of domestic violence in Davie, Florida, can be considered as a single case if the objective is to understand domestic violence as a community phenomenon in Davie. The same phenomenon can also be approached as multiple if the objective is to understand the dynamics of violence in domestic units and compare these among residents of Davie. In one case you treat Davie as a single unit while in the other, the units are the domestic arrangements and Davie forms the space boundary.

An example of a single case study in conflict is *Essence of Decision: Explaining the Cuban Missile Crisis*, in which Allison and Zelikow (1999) studied the decision making process during the crisis as a case study, presenting and critiquing the accepted rational actor model and suggesting that a better and deeper understanding would be achieved from a multiple perspective approach that would include more interpretive models. A case study approach enabled the use of multiple models of explanation because the single unit of analysis remained the main focus of multiple explanations, namely decision making during the Cuban missile crisis.

An example of a single but embedded study is Kaae, Søndergaard, Haugbølle, and Traulsen's (2010), study of cognitive service delivery in Denmark. The researchers used a qualitative exploratory multicase study based on a combination of "field observations, semi-structured interviews, group interviews as well as collection of documentary material" (p. 36) to study the provision of specified cognitive services in Denmark. In-depth knowledge was required in order to ensure targeted service provision and a number of sites were needed so as to gather evidence across a wider population.

A longitudinal case study tracks changes or constants in the same case over time. Kiely's (2004) seven year long case study for example, examined how 22 mostly U.S., undergraduate students experienced perspective transformation from participating in an international service-learning program which had an explicit social justice orientation. Aside from seeking to contribute to service-learning theory and practice, the study was aimed at initiating discussion on the practical and ethical implications of international service-learning. Using case study methodology allowed the presentation of the students' common experiences from a phenomenological perspective over time while at the same time, it allowed exploration of the "forms, processes, actions, and programmatic factors that enhanced and/or hindered students' transformational learning" (p. 18) There are numerous challenges with longitudinal studies despite their many benefits. Benefits of tracking real time change give us more than a snapshot at phenomenon. A challenge is the time and resource investment that a longitudinal study requires. Many students and faculty simply may not afford longitudinal studies because of financial and time constraints. There is also a danger with real-time longitudinal study that the researcher can lose relative objectivity and become involved with and/or empathetic to the organization, the people, and the process that she is tracking. Objectivity is not a requirement in qualitative research, but the research still must avoid bias and not simply become an advocacy piece for the subjects.

A multiple case study is used to compare cases that share commonalities or have interesting differences. An example is Andrea Pérez and Ignacio Rodríguez del Bosque's (2012) study of corporate social responsibility in a European country based on an examination of six banks. The study was comparative, instrumental, descriptive, and illustrative in that it sought to reveal the practices and the motives of banks adopting corporate social responsibility by seeking affirmation or difference. Findings indicated aspects of business practices that facilitated and detracted from effective corporate social responsibility across a small spectrum of banks.

If one uses the categories postulated by Stake (1995, 2000), then an intrinsic case study is when one wishes to gain and provide better understanding of the case. The understanding sought is of the particular case itself. Duckworth's (2011) case study analyzing the indigenous land rights movement in Paraguay, for example, is intrinsic given that not enough was known about indigenous leadership decision making as regards social movement strategy in Paraguay. For example, how did the historical, cultural and economic context shape their choices about how to advance and frame their movement? How did they assess resources and opportunities? How did they frame their movement to the media, opponents and allies? Most of the literature treating contemporary Paraguay as a "case" focused on the fall of Paraguay's late dictator, General Strossner, for example, or on Paraguay's subsequent challenged transition to democracy. This gap necessitated a more detailed understanding of the land rights conflict from the perspective of indigenous leaders; thus Duckworth's case study could be considered intrinsic. Most case studies are in some sense "intrinsic" in that they have this objective of providing an enhanced understanding of the case, in conjunction with the other objectives.

An instrumental case is one where the objective is understanding or usage of lessons learned beyond the particular case itself. The case in this instance is not the end goal, but rather the means to another end which might be the formulation or refinement of a theory or an intervention model. In this sense, Andrea Pérez and Ignacio Rodríguez del Bosque's (2012) corporate social responsibility case was instrumental as it also sought to find best practices and detractors to corporate social responsibility. Susanne Kaae's (2010) study of cognitive services would also qualify as instrumental since the ultimate objective was better provision of cognitive services in Denmark.

DOING CASE STUDY IN CONFLICT RESOLUTION

Setting the Parameters

So how then does one define a case in conflict or conflict resolution? As Baxter and Jack (2008, pp. 545) point out, defining a case is no easy task. Miles and Huberman (1994) offer a good starting point; that your unit of analysis is the case which must comprise in some phenomenon that takes place in a bounded context. The phenomenon can be an individual, an organization or even a group, and it can also be a process. Cases can be instances of decision making for example a trade negotiation, or an application of economic sanctions (Odell, 2000). Examples of conflict cases could be domestic violence in a specified segment of society, a genocide, a revolution, a school shooting, and so on. Process can be a campaign, a negotiation such as the Israeli-Palestinian Camp David Oslo negotiations, a mediation whether on a domestic or an intergroup conflict. Cases are as much determined by what they are as by what they are not. Student researchers often try to be comprehensive by being broad in their definition of case which almost always leads to difficulty focusing the study. The fuzzier the boundaries of a case, the more likely that the research project will be unfocused and time consuming.

There are several ways of binding a case, again depending on the nature of the inquiry. A case can be bounded by identity of subjects, for example, a motor cycle gang, or a religious community, and so on. It can also be limited in terms of place as a separate or additional parameter, for example, a motor cycle gang in Seattle. Further or alternative binding can be on the basis of time such as the violence unleashed by a motor cycle gang in Seattle in 2002. The focus can be "why" the violence or "how" the violence was perpetrated or even "how" the community and the bikers resolved their conflicts. Creswell (2013) discusses binding by time and place, Stake (2000) by time and activity, Miles and Huberman (1994) by definition and context. Additional ways of demarcating boundedness abound, but the objective remains that of making the research project a reasonably defined and doable one in terms of scope. Boundedness is not synonymous with sampling. Within the boundaries of the case, one still has to make sampling decisions as, in most cases it is impossible to talk to or listen to everyone. Researchers can choose, for example, purposive sampling, in which subjects are selected due to their membership in a particular group, organization or their history with a particular experience under study. "Snowball" sampling, in which researchers ask interviewees for suggestions on other possible persons to interview, is another possibility with case study (as well as other qualitative research designs). Students will find that a clear sense of the "boundaries" of the case will assist with sampling, as well as other data collection and analysis, decisions.

FORMULATING THE QUESTION OR ISSUE

Although this topic is placed after setting the boundaries in this chapter, note that the issue formulation and boundary setting are normally intrinsic to each other and the process is iterative and reciprocating. One's propositions may well give direction to the case type and the conceptual framework as well as the reasoning or logic that will likely link the data to the propositions. The propositions are very important as they will act as the guidelines to the research. One can formulate propositions intuitively, from familiarity with the case, from the existing literature, or from theories that are of interest. An example of a proposition can be that conflicts escalate due to lack of listening skills among conflict parties. Listening skills then becomes the guiding research focus and one can use multiple cases, observing or interviewing conflict parties and evaluating whether listening or lack thereof was or is a relevant element in the success or otherwise of the process, whether it be mediation or negotiation or something else. Another example of a proposition may be related to conflict causes. One of our students' proposition about the continuing war in the Democratic Republic of Congo was that motives for fighting were not only the pursuit of natural resources, but also the desire for an ethnic based state in Eastern Congo by one of the fighting groups . To find out if this is so, the research would then involve an analysis of the statements by leaders of the "separatist" group, to unearth the meanings behind the statements and then link that to the fact that despite the larger state of Congo acceding to all the other demands of the group, fighting rages on. The case here is bounded by space (Eastern DRC), and theme (ethnic nationalism). As is clear from this example, there can and often are a number of interlinked propositions, and the propositions help guide the scope of the research. In

Duckworth's (2011) case study regarding the Paraguayan indigenous land rights movement, for example, her research was guided by a proposition that the political, sociocultural, historical and economic context would all be factors shaping how indigenous leaders chose to frame their movement. To assess this proposition, she then gathered data by observing civil society meetings, interviewing indigenous leaders, development experts, land-owning ranchers, government officials and human rights advocates, as well as gathering data from ethnographies on indigenous people in Paraguay, political science literature on Paraguay's transition to democracy, media coverage of the land rights conflict, NGO organizational literature and economic data from sources such as *Banco Mundial* and BID (the Inter-American Development Bank). This wide variety of sectors, methods and sources of data (again known as triangulation of data) is common to case study research. Propositions are additionally important because, from the propositions, the researcher can work out a framework or structure for the study. Duckworth, for example, coded and analyzed her data to ultimately develop the framework that she termed the "Dignity Frame." That is, based on her original proposition that Paraguay's specific historical, cultural and politico-economic context would play a role in how the indigenous land rights movement manifested, she ultimately argued that the Dignity Frame was uniquely able to facilitate indigenous outreach to human rights allies, address urgent basic human needs of food and water security which arose after a community lost their ancestral land and above all, the Dignity Frame was able to speak directly to the indigenous sense of having been invisible and dehumanized for centuries throughout Paraguay's history. Other frames had failed to resonate with this social identity need. This provides an example of how a proposition can develop into an overall framework for analysis. Note that whereas Yin (2009) uses the term propositions, Stake (1995, 2000) refers to the same thing as "issues."

FRAMEWORKS AND DATA SOURCES

We referenced a framework of study above. Miles and Huberman (1994) provide guidelines to a conceptual framework as (a) identifying the subjects of study, (b) formulating or describing the relationships among the subjects (often a component of the proposition) and (c) creating coding structures so as to start making sense of the data. A framework is a useful instrument but it remains always a work in progress, open and subject to themes emerging from the data. A framework is therefore a balancing act: if it is too rigid, if forecloses discovery and openness to the perspectives of the subjects, but a more structured framework makes for a more structured study. Too rigid a framework runs the risk of making the study more deductive than inductive, defeating one of the major objectives of qualitative research.

Where the research entails primary data from human subjects, sampling naturally takes great importance. By definition, the case already sets boundaries on who gets included, but even within the case, sampling issues require decision. Sampling in the qualitative form of conflict case study research follows the same prescriptions as in other qualitative research. Purposive sampling is used based on the basis of predetermined criteria that allow for an exhaustive and in-depth analysis of the issues or problems under study. Pérez and del Bosque (2012) for example chose three criteria to select the cases to represent the greatest heterogeneity in terms of company size, location, legal status, and management styles in the six banking corporations they used as a basis for studying corporate social responsibility. Within the cases, they then chose the people to interview on the basis of their knowledge or expertise of corporate social responsibility.

In deciding who should be the object of research, an important practical element is the availability of data. In qualitative research, multiple sources of data are desirable; in case study, they are a must. There is no point in formulating a great research proposition and coming up with a framework if data cannot be accessed. Part of the decision on who is to be included is necessarily about what can be accessed. This can be especially difficult, depending on the nature of the case one is studying when researching conflict, so researchers will need to think carefully about data access. Conflict parties (research participants) may well be leery of speaking to someone not a member of their trusted group. Depending on the nature of the conflict, the environment in which one is seeking to gather data may well be dangerous for both researchers and potential research participants. Finally, those we interview for conflict resolution case studies will almost certainly be advocating for their group's narrative of the conflict. Researchers must be aware of this potential for bias. Case studies are especially useful to researchers in navigating this reality as they provide for broad flexibility in gathering data from a number of sources and a variety of methods. Hence the researcher can cross-check facts and provide for "multivocal" portrait of the conflict which represents the diversity of perspectives which parties to the conflict are certain to have. Grounded theory and phenomenology, for example, while they of course have their utilities for researching conflict, are somewhat less able to offer this multivocality which can be so important to understanding the narratives and worldviews of the conflict parties.

Case study requires and enables the use of multiple data sources including observation, interview, conversation, documentation (part of which can be quantitative), archives and reports. The greater the sources of data, the stronger the research project because it allows for triangulation and confirmation from various sources. This is illustrated well in the importance of context and observation. It is a feature of group dynamics that groups will project positive or desirable images of themselves (Brewer in Ashmore, 2001; Pruitt & Kim, 2003). The subjects may even have strongly held beliefs and narratives as to how things are, which is what they may tell a researcher. Observation however, may reveal different or additional perspectives on how things really are. Through observation, one can detect how things happen, while through interviews the researcher explores how things are perceived by the subjects. However, the drawback of multiple sources of data is the danger of data overload and the challenges of analyzing massive amounts of data. Again, this makes defining the boundaries of the case necessary. Similarly again as with all qualitative research, case study research utilizes multiple sources of data so as to verify and validate perceptions, or at least to represent or interpret the variety of contested narratives about the conflict which might exist. In the corporate social responsibility case study above (Pérez & del Bosque, 2012) the authors combined in-depth analysis of secondary information gathered from company-controlled reports, communications and academic participations, noncontrolled sources such as stock market indices, public awards, and media publications in addition to in-depth interviews. This enabled them to enhance the credibility of their case study.

ANALYSIS

Analysis comprises in how a researcher arrives at the final conclusions or presentations from the large volume of field notes that are typical of qualitative research. Analysis is treated separately in presentation but in reality, analysis and data collection are often concurrent processes in qualitative research. Most qualitative analysis starts with coding and a full presentation of coding is beyond the scope of this chapter. Coding is the initiation of or transition to more in-depth analysis. There are several excellent texts on coding such as Saldana's (2009) *Coding Manual* which give the novice researcher an introduction to coding. As Saldana defines it, "A code in qualitative inquiry is most often a word or short phrase that symbolically assigns a summative, salient, essence-capturing, and/or evocative attribute for a portion of language-based or visual data" (p. 3). Coding often requires numerous iterations with refinement at each iteration. The coding can be of numerous forms of data, especially but not exclusively interviews. Each code tries to capture the message, main topic or drift of each chunk of data related, in case study, to the guiding question and/or the propositions. In its simplest form, a code reduces or summarizes the data, but that already is a form of analysis as codes evoke meanings to data. As one works through the data, codes repeat and start to suggest patterns which can then be developed into themes. Patterns need not only emerge from the data; some codes are intentionally formulated by the researcher or suggested by the participants. The themes that emerge from patterns can be based on similarities, differences, sequence, frequency, and cause, and through intuitive reasoning lead to categories, ideas and linkages of data to propositions and theories. It is a process of consolidating meaning and explanation. Different texts have different suggestions for how the researcher then compares and contrasts data.

Yin (2009) offers five analytical techniques: pattern matching, linking data to propositions, explanation binding, time-series analysis, logic models and cross case analysis. Stake (1995, 2000) proposes two analysis models, categorical aggregation and direct interpretation. Although Yin presents linking data to propositions as a distinct technique, the linking of data to the initial and developing propositions is inherent in all case study analytical approaches. This is what gives focus to the analysis. The multiplicity of data sourcing in qualitative analysis also entails a need to converge the data so as to build one case rather than a fragmentary presentation of each data set. This is part of what gives strength to the qualitative research.

Creswell (2013) has an additional analytical step that is similar with ethnographic research; a detailed description of the case indicating the main parties, the sequence and the sites of events which are then followed by categorizations of data, development of themes and comparisons with existing literature. This illustrates a common feature of case study research that is, the use of multiple analytical techniques in an effort to converge data so as to yield an in depth understanding of the studied phenomenon. This "thick" description is especially useful for conflict research as it enables scholars and practitioners to analyze, deeply and in localized, contextualized detail, the conflict at hand, which is naturally key to a successful attempt at resolution.

REPORTING

Presenting the findings to the external world is a critical component of the research as that is ultimately the objective of the whole exercise. Because of the detail entailed by case study and the depth which is inherent in qualitative research, one of the major challenges is in providing a concise report. There is no one good way of reporting as that will depend on the nature of the research. In written reports some key elements include presentation of context, description of the phenomenon itself, explanation of the analysis of data and persuasive and integrated presentation.

Rather than reliability, generalizability and replication, one tries to ensure trustworthiness and credibility in qualitative research in general.

This is because more quantitative concepts, such as reliability and validity, have limited utility in providing a framework by which we can assess the quality of a piece of qualitative research (Creswell, 2013, pp. 243–269). There are several ways in which trustworthiness or credibility can be achieved. Miles and Huberman (1994) have several suggestions for all qualitative research: (a) that the study's general methods and procedures should be described in detail, (b) that the process of analysis be possible to follow, (c) that the conclusions should be explicitly linked preferably with exhibits of displayed data, and (d) the data from the study should be available for analysis by others. In case study research, this can be strengthened by making the research issue or question and the propositions as clear as possible. Further, the philosophical approach, the theories relied on and the methodology should be synchronized. One should also be clear as to how the researcher(s) choose who is to be included in the study and explain clearly the logic of their sampling methods. While the use of multiple methods of data collection and analysis adds rigor, breadth and depth to research (Flick, 2002), the data collection process should be well laid out and the analysis of the data needs to show integrity. That is, the research ought to clearly detail and justify, for example, what sort of coding and other analytical methods were used. How were themes developed? Did the researcher use member checks? Did he or she keep an "audit trail" of data gathered in the field? This being qualitative research, triangulation will strengthen the research, but that only adds value when the data converges rather than remaining disparate. This is especially true when researching conflict, which will naturally involve tensions and contestations of what occurred and the meaning of those events.

LIMITATIONS OF THE CASE STUDY

We should bring this chapter to a close by reflecting on some key limitations of the case study. As with any other methodology, case studies, being in general more "broad" than "deep," cannot as readily speak to the nature of a particular human experience. If this is a goal, the student would want to consider a phenomenology. Phenomenology, while it sacrifices some context, immerses the researcher and reader in the experience under study. Similarly, while case studies can certainly speak to "lessons learned" of, say, a particular series of dialogues or negotiations, they are not specifically suited for developing theory. Grounded theory would be the best choice for such a research goal. Because of the "constant comparative" nature of data analysis in grounded theory, data collection and analysis becomes robust enough to develop formal theory. One would really need a number of similar case studies, on the other hand, to begin to develop theory from case studies. "Boundedness" of course is a classic feature of the case study (Creswell, 2007; Yin, 2009). While this makes the case study a good fit for studying particular conflict, or events or processes within a conflict, such as perhaps a specific negotiation or series of dialogues, the case study may not be as solid a fit for larger, macroprocesses that are essential to understand (such as the so-called "Arab Spring," environmental conflict or neoliberal globalization).

One other key limitation of the case study is that, while we can *thematically* generalize from a case study, we cannot *statistically* generalize from a case study. Yin (2009) refers to this as "analytic generalization" (p. 38). That is, if 70% of students on one particular campus say they have experienced (for example) religious conflict between themselves and another student, we cannot assume that the numbers on another campus will be the same. However, we can thematically generalize, and this is useful. If a campus with a fair amount of interreligious conflict published a case study on successes and lessons learned from an interfaith dialogue program on campus, a reasonably similar campus would be on solid ground to shape their own program around those insights. Certainly the second campus might discover differences as they implement their program, but few would argue that the experiences of another similar case were irrelevant.

Finally, researchers might wish to be aware of some of the logistical challenges of a case study; every methodology has them. Case studies, for example, involve exhaustive data collection from a wide variety of sources. Researchers should be prepared for this. By their nature they demand current data. As with other qualitative methodologies, they also require the researcher to develop effective and trusting working relationships with their research participants, especially any relevant gate-keepers. This is a further challenge of the case study (and much research in general) that researchers should be prepared for.

CONCLUSION

Case study methodology is not simply the study of a particular case, but rather a methodology with well-defined procedures for formulation of the question and propositions, framing the study, gathering the data, interpreting and reporting it. When it is done properly, it makes for rigorous and trustworthy research. Conducting case study research requires training and an investment in terms of time and resources and when it is done well, it adds significantly to knowledge creation. It represents an essential means of researching conflicts for several reasons. One, conflicts can often be bounded by geography, incident or time. Second, as we have been emphasizing, its flexible and varied methods of design, data collection and data analysis enable the researcher(s) and research participants (the parties to the conflict, presumably) to explore and represent a variety of differing views as to what happened and what those events mean. Given that conflicts so often feature contested narratives (Cheldelin, 2008), the ability of the case study to present differing perspectives is a significant boon to those of us researching conflict. This enables us as researchers, in partnership with our research participants, to indeed practice research as intervention.

REFERENCES

Adano, W. R., Dietz, T., Witsenburg, K., & Zaal, F. (2012). Climate change, violent conflict and local institutions in Kenya's drylands. *Journal of Peace Research, 49*(1), 65–80

Allison, G., & Zelikow, P. (1999). *Essence of decision: Explaining the Cuban Missile Crisis* (2nd ed.). New York, NY: Longman.

Baxter, P., & Jack, S. (2008). Qualitative case study methodology: Study design and implementation for novice researchers. *The Qualitative Report, 13*(4), 544–559.

Brewer, M. B. (2001). Ingroup identification and intergroup conflict: Where does ingroup love become outgroup hate? In R. D. Ashmore, L. Jussim, & D. Wilder (Eds.), *Social identity, intergroup conflict and conflict reduction* (pp. 17–41). New York, NY: Oxford University Press.

Cheldelin, S., Druckman, D., & Fast, L. (2008). *Conflict* (2nd ed). New York NY: Continuum.

Cole, S. (April, 2012). A political ecology of water equity and tourism: A Case Study From Bali. *Annals of Tourism Research, 39*(2), 1221–1241.

Creswell, J. W. (2013). *Qualitative inquiry and research design: Choosing among five approaches* (3rd ed.). Los Angeles, CA: Sage.

Duckworth, C. (2011). *Land and dignity in Paraguay*. New York, NY: Continuum Press.

Flick, U. (2002). *An introduction to qualitative research*. London, England: Sage.

Harper, D. (1992). Small N's and community case studies. In C.C. Ragin & H. S. Becker (Eds.), *What is a case? Exploring the foundations of social inquiry* (p. 139). New York, NY: Cambridge University Press.

Jacob, E. (1988). Clarifying qualitative research: A focus on traditions. *Educational Researcher, 17*(1), 16–19, 22–24

Kim, J. (2005). Democratic peace and covert war: A case study of the US covert war in Chile. *Journal of International and Area Studies, 12*(1), 25–47.

Kaae, S., Søndergaard, B., Haugbølle, L. S., & Traulsen, J.M. (2010). Development of a qualitative exploratory case study research method to explore sustained delivery of cognitive services. *Pharm World Sci, 32*, 36–42.

Kiely, R. (2004, Spring). A Chameleon with a Complex: Searching for Transformation in International Service-Learning. *Michigan Journal of Community Service Learning*, 5–20.

Miles, M. B., & Huberman, A. M. (1994). *Qualitative data analysis: An expanded sourcebook* (2nd ed.). Los Angeles, CA: Sage.

Muvingi, I. (2008). *Oil, diamonds, and human rights in the marketplace: Campaigning to stop the capitalization of Sudanese oil development and the international trade in conflict diamonds*. Verlag, Saarbrücken, Germany: VDM.

Odell, J. S. (2000, March). *Case study methods in international political economy*. International Studies Association: 41st Annual Convention Los Angeles, CA. (CIAO Working Papers). Retrieved from, http://www.ciaonet.org.ezproxylocal. library.nova.edu/isa/odj01/

Pérez, A., & del Bosque, I. R. (2012). The role of CSR in the corporate identity of banking. *Journal of Business Ethics, 108*(2), 145–166.

Pruitt, D., & Kim, S. H. (2003). *Social conflict: Escalation, stalemate and settlement* (3rd ed.). New York, NY: McGraw Hill.

Ragin, C. C. (1992). Introduction: Cases of "What is a case?" In C. C. Ragin & H. S. Becker (Eds.), *What is a case? Exploring the foundations of social inquiry*. New York, NY: Cambridge University Press.

Saldana, J. (2009). *The coding manual for qualitative researchers* (2012 reprint). Thousand Oaks CA: Sage.

Sentama, E. (2009). Peacebuilding in post-genocide Rwanda: The role of cooperatives in the restoration of interpersonal relationships. Dissertation, Department of Peace and Development Research, School of Global Studies. Göteborg, Sweden: University of Gothenburg.

Stake, R. E. (1995). *The art of case study research*. Thousand Oaks, CA: Sage.

Stake, R. E. (2000). Case studies. In N. K. Denzin & Y. S. Lincoln (Eds.), *Handbook of qualitative research* (pp. 435–453). Thousand Oaks, CA: Sage.

Urban, L. S., Markway, J., & Crockett, K. (2011). Evaluating victim–offender dialogue (VOD) for serious cases using Umbreit's 2001 handbook: A case study. *Conflict Resolution Quarterly, 29*, 3–23. doi:10.1002/crq.21034

Yin, R. K. (2009). *Case study research: Design and methods* (4th ed.). Thousand Oaks, CA: Sage.

CHAPTER 6

276 CUPS OF TEA

Ethnography in Peace and Conflict Research

Emily E. Welty

When explaining my ethnographic PhD research, I am often tempted to describe it in terms of the numbers of cups of tea I drank during my year of research in Uganda and Kenya. Greg Mortenson popularly characterized development in terms of cups of tea in his book *Three Cups of Tea* (2006) exploring education in Afghanistan and Pakistan. While I do not share Mortensen's approach or many of his conclusions, I do feel that my "cup of tea count" meaningfully captures the ethnographic nature of my research. Much of my participant observation involved cups of tea (and coffee and juice) with Mennonite Central Committee (MCC) volunteers and partners—sitting in meetings, in offices and in their homes speaking informally about what they were doing, thinking and feeling. The approximately 276 cups of tea I drank represent the methodology I used to understand the work of an international faith-based peacebuilding and development organization operating in East Africa.

Ethnography is a methodology particularly well-suited for the growing field of peace and conflict studies. While traditionally seen as the domain

Peace and Conflict Studies Research: A Qualitative Perspective, pp. 111–135

of anthropologists, ethnography is increasingly being used by many disciplines including religious studies, political science, sociology, and psychology. As an interdisciplinary field, peace and conflict studies must explore and utilize a wide range of methodological practices. I argue that ethnography is particularly suited for peace and conflict studies because of its careful attention to power dynamics, focus on the local/grassroots level and tendency to seek understanding rather than simply explanation. In this chapter, I first highlight some of the core issues in ethnographic research and draw upon my own research of a faith-based humanitarian organization working in Kenya and Uganda to demonstrate ethnographic principles in practice.

ETHNOGRAPHY IN PEACE AND CONFLICT LITERATURE

Many scholars working in peace and conflict studies use ethnography as a methodology. Canonical peace studies professor and scholar John Paul Lederach (1996) describes the *in situ* and *emic* approach of ethnography as particularly well-suited to the field due to its "enormous respect for how people in a given setting understand themselves and events" and "careful attention to everyday talk and taken-for-granted meaning" (p. 30).

A twofold categorization of ethnography in this field might be (1) research which examines violence and/or conflict and (2) research which looks at postconflict peacebuilding efforts and/or organizations working on conflict transformation. The first category of ethnography primarily considers the meanings attached to conflict or violence as understood by perpetrators, survivors and bystanders. The second category seeks to understand the processes of reconciliation, peacebuilding and healing in the wake of violence or those working for peace in the midst of violence.

Ethnography is a good avenue for examining the deeper personal, political and social meanings of conflict. Even ethnographies which are not primarily about social conflicts still typically address the issue of conflict in some way. One of the most prominent ethnographers of violence is Carolyn Nordstrom and her investigations of war-profiteers (2004), transnational networks of illicit trade (2007), political violence in Mozambique (1997), UN peacekeeping (Fetherston & Nordstrom, 1995) and fieldwork in violent contexts (1995). Anthologies such as *No Peace, No War: An Anthropology of Contemporary Armed Conflicts* (Richards, 2005) and *Violence in War and Peace* (Scheper-Hughes & Bourgois, 2004) include anthropological perspectives and ethnographies of violent conflict in Africa, Asia, Europe and Latin America. Kevin Avruch (2001) adeptly surveyed and analyzed a collection of ethnographies of violence and concluded that such studies offer key insights into the causes and consequences of conflict.

The recent and relatively rapid increase in the number of nongovernmental organizations (NGOs) engaged in peacebuilding and development
work, has been followed by a corresponding increase in the ethnographic
studies of such organizations (Fisher, 1997; Mosse & Lewis, 2005, 2006).
David Mosse (2005) is one of the best-known ethnographers of develop-
ment aid; his long-term participant-insider research examined a DFID
(Department for International Development) project in rural India.
Recent ethnographies of contemporary peace movements include Occupy
Wall Street (Welty, Bolton, Nayak, & Malone, 2012), anarchists in Israel
(Gordon, 2010), peacebuilding and development in Haiti postearthquake
(Marcelin, 2011), and direct action in global justice movements (Graeber,
2009). While diverse in their subject matter, all of these works share a methodological commitment to understanding phenomena through ongoing
direct observation, participation and analysis of the struggle for peace and
justice.

My research project examined how particular Mennonite values guided
the work of the Mennonite Central Committee (MCC) in its peacebuilding
and development projects in Uganda and Kenya. I created a theoretical
framework of distinctively Mennonite values which highlighted the central-
ity of peace, community, simplicity and humility, and then, during a year
of ethnographic fieldwork, I observed the work of the MCC team in East
Africa to understand the role of these values and how they were perceived
by MCC's personnel, local partners and beneficiaries. I argued that MCC
draws on these particularly Mennonite symbols to organize and explain
its experiences. Such analysis of meaning-making within an institution is
grounded in previous research in identity, culture, social realities and construction of meaning within organizations (Dandridge, Mitroff, & Joyce,
1980; Jones, 1996; Yanow, 1996). Methodologically, I framed my study
of the Mennonite Central Committee as an organizational ethnography
drawing on participant observation or, in apt description of Clifford Geertz
(1998), "deep hanging out." I spent two and a half months working as
an intern in the MCC Washington Office, seven months observing MCC-
Uganda and six months observing MCC-Kenya.

ETHNOGRAPHY—TYPES AND CHARACTERISTICS

While I was planning the fieldwork for my PhD, I was certain that I wanted
to understand how Mennonite values were understood by MCC workers
and beneficiaries in Uganda and Kenya. I suggested to several mentors that
I was considering an ethnography as the most suitable methodology for my
research. One person cautioned me that "anthropologists believe they own
ethnography" and that examiners might crush my work before even con-

sidering it if I appeared to be appropriating ethnography for a discipline other than anthropology. I am pleased to report that I was not demolished by my examiners but I share the concern of some anthropologists that the increasing popularity of ethnography means that many researchers describe their work as "ethnographic" after spending mere hours with their research subjects. This echoes Wolcott's (1995) worry that ethnography is "the label of choice for much of the qualitative/descriptive work currently being reported" (p. 79) and not all of it meets the general description of "deeply hanging out" that he employs (Wolcott, 1999). It is worthwhile, therefore to be clear about exactly what ethnography means. As described by John Brewer (2000), ethnography is defined by three characteristics:

> the object of the research, which is to study people in naturally occurring settings; the researcher's role in that setting, which is to understand and explain what people are doing in that setting by means of participating directly in it; and the data to be collected, which must be naturally occurring and captured in such a way that meaning is not imposed on them from outside. (p. 18)

Some of the hallmarks of ethnography are direct or participant observation, interviews, surveys and other qualitative data collection. All of these methods share the primary objective of understanding how systems of meaning are created by the individuals, organizations or larger groups. The advent of the Internet challenged previously conceived notions of bounded geographic sites for ethnographic research as researchers began to consider to how to study online behavior in gaming and other virtual worlds. Thus, web-based ethnography has expanded as the work of Tom Boellstorff (2010, 2012), Bonnie Nardi (2010), Celia Pierce (2011), and T. L. Taylor (2009) demonstrates.

Rather than a strictly inductive or deductive positivist approach, a constructivist-interpretive approach may be the most appropriate for an ethnographic investigation (Yanow & Schwartz-Shea, 2006; Ybema, Yanow, Wels, & Kamsteeg, 2009; Schwartz-Shea & Yanow, 2009). My multidisciplinary study was not positivist in nature but included the epistemic communities of religious studies, peace studies, development studies and social anthropology.

ORGANIZATIONAL ETHNOGRAPHY

Organizational ethnography provides an excellent way to observe the values and relationships between individuals as well as group identity (Kostera, 2007; Neyland, 2008; Schwartzman, 1993; Ybema, Yanow, Wels, & Kamsteeg, 2009). Recent methodological theory confirms the appropriateness of ethnographies in conducting qualitative studies of organizations

(Czarniawska-Jorges, 1992; Gellner & Hirsch, 2001; Moeran, 2005; Prasad, 2005; Van Maanen, 1995). Investigation of organizations involves a bifurcated focus—an examination of the work of the organization as well as an investigation of the culture within the organization because "more things are going on in organizations than getting the job done" (Pacanowsky & O'Donnell-Trujillo, 1982, p. 16). Such research entails careful observation of organizational myths, stories, jokes, symbols, daily routines and gossip to discover deeper shared meanings, values and beliefs and listening to how participants explain their experience of the organization. My ethnography of MCC addressed both of these levels—the values communicated by MCC's work in Uganda and Kenya as well as the values present in MCC's organizational culture.

While NGOs present fertile grounds for ethnographic study, nonetheless, surprisingly few have been conducted and even fewer investigate NGOs working in conflict zones. One of the reasons, as noted by David Mosse (2005), may be:

> Development organisations are in the habit of dealing with criticism and the questioning of their claims and actions (e.g. through reviews and evaluations). However, they are less tolerant of research that falls outside design frameworks, that does not appear to be of practical relevance, is wasteful of time or adds complexity and makes the task of management harder. (p. 12)

This was true for my research and necessitated my selection of participant observation as a way to justify my presence to MCC. In her description of the difficulty of NGO ethnography, Lisa Markowitz (2001) writes: "Studying NGOs thus requires doing local fieldwork within a web of relationships that are inherently unstable among groups of people with whom one has widely varying relationships" (p. 41). She highlights the necessity of "situating oneself as a researcher within a nexus of fluid interpersonal and institutional relationships" and "identifying and tracking the multidirectional flows of information, ideas, and material" (p. 42).

Critical Ethnography

The need to responsibly observe and contend with the unequal distribution of power which is inherent to the ethnographic methodology gave rise to critical ethnography—a way to "not choose between critical theory and ethnography" (Noblit, Flores, & Murillo, 2004, p. 4). Critical ethnography emphasizes the positionality of the researcher, the socially unjust conditions of the subjects and involves "a moral obligation to make a contribution towards changing those conditions toward greater freedom and equity"

(Madison, 2005, p. 5). This approach rejects the supposed "neutrality" of the researcher and recognizes the impossibility of achieving the perfect objectivity that empiricism or positivism promotes. The critical ethnographer must take seriously the encounter with Otherness and profoundly engage with it while also transparently acknowledging one's own positionality and the ways one's social location influences the encounter. Peace and conflict studies demands that the researchers demonstrate awareness of their own power and privilege and the particular lens that it brings to their work in order to remain consistent with the bedrock values of liberatory peace education (Bajaj & Brantmeier, 2011; Brantmeier, 2007). Critical methodologies can guide researchers and educators in the production of knowledge that reflects the larger values of peace and social justice.

Phil Carspecken (1996) argues that critical ethnography (or critical qualitative research) as a methodology highlights the relationship between the findings or outcomes of research and values. For critical ethnographers, research is not a value-free enterprise but rather a reflection of deeply held beliefs and worldviews. Critical epistemologies highlight social inequality and lay the groundwork for social change. The desire to end oppression and build sustainable societies does not predetermine the findings of research but it sets the agenda and directs the ethnographer's gaze. This is precisely why critical ethnographies compliment peace and social justice research and education.

REFLEXIVITY AND SOCIAL LOCATION

The social location and multiple identity categories of the ethnographer have significant bearing on fieldwork, and researchers must be aware that they are "part and parcel of the setting, context and culture" they are researching (Brewer, 2000, p. 127). My research was influenced both by demographic aspects of my identity (gender, marital status, age) as well as phenomenological elements of my identity (education, training, religious background, previous experience working in Africa). This positionality affected my access, interactions with informants and analysis. As a White North American married female researcher with both Mennonite and Presbyterian heritage, I had unique insider and outsider status which allowed me to acquire both *emic* and *etic* understandings of the organization and its participants (Lett, 1990).

Being approximately the same age as most of the MCC-Uganda volunteers enhanced my relationships with them and made the "deep hanging out" easier. Interestingly, this was the aspect of my social location that was the deepest source of bonding, a concept familiar to the East African context in the institution of the age-mate system, the horizontal bonding that occurs within people in the same age group.

Being married and having my spouse in the field with me enhanced my interactions with the Ugandan and Kenyan partners by allowing me to appear less strange and more culturally appropriate when travelling in the region. As a woman, while I sometimes resented the fact that marriage gave me more credibility, it also made my fieldwork easier than earlier work conducted in the region.

Operating as a White person in East Africa came with its own set of power dynamics. Because of the perceived differences in power, I sometimes felt that Ugandans and Kenyans reported what they thought I wanted to hear in interviews. Participatory development critic Ilan Kapoor (2004) writes:

> even *if* the subalterns speak, they (like anyone) may perform the roles they think are expected of them (by their own communities, the facilitator, the funding agency). They may modify their speech when under pressure, or exaggerate their praise to please the funder. (p. 636)

To attempt to mitigate this dynamic, I only interviewed Kenyans and Ugandans after establishing a relationship and observing their work. I cannot claim that a preexisting relationship compensated for the powerful dynamics at work between us. However, I believed that if trust and familiarity were established before the interview, the interviewees would feel more comfortable and able to speak freely rather than to try to please me or satisfy my research goals.

My academic training in international peacebuilding and experience in humanitarian aid work made me a better participant observer with more skills to offer MCC. It was this background that helped me obtain a summer internship at the Washington office. This identity also allowed me to reach beyond the Mennonite world and connect the literature from peace studies, development studies and African studies in order to understand the relevance and relationship of MCC's work to the secular world of humanitarian aid work.

One's very identity as a researcher may be read different ways by different people—some may experience it as a threat and others may be flattered to be the subject of study. When introduced by Ugandans or Kenyans, my academic work was usually seen as a sign of prestige. Some introduced me as "professor" and others congratulated themselves on the honor of having their work recognized as worthy of study. For many Ugandans and Kenyans, my presence represented a form of "symbolic capital" which validated the importance of their work (Bourdieu, 1984). However, it was still often unclear to Kenyans and Ugandans that while I often accompanied MCC staff, I was not officially associated with MCC and had no power over funding or programmatic decisions. My race, nationality and accent all contributed to this confusion. Eventually, MCC leaders in both countries introduced me to partners and beneficiaries as "a friend of MCC," an explanation that positioned me in the MCC landscape as an outside observer rather than a staff member. While the term "friend" is problematic in ethnographic fieldwork, particularly with regard to critical distance, in this case, MCC staff used "friend" not to imply my involvement *within* the organization but rather to establish my position *outside* of it.

One of the most difficult identities to manage in the course of ethnographic fieldwork may be the identity that one shares with one's research subjects (Chock, 1986; Geertz, 1973; Mosse, 2006; Ybema & Kamsteeg, 2009). This was certainly the case for me as I struggled to manage my role as both an insider and an outsider to the Mennonite faith. I come from a mixed Presbyterian-Mennonite background. My surname, Welty, is a traditional Mennonite name but I was not raised in a Mennonite church nor did I attend a Mennonite university. I was part of Mennonite communities in both the United Kingdom and the United States but officially joined the church as an adult in New York City. This often created confusion as Mennonite volunteers struggled to place me in "the Mennonite name game" by mentioning relatives that they imagined I might know. My inevitable failure to participate in this game in a satisfying way sometimes seemed to raise suspicions about the legitimacy of my work. I was fortunate to have four powerful and well-respected Mennonite patrons whose friendship gave my work a greater degree of Mennonite credibility. They served as important MCC gatekeepers and created a pseudo-family by which other Mennonites could understand how I fit into the Mennonite world.

In classical anthropology, ethnographic research implies that the researcher is able to "eat like they eat, speak like they speak and do as they do" (Brewer, 2000). While I did not need to speak a different language or adopt a foreign set of customs to relate to my primary informants, I did think carefully about how I was perceived in terms of dress, diet and customs. My research concluded that Mennonite values operate so strongly within MCC that the organization excludes those it judges to be outside the Mennonite value system. However, this meant that during my fieldwork I also had to reinforce to MCC staff that I shared their values in order to maintain my level of access.

In ethnography, the researcher is both the observer and the observed. I was conscious of MCC volunteers scrutinizing my lifestyle and judging whether I sufficiently embraced Mennonite values. I needed to carefully consider how my spouse and I spent our leisure time when I was not with the MCC team and felt pressure to gain the social approval of my informants. For example, when we celebrated Valentine's Day at an expensive restaurant in Kampala, I kept this secret from the MCC-Uganda team, knowing that it contravened the Mennonite emphasis on simplicity and frugality. I found it difficult when MCC volunteers criticized my life outside MCC. One particularly awkward moment occurred when I spent a Saturday at a pool popular with the expatriate community and became sunburned. My sunburn aroused the attention of MCC leaders who made it known that this activity was "frivolous" and not in line with Mennonite values. Because I was so worried about offending the team, I actually found it easier to spend most of my time in the company of MCC volunteers and thus avoid reproach.

It is important to observe how one's presence in the field influences the behavior of one's informants (Hammersley & Atkinson, 1995). When I first shadowed MCC volunteers, I noticed that they sometimes went out of their way to behave in particular ways. For example, upon hearing that I was interested in the presence/absence of faith in religious NGOs, I noticed one worker began to pray more visibly and often. Another overemphasized her humility to the partner organization she worked with while I was nearby. These manifestations seemed prompted by my presence but as MCC volunteers became more comfortable with me, behavior became more natural and less forced.

A Short Guide to Peace and Conflict Ethnography:

- Carefully consider case study selection—how might this case study illustrate something interesting about a larger issue?
- Before, during and after fieldwork consider how your social location and identity affects fieldwork, informants, data and analysis
- Do No Harm—if working in the midst of violent conflict, it is important to consider how your presence might contribute to the conflict and to remember that you may be interacting with traumatized people
- Identify and win the trust of key gatekeepers
- Make use of participant observation to understand more about how it feels and what it means to be a part of this community/ organization
- Take careful and thorough notes throughout fieldwork

RESEARCH DESIGN AND CASE STUDY SELECTION

Academic research in the social sciences is typically driven by the desire to answer research questions about complex social phenomena. The decision to use an ethnography as one's methodology reflects the idea that close observation of particular contexts can provide insight into more general areas of knowledge. Therefore, careful attention should be given to the selection of case studies and research sites.

While ethnographers may appear myopically focused on a single context, the selected case study is intended to represent and explore broader issues (Gerring, 2004; Yin, 1994; Feagin, Orum, & Sjoberg, 1991). The case study selected may dictate focus on one particular site for research or may include multiple sites which allow the researcher to explore the ethnographic subject in greater depth (Gellner & Hirsch, 2001; Hannerz, 2003; Marcus, 1995, 1998). Triangulation across more than one site allows the ethnographer to corroborate her findings and lessens the possibility that her findings represent an exceptional case.

My primary research interest is in faith-based NGOs (FBNGOs) but I decided that analysis of a single case study, MCC, would provide the most interesting avenue into understanding a larger phenomenon and yield the most useful data for my examination of FBNGOs. I selected two subunits of MCC, MCC-Kenya and MCC-Uganda, to execute a multisited ethnography of MCC's work in East Africa. I felt selecting only one site risked the chance that the program selected might represent an outlier rather than a typical example of MCC work. Therefore, I selected MCC's programs in both Kenya and Uganda—two countries sharing a border, a common history of British colonization and English as a common language. I felt that by comparing how MCC functioned in two settings, I could better understand the organization's work and meaning to its African partners as well as its North American staff and donors.

I primarily based myself in Kampala and Nairobi, the headquarters of MCC's country programs in Uganda and Kenya which provided physical proximity to the country representatives who were my primary informants as well as gatekeepers for MCC volunteers and partners. Being based near the country offices was a strategic decision which helped me understand the overall program as well as maintain a daily presence in the MCC offices when not travelling to meet other MCC staff or visit program sites.

When defining the terms of one's fieldwork, consider the many different types of available data including primary and secondary sources, participant observation and interviews. My research demanded studying MCC volunteers, MCC partners and beneficiaries *in situ*, closely observing their work, relationships and routines using multiple ethnographic methods including interviews, observation of meetings and informal conversations with my research subjects. Another valuable source of research data was the "grey" literature I accessed during my time in the MCC Washington Office, and MCC country headquarters in Kampala and Nairobi. I read reams of internal reports, correspondence, newsletters and other unpublished information related to MCC's work.

The expansion of digital technology and social media continues to open new avenues for ethnographic investigation. While I was not conducting a web-based ethnography, new media such as blogs and social networking sites such as Facebook proved useful to my research. Through my virtual interactions and observations of MCC volunteers' thoughts and feelings, I was better able to map, follow and understand the 25 people whose lives and work formed the backbone of my research. I never quoted Facebook information in my final dissertation as I felt this represented a grey area since it was shared under the pretext of friendship rather than research. However, I did find it useful to guide my questions and check my understandings of information shared at times when the volunteers knew themselves to be "on record."

CHOOSING KEY INFORMANTS

From the perspective of the researched, too often research by the outsider has "told us things already known, suggested things that would not work, and made careers for people who already had jobs" (Smith, 2012, p. 3). Conscious of this pervasive dynamic, I focused on the Ugandans and Kenyans who were both coworkers and beneficiaries as active subjects who shaped the meaning of MCC and its work rather than objects to which aid was delivered. It was essential to me to witness MCC through the eyes of MCC volunteers but I quickly realized it was equally important to understand what MCC looked like from the perspective of local partner organizations and beneficiaries.

Beneficiaries were more difficult to observe and most of my interviews at this level were informal and spontaneous. I felt that gathering beneficiaries (who were already facing devastating problems such as violence, food insecurity and HIV/AIDS) for interviews was a needless inconvenience that would only deepen my privileged position and not offer concrete benefits. Thus, I accompanied partners and spoke with beneficiaries in the course of their interactions with the partner.

ACCESS AND ENTRY

Gaining access to a group of people for lengthy ethnographic observation requires considerable negotiation. It is important to carefully consider the wider implications of one's request for access and it may be useful to think about how to use existing contacts. Like many researchers, my case study was selected in part due to my identity and access to a particular group of people (Crang & Cook, 2007; Brewer, 2000; Schwartzman, 1993; van der

Waal, 2009). I had contacts within MCC based on earlier work in South Africa and Sudan and I used these relationships to initially assess whether MCC was a viable research site.

Ethnography requires particularly careful attention to the issues of gate-keeping and management of powerful connections, as access to the entire organization or community may be predicated on the approval of a few select individuals (Moeran, 2009). Developing key contacts within a community or organization and identifying the key gatekeepers whose permission and buy-in matters is essential. Negotiating access is an ongoing process and conversations about access are a routine part of fieldwork (Smith, 2007). Even once I had permission to observe MCC in Uganda and Kenya, I was still often unclear about which meetings or trips I was welcome to join and which were closed. While I periodically felt uncomfortable about the need for conversations about what I was allowed to do, I also recognized that this boundary-keeping represented due diligence and responsible leadership on the part of the leadership.

The trust and goodwill of the MCC leadership in both Uganda and Kenya was crucial as they had the power to cut off my access to all MCC partners and volunteers. Because MCC does not publish the contact details of any partner organizations or staff, without the acquiescence of these gatekeepers, the research would not have been possible. The country representatives in both Uganda and Kenya demonstrated cautious optimism about my research but were guarded about the project's usefulness and worried about the impact my presence might have on their work. Thinking carefully about how I described my research to MCC alerted me to the hesitation the organization felt about an outsider doing an "evaluation" of their work. I emphasized my ethnographic approach and stressed that I wanted to see the institution in a deep, complete way. I acknowledged that, at times, my presence might feel inconvenient but that I was sensitive to the issue of burdening them and would try to be as helpful as possible as a participant observer.

Access opened up slowly and increased as I spent more time with MCC. My internship at the Washington Office in the beginning of my fieldwork was essential to securing a wider network of contacts within MCC. During my time with MCC-Uganda, I met many members of the MCC-Kenya team at meetings and retreats before shifting the site of my fieldwork from Kampala to Nairobi. This familiarity considerably eased my transition from one site to another. As the fieldwork progressed, more doors opened and I stopped worrying that I did not have enough informants and began to limit the number of people included as research subjects.

In the midst of negotiating these terms of access, I was grateful to have self-designed my study and to be free from institutional constraints or terms of reference beyond those of reasonable and ethical research. I chose my own methodology and questioned existing institutional assumptions without needing anyone to sign off on my conclusions, a freedom which allowed me think quite widely about what I experienced in the field.

Many people warned me that Uganda and Kenya were saturated with researchers and that many people might be reluctant to speak with me without compensation. As a matter of principle, I refused to buy my informants' time. I worked out this ethical dilemma by volunteering as a lecturer at Makerere University in the Religion and Peace Studies Department. Thus, when asked how this research would benefit Ugandans or Kenyans, I honestly said that it might not help particular individuals but that as part of my presence in the country, I was making an intellectual contribution to the education of university students. This answer seemed satisfactory to those who asked.

INTERVIEWS

Interviews often form one of the most important parts of the ethnographic study. These encounters between the ethnographer and her research subjects create a space in which deeper understanding of the motivations, feelings, perceptions and meanings can be explored. While interviews may be fairly unstructured, the researcher should carefully consider what types of information she hopes to learn in order to ask questions about impressions, motivations and feelings rather than collecting biographical data (Burgess, 1984; Weiss, 1994).

The semistructured interview allows the researcher to follow a delineated pathway of inquiry but also to remain open and guided by the insights, feelings and impressions of the informant. In my fieldwork, I asked open, nondirective questions and interviews occurred in a setting chosen by the interviewee. Robert Burgess (1984) describes this process of interviewing as "conversations with purpose," which appropriately highlights a dialogical encounter rather than an interrogatory one. By developing rapport and trust with my informants before I interviewed them, I was able to probe more deeply into the inner lives and complexities of people's feelings about MCC. Some of my informants indicated that these conversations were mutually beneficial, and one research subject commented to another before an interview with me, "Don't worry about the interview, talking to Emily was actually kind of therapeutic—just to think about all of these issues and what they mean. I felt like I should be thanking her!"

Research within Peace and Conflict Studies often means that fieldwork is carried out in a place with active or recent violent conflict. There is an even higher duty of care that should be exercised by a researcher in these circumstances as one's informants may be traumatized. Carefully considering Mary Anderson's (1999) *Do No Harm* approach to work in a conflict zone is a good ethical starting place.

Interviews alone will not sufficiently capture the nuance and complexity of the selected community or organization. In the course of my research, while I do not believe anyone intentionally manipulated me or lied, I certainly observed cases in which professed values differed from values in practice. As in any social setting, people can be inconsistent or seek social approval in interviews. Therefore, observation beyond interviews is important to verify and triangulate findings.

PARTICIPANT OBSERVATION

Participant observation is a staple ethnographic technique but the depth or degree of participation/observation may vary greatly. Raymond Gold (1958) described four levels of participant observation: complete participation (covert research of a group of which one is a member), participant as observer (research while also acting as a full group member), observer as participant (research as the primary role with limited participation) and complete observer (no participation, only observation). Generally participant observation means the researcher is actively participating in the life of the community or social group while also engaged in research of the same group. This process requires careful thought about issues of access, entry, relationships, observation, field notes and ethics (DeWalt & DeWalt, 2011).

My methodology was based on gathering data through participation in and observation of the lives of my informants as I observed and questioned how my subjects interacted, interpreted their context and explained the social meanings of the MCC. My participation included observation of meetings (sometimes acting as the notetaker and offering input when asked), reorganization of the MCC library and filing system in Uganda, and occasional leadership of peacebuilding training sessions. I often learned as much as a participant observer by accompanying MCC volunteers on their weekly grocery shopping as I did observing their organizational meetings. I encouraged them to share not only their current work experiences but how this related to who they had been at home in North America. Everything from what they chose to wear to how they decorated their homes and who their friends were helped me to understand the values that shaped their lives as MCC volunteers.

I was present with MCC volunteers as they transitioned in and out of their jobs, through changing relationships with spouses and significant others, through births and deaths. Playing late night games of speed Scrabble or Uno, witnessing the piercing of noses and ears, doing yoga, hiking and sharing meals in my apartment were all at least as significant as the time I spent in meetings, interviews and shadowing MCC workers in their jobs. I became bound up in their lives and they became bound up in mine, at times blurring the line between the times I was acting as a researcher and the times I was acting as their friend. My life also changed over the course of my fieldwork and some of the "characters" in my thesis became involved in my life outside the PhD work. This was most clearly demonstrated when I was hospitalized in Nairobi and several of my informants visited me in the hospital and were interviewed from my sick bed while I was still too ill to leave the house.

Sudhir Venkatesh (2008) described his fieldwork among gangs in Chicago as managing the tension between being "the hustler" and being "the hustled." One informant tells Venkatesh, "They *know* you can do something for them.... You're a hustler, I can see it. You'll do anything to get what you want" (p. 188, emphasis in original). In their discussion of ethical issues, Gary Fine and David Shulman (2009) describe ethnographers as "manipulative suitors," prone to "flatter to develop a rapport to acquire suitors and whisper sweet nothings to ferret out the truth" (p. 178). Sometimes when I hung out with volunteers, I worried that I was "hustling" them—presenting myself as a friend when I was actually carefully observing and writing about everything they did or said. Managing my own expectations as well as theirs about our relationship was difficult, particularly as I naturally came to form my own personal opinions and preferences— feeling drawn to some and irritated by others but still needing to maintain relationship with all of them. I was concerned that the framework and expectations of friendship concealed the fact that I was still very much a researcher (Beech, Hibbert, MacIntosh, & McInnes, 2009). Once the research was over, I remained close friends with some informants but the relationship faded with others. Interestingly, one of my best friends today is one of my research subjects from my time in Uganda and I sometimes wonder how our initial roles as researcher and researched enhances or hinders our relationship now.

While emotional closeness provides many benefits to research, it also has drawbacks. Like many anthropologists, I sometimes struggled with the fine (and sometimes nonexistent) line between participant observation and emotional involvement in the lives of my subjects. At times, I was privy to some intimate details of their lives, information which I did not share in the final project out of respect for their privacy even when the information was clearly relevant. Maintaining a critical distance from my research subjects was difficult. Yet I recognized that even the idea of critical distance privileged certain ways of knowing and created artificial divisions between thinking and feeling or researcher and researched.

As a participant observer, there are often contesting narratives presented by multiple informants which will vie to become "the" official version of events depicted in one's research. I sometimes felt pulled between multiple allegiances within MCC and the larger Mennonite community in East Africa. As informants shared simmering organizational conflicts, some people made clear bids for my sympathy and support. These attempts at triangulation were difficult to resist but would have threatened my ability to see dynamics through multiple perspectives. At times, I witnessed underlying conflicts between Mennonite leadership and other staff, between MCC and a regional Mennonite mission organization, between local partners and MCC and between current and former MCC volunteers.

While impossible to quantify and difficult to describe, building and maintaining trust is one of the most salient aspects of fieldwork (van Maanen, 1982). I felt enormous pressure to be trustworthy and to demonstrate to my informants how deeply committed I was to a responsible and authentic representation of their lives and their work, even though I was also not a genuine member of their team. I sensed initial hesitation on the part of MCC leadership in both countries to my presence. As a Mennonite myself, the Mennonite communitarian ethos somewhat obligated MCC to allow me access. However, some informants indicated hesitancy about the implications of my presence. One MCC leader repeatedly joked about reporting "only the good things," a quip with a note of seriousness beneath it. At one MCC gathering, a volunteer cautioned: "we need to watch what we say, there's a researcher around." Remarks like this demonstrated informants' awareness of my presence and the bearing that my research might have on their work.

It is important to observe how one's work and presence is being perceived and experienced by one's informants. MCC volunteers often emphasized that my time in the region was "short" and "just for study"—an observation indicative of their belief that their own work is both "long term" and "meaningful." The mild Mennonite bias against higher education and preference for service was sometimes evident when volunteers explained my work to each other or to outsiders. Occasionally I witnessed "insider talk" which indicated that I was seen as engaging in something that was a "luxury" or "superficial" and "not as important" as volunteer work.

ANALYSIS, WRITING, AND DISTRIBUTION

When beginning the writing process, the sheer amount of data collected during the course of fieldwork can feel overwhelming. Finding common themes and identifying key moments that stand out can bring a sense of structure to one's overall research project. I analyzed my data using a coding process to link information gathered in the field with values found in my literature review of Mennonite ethics and theology.

One of the advantages of the ethnographic methodology is the use of "thick description" to illustrate complex and often subtle social dynamics (Geertz, 1973). The ethnographer should not shy away from thorough description of the context of one's work—often even the most minute details can be analyzed to help argue a larger point. This writing will be greatly aided if the researcher has taken careful and detailed notes throughout fieldwork. It is easy to edit "thick description" out but difficult to add it in if one has not taken note of it initially.

Confidentiality was not a concern for most MCC volunteers, most of whom would no longer be with MCC by the time my writing was complete. Nonetheless, I was aware that MCC partners in particular were taking a risk in criticizing MCC, an institution upon which their livelihood depended. I respected this confidence by using intentionally vague footnotes which made tracing comments to a particular informant difficult, thereby protecting their identity. When necessary, I also protected my informants by withholding certain identifying features (such as gender) when using their words.

A "member checking" process in which the researcher shares impressions with the informants helps to present a more nuanced and accurate picture of the fieldwork while also allowing room for one's own interpretations of the data (Lincoln & Guba, 1985; Maxwell, 1996; Schwartz-Shea & Yanow, 2009). As I began the writing process, I continued to correspond with nearly all of my MCC informants which proved an important source of participant validation. I understood my fieldwork to be a collaborative effort between myself and my research informants and while the analysis was mine alone, I wanted to accurately reflect the opinions and stories shared with me.

When the research project was complete, I sent electronic copies of the work (my completed PhD dissertation) to all of my informants and offered to send paper copies to a few of the locations in Uganda and Kenya with limited internet connectivity. I was quite anxious to hear how my research subjects responded to my final portrait of them. The responses were generally positive though most informants noted that reading a 200 page academic paper was not a high priority. Those who both read it and continued to correspond with me about it felt pleased that I had taken care to really understand them, even if they may have disagreed with some of my analysis. I was initially unnerved that a few of the informants did not agree with everything that I had written. Did this mean I had failed to represent them faithfully? Was my ethnography somehow flawed if they did not universally celebrate my depictions? Ultimately, I decided that this was what separated my scholarly research project from merely recording and describing data. While my methodology was ethnographic, it still required analysis and interpretation from me. My objective was not simply to depict the lives, beliefs and practices of a group of aid workers and beneficiaries but ultimately to analyze and evaluate MCC's contributions to peacebuilding and development work. This may be a key difference between an ethnography conducted in the discipline of anthropology and an ethnography in peace and conflict studies.

ADVANTAGES AND DISADVANTAGES OF THE ETHNOGRAPHIC APPROACH

Just as peace and conflict studies as an interdisciplinary field draws upon many disciplines, it must also draw upon multiple research methodologies. While my experience using critical ethnography to analyze and understand both power dynamics and religious meaning in a NGO argues for the usefulness of this methodology, I do not discount the utility and appropriateness of other methodologies in this field. I believe ethnography offers multiple benefits to many research endeavors (Clifford & Marcus, 1986; Hammersley & Atkinson, 1995; Marcus, 1998; van Maanen, 1988) including several particular advantages to the researcher focusing on peace and conflict studies.

UNDERSTANDING THE LOCAL

One of the ways in which ethnography is a methodology well-suited for peace and conflict studies is ethnography's focus on the particularities of context. Epistemologically, peace and conflict studies tends to privilege the local and the particular while also trying to understand and develop broader theory. While the Westphalian model of state-centric international relations is still seen as a valid way of understanding the world, much of peace and conflict studies has tended to challenge this paradigm by emphasizing the need to take the local/grassroots level of politics into account. Ethnography's focus on deep, textured understanding of a particular context at a particular moment in time with particular actors reinforces this approach.

Peace and conflict studies attempts to understand and value approaches to conflict resolution and reconciliation that are grounded in the local context of the actors. Practices such as *mato oput* in Uganda or *sulha* in Palestine are seen as valuable even though most practitioners would not suggest trying to graft them onto other cultural contexts. Such approaches are sometimes referred to as "cultural practices," which is mistaken nomenclature as it subtly normalizes Western practices as standard and non-Western practices as "cultural." Nonetheless, the ethnographic study of how different societies resolve and manage difference provides information that is both culturally-specific and theoretically useful. While Sri Lankans may not be able to relate to the details of an Acholi reconciliation ritual in Uganda, they may benefit from understanding how a cultural ritual can provide a meaningful platform for reintegration of combatants into postconflict society.

Conflict theory emphasizes the importance of understanding the time-frame or stages in a conflict. The model is admittedly imperfect and most conflicts cannot be easily divided into the traditional conflict curve of difference, violence, escalation, peak/stalemate, ceasefire, reconstruction and reconciliation; however, ripeness theory, the idea that conflicts have phases during which different peacemaking techniques are most appropriate, is still salient. Ethnography highlights this dynamic as ethnographers do not produce universally valid knowledge but rather narrow their focus to a defined set of actors interacting in specific time and place.

Some scholars (Milne, 2010) have noted that this specificity or micro-focus runs counter to a field that has tended to privilege overarching, broadly applicable theories. The relative newness of peace and conflict studies as a recognized field of study may mean that scholars working within it are under pressure to "prove" that they can contribute to the more positivist traditions of research in international relations or political science. My experience in attempting to publish my ethnographic dissertation thesis was often frustrating as publishers kindly but firmly explained that the market demand was not for ethnography but for broad, comparative studies which reinforce or challenge generalized theories. Policy think-tanks and peacebuilding research institutes tend to prefer research with clear practical applications, generalized theory which can easily be used elsewhere. Unlike the critical peace education approach (Brantmeier, 2007), such institutions are not in the business of examining the detailed complexities of local contexts which is what ethnography tends to produce. The "validity" of the ethnography tends to be production and interpretation of data in an authentic way that is consistent with the lived realities of the research subject.

Nonetheless, even as the social sciences (including but not limited to political science, economics, sociology and psychology—traditional home disciplines of peace and conflict studies) continue to be influenced by poststructuralism, feminism, postmodernism, postcolonialism and critical theory, the reliability and valorized status of the broad-based theory begins to fray. Ethnography may not produce general theory but the detailed descriptions and observations it generates offer a more nuanced, careful understanding of the subject under consideration.

REFLEXIVITY AND SOCIAL LOCATION
HIGHLIGHTING POWER AND PRIVILEGE

Ethnography also challenges the positivist framework of research which attempts to delineate a clear separation between the researcher and the researched. Social science research increasingly demands that the researcher consider how s/he influenced the results of the study. Ethnography highlights this dynamic by forcing the researcher to contemplate how his/her own social location affected how information was observed and interpreted. In this way, ethnography challenges the sterile division of people into actors and acted upon. Clear identification of the researcher's social location and positionality helps to reveal the power dynamics shaping the final conclusions of any research project (Pachirat, 2009; Popoviciu, Haywood, & Ghaill, 2006; Shehata, 2006).

Studies of conflict have moved beyond a narrow division of actors into perpetrators and victims by recognizing that bystanders—both internal and externa—play an influential role in the evolution and aftermath of violence. Participant observation highlights the active agency of the ethnographer and challenges the idea that the researcher is a passive bystander removed from any responsibility for or participation in the events around them.

By urging the researcher to name his/her own identities and examine how these social categories influence both the phenomenon observed as well as the discourses produced, ethnography can make research more careful. There is a relationship between the methodology we use, the power we exercise, the epistemology we privilege, the data we observe and the theory we generate.

ENCOUNTERING THE OTHER

Peace and conflict studies and critical peace education recognize the importance of power and seeks to understand how actors exercise power over or with one another during conflict and in its aftermath. The need to highlight the voices of the voiceless and to de-center the traditional focus on understanding (and thus privileging) the powerful is one of the undergirding normative frameworks of the field. This focus on alterity and magnifying the experiences of the subaltern can be reinforced by an ethnographic approach which takes seriously the validity of the lived knowledge of individuals rather than trying to fit individual narratives into an existing theory.

However, as anthropologists have long-known, the extended focus on Otherness also carries risks of exoticizing and marginalizing the Other (Smith, 2012). The ethnographer must carefully balance the need to emphasize the familiarity and common humanity of the research subjects while also carefully highlighting difference. To forget this balance is to risk deepening the gap between the self and the Other, an endeavor which paves the way for dehumanization. While still imperfect, ethnography recognizes that research methodologies have both epistemological as well as moral implications.

CONCLUSION

One of the core features of the field of peace and conflict studies is its interdisciplinary nature. This means that, by definition, the field must embrace multiple methodologies and disciplinary approaches to knowledge. I believe that ethnography is a particularly appropriate qualitative methodology due to its careful attention to power dynamics, multiple epistemologies and emphasis on coming to understand the Other, not as a poor imitation of the self but as a subject with valid beliefs, practices and worldviews. Ethnography offers the researchers an opportunity to immerse themselves in new contexts to understand the complexities of both conflict and postconflict peacebuilding.

My own experience with ethnography helped me to understand Ugandans and Kenyans working with MCC on humanitarian relief, development and peacebuilding projects and gave me the opportunity to understand how the work of a North American NGO appears from multiple perspectives. However, equally importantly, my ethnographic study was able to help me see groups which I am intimately connected to (Mennonites, Americans, aid workers) as Other by providing a way for me to observe and study them. As the line between self and Other, between helper and helped, between "West" and "the rest" continues to fray, ethnography as a research methodology will remain a valuable way to understand both ourselves and Others—a core goal also shared by peace and conflict studies.

REFERENCES

Anderson, M. (1999). *Do no harm: How aid can support peace—or war.* Boulder, CO: Lynne Rienner.

Avruch, K. (2001) Notes Towards Ethnographies of Conflict and Violence. *Journal of Contemporary Ethnography, 30*(5), 637–648.

Bajaj, M., & Brantmeier, E. J. (2011). The politics, praxis, and possibilities of critical peace education. *Journal of Peace Education, 8*(3), 221–224.

Beech, N., Hibbert, P., MacIntosh, R., & McInnes, P. (2009). "But I thought we were friends?" Life cycles and research relationships. In S. Ybema, D. Yanow, H.

Wels, & F. Kamsteeg (Eds.), *Organizational ethnography: Studying the complexities of everyday life* (pp. 196–214). London, England: Sage.

Boellstorff, T. (2010). *Coming of age in second life: An anthropologist explores the virtually human.* Princeton, NJ: Princeton University Press.

Boellstorff, T., Nardi, B., Pierce, C., & Taylor, T.L. (2012). *Ethnography and Virtual Worlds: A handbook of method.* Princeton, NJ: Princeton University Press.

Bourdieu, P. (1984) *Distinction: A social critique of the judgement of taste.* London, England: Routledge.

Brantmeier, E. (2007). Everyday understandings of peace and non-peace: peace-keeping and peacebuilding at a US Midwestern high school. *Journal of Peace Education, 4*(2), 127–148.

Brewer, J. (2000). *Ethnography.* Buckingham, England: Open University Press.

Burgess, R. (1984). Conversations with a purpose: the ethnographic interview in educational research. In R. Burgess (Ed.), *Studies in qualitative methodology: A Research Annual* (pp. 137–155). London, England: JAI Press.

Carspecken, P. (1996). *Critical ethnography in educational research: A theoretical and practical guide.* New York, NY: Routledge.

Chock, P. (1986). Irony and Ethnography: on cultural analysis of one's own culture. *Anthropology Quarterly, 59*(2), 87–96.

Clifford, J., & Marcus, G. (Eds.). (1986). *Writing culture: The poetics and politics of ethnography.* Berkeley, CA: University of California Press.

Crang, M., & Cook, I. (2007). *Doing ethnographies.* London, England: Sage.

Czarniawska-Joerges, B. (1992). *Exploring complex organizations: A cultural perspective.* London, England: Sage.

Dandridge, T., Mitroff, I., & Joyce, W. (1980) Organizational symbolism: A topic to expand organizational analysis. *Academy of Management Review, 5,* 77–82.

DeWalt, K., & DeWalt, B. (2011) *Participant observation: A guide for fieldworkers.* Lanham, MD: AltaMira Press.

Feagin, J., Orum, A., & Sjoberg, G. (1991). *A case for the case study.* Chapel Hill, NC: University of North Carolina Press.

Fetherston, A. B., & Nordstrom, C. (1995) Overcoming *Habitus* in Conflict Management: UN peacekeeping and war zone ethnography. *Peace and Change, 20*(1), 94–119.

Fine, G., & Shulman, D. (2009). Lies from the field: Ethical issues in organizational ethnography. In S. Ybema, D. Yanow, H. Wels, & F. Kamsteeg (Eds.), *Organizational ethnography: Studying the complexities of everyday life* (pp. 177–196). London: SAGE

Fisher, W. (1997) Doing good? The politics and anti-politics of NGO practices. *Annual Review of Anthropology, 26,* 439–464.

Geertz, C. (1973). *The interpretation of cultures.* New York, NY: Basic Books.

Geertz, C. (1998). Deep hanging out (Review of the book *Routes: Travel and Translation in the Late Twentieth Century,* by James Clifford). *New York Review of Books, 46*(16), 69–72.

Gellner, D., & Hirsch, E. (Eds.). (2001). *Inside organisations: Anthropologists at work.* Oxford, England: Berg.

Gerring, J. (2004). What is a case study and what is it good for? *American Political Science Review, 98*(2), 341–354.

Gold, R. (1958). Roles in sociological field observations. *Social Forces, 36*(3), 217–223.

Gordon, U. (2010). Against the wall: Anarchist mobilization in the Israeli-Palestinian Conflict. *Peace and Change, 35*(3), 412–433.

Graeber, D. (2009). *Direct action: An ethnography.* Oakland, CA: AK Press.

Hammersley, M., & Atkinson, P. (1995). *Ethnography: Principles in practice* (2nd ed.). London, Englanc: Routledge.

Hannerz, U. (2003). Being there … and there … and there! Reflections on multi-site ethnography *Ethnography, 4,* 201–216.

Jones, M. (1996). *Studying organizational symbolism.* London, England: Sage.

Kapoor, I. (2004). Hyper-self-reflexive development? Spivak on representing the Third World Other. *Third World Quarterly, 25,* 627–647.

Kostera, M. (2007). *Organisational ethnography: Methods and inspirations.* Lund: Studentlitteratur AB.

Lederach, J. P. (1996). *Preparing for peace: Conflict transformation across culture.* Syracuse, NY: Syracuse University Press.

Lett, J. (1990). Emics and Etics: Notes on the epistemology of anthropology. In T. Headland, K. Pike, & M. Harris, (Eds.), *Emics and etics: The insider/outsider debate* (pp. 127–142). Newbury Park, CA: Sage.

Lincoln, Y., & Guba, E. (1985). *Naturalistic inquiry.* Newbury Park, CA: Sage.

Madison. D. S. (2005). *Critical ethnography: Method, ethics and performance.* Thousand Oaks, CA: Sage.

Marcelin, H. (2011) Cooperation, peace and (re)construction? A tale from the shanties. *Journal of Peacebuilding and Developmen, 6*(3), 17–31.

Marcus, G. (1995) Ethnography in/of the world system: the emergence of multi-sited ethnography *Annual Review of Anthropology, 24,* 95–117.

Marcus, G. (1998) *Ethnography through thick and thin.* Princeton, NJ: Princeton University Press.

Markowitz, L. (2001). Finding the Field: Notes on the ethnography of NGOs. *Human Organization, 60*(1), 40–46.

Maxwell, J. (1996). *Qualitative research design: An interactive approach.* London, England: Sage.

Milne, J. V. (2010). Method: Theory and ethnography in peace and conflict studies. In O. Richmond (Ed.), *Palgrave advances in peacebuilding: Critical developments and approaches* (pp. 74–98). London, England: Palgrave Macmillan.

Moeran, B. (2005). *The business of ethnography.* Oxford, England: Berg.

Moeran, B. (2009). From participant observation to observant participation. In S. Ybema, D. Yanow, H. Wels, & F. Kamsteeg (Eds.), *Organizational ethnography: Studying the complexities of everyday life* (pp. 139–155). London, England: Sage.

Mortenson, G. (2006). *Three cups of tea.* New York, NY: Viking.

Mosse, D. (2005). *Cultivating development: An ethnography of aid policy and practice.* London, England: Pluto Press.

Mosse, D. (2006). Anti-social anthropology? Objectivity, objection and the ethnography of public policy and professional communities. *Journal of the Royal Anthropological Institute, 12*(4), 935–956.

Mosse, D., & Lewis, D. (Eds.). (2005). *The aid effect: Giving and governing in international development.* London, England: Pluto Press.

Mosse, D., & Lewis, D. (Eds.). (2006). *Development brokers and translators. The ethnography of aid and agencies.* Bloomfield, CT: Kumarian Press.

Nardi, B. (2010). *My life as a night elf priest: An anthropological account of World of Warcraft.* Ann Arbor, MI: University of Michigan Press.

Neyland, D. (2008). *Organizational ethnography.* London, England: Sage.

Noblit, G., Flores, S., & Murillo, E. (Eds.). (2004). *Post critical ethnography: Reinscribing critique.* Cress, NJ: Hampton Press.

Nordstrom, C., & Robben, A. (Eds.). (1995). *Fieldwork under fire: Contemporary studies of violence and survival.* Berkley, CA: University of California Press.

Nordstrom, C. (1997). *A different kind of war story.* Philadelphia, PA: University of Pennsylvania Press.

Nordstrom, C. (2004). *Shadows of war: Violence, war and international profiteering in the twenty-first century.* Berkeley, CA: University of California Press.

Nordstrom, C. (2007). *Global outlaws: Crime, money and power in the contemporary world.* Berkley, CA: University of California Press.

Pacanowsky, M., & O'Donnell-Trujillo, N. (1982). Communication and organizational culture. *Western Journal of Speech Communication, 46,* 115–130.

Pachirat, T. (2009). The political in political ethnography: Reflections from an industrialized slaughterhouse on perspective, power and sight. In E. Schatz (Ed.), *Political ethnography: What immersion contributes to the study of politics.* Chicago, IL: University of Chicago Press.

Pierce, C. (2011). *Communities of play: Emergent cultures in multiplayer games and virtual worlds.* Cambridge, MA: MIT Press.

Popoviciu, L., Haywood, C., & Ghaill, M. (2006) The promise of post-structuralist methodology: Ethnographic representation of education and masculinity, *Ethnography and Education, 1*(3), 393–412.

Prasad, P. (2005). *Crafting qualitative research: Working in the postpositivist traditions.* Armonk, NY: M.E. Sharpe.

Richards, P. (Ed.). (2005). *No peace, No war: An anthropology of contemporary armed conflicts.* Athens, OH: Ohio University Press.

Scheper-Hughes, N., & Bourgois, P. (Eds.). (2004). *Violence in war and peace: An anthology.* Oxford, Englanc: Blackwell.

Schwartz-Shea, P., & Yanow, D. (2009). Reading and writing as method: in search of trustworthy texts. In S. Ybema, D. Yanow, H. Wels, & F. Kamsteeg (Eds.), *Organizational ethnography: Studying the complexities of everyday life* (pp. 56–82). London, Englanc: Sage.

Schwartzman, H. (1993). *Ethnography in organizations.* London, England: Sage.

Shehata, S. (2006). Ethnography, identity, and the production of knowledge. In D. Yanow & P. Schwartz-Shea (Eds.), *Interpretation and method: Empirical research methods and the interpretative turn* (pp. 244–263). Armonk, NY: M.E. Sharpe.

Smith, L. T. (2012). *Decolonizing methodologies: Research and indigenous people.* New York, NY: Palgrave Macmillan.

Smith, V. (2007). Ethnographies of work and the work of ethnographers. In P. Atkinson, A. Coffey, S. Delamont, J. Lofland, & L. Lofland (Eds.), *Handbook of ethnography* (pp. 220–233). London, England: Sage.

Taylor, T. L. (2009). *Play between worlds: Exploring online game culture.* Cambridge, MA: MIT Press.

Van Maanen, J. (1982). *Varieties of qualitative research*. Beverly Hills, CA: Sage.

Van Maanen, J. (1988). *Tales of the field: On writing ethnography*. Chicago, IL: University of Chicago Press.

Van Maanen, J. (Ed.). (1995). *Representation in ethnography*. London, England: Sage.

van der Waal, K. (2009). Getting Going: organizing ethnographic fieldwork. In S. Ybema, D. Yanow, H. Wels, & F. Kamsteeg (Eds.), *Organizational ethnography: Studying the complexities of everyday life* (pp. 23–39). London, England: Sage.

Venkatesh, S. (2008). *Gang leader for a day: A rogue sociologist takes to the streets*. London, England: Penguin.

Weiss, R. (1994). *Learning from strangers: The art and method of qualitative interview studies*. New York, NY: Free Press.

Welty, E., Bolton, M., Nayak, M., & Malone, C. (Eds.). (2012). *Occupying political science: The Occupy Wall Street Movement from New York to the World*. New York, NY: Palgrave Macmillan.

Wolcott, H. (1995). Making a study "More ethnographic." In J. Van Maanen (Ed.), *Representation in ethnography* (pp. 79–111). Thousand Oaks, CA: Sage.

Wolcott, H. (1999). *Ethnography: A way of seeing*. Long Beach, CA: AltaMira Press.

Yanow, D. (1996). *How does a policy mean? Interpreting policy and organizational actions*. Washington DC: Georgetown University Press.

Yanow, D., & Schwartz-Shea, P. (Eds.). (2006). *Interpretation and method: Empirical research methods and the interpretive turn*. Armonk, NY: M.E. Sharpe.

Ybema, S., & Kamsteeg, F. (2009). Making the familiar strange: A case for disengaged organizational ethnography. In S. Ybema, D. Yanow, H. Wels, & F. Kamsteeg (Eds.), *Organizational ethnography: Studying the complexities of everyday life* (pp. 101–119). London, England: Sage.

Ybema, S., Yanow, D., Wels, H., & Kamsteeg, F. (Eds.). (2009). *Organizational ethnography: Studying the complexities of everyday life*. London, Englanc: Sage.

Yin, R. (1994). *Case study research: Design and methods*. Newbury Park, CA: Sage.

CHAPTER 7

THEIR LIVES, OUR PEACE

Narrative Inquiry in
Peace and Conflict Studies

Patrick T. Hiller and Julia Chaitin

Introduction

I actually saw the moon landing, in 1969, in a tenement apartment, we didn't have a TV so we went to one of the gang member's family house, and on this TV screen we saw the landing on the moon, and there was a rat running across the floor, and to a person in that room, the people of color didn't really believe we landed on the moon, they thought it was somehow staged in the Western part of the country, because they didn't wanna believe that their government would be so careless that they would live in these conditions and spend a billion dollars to put some fool up on the moon while they lived like this, and so that really helped learn to get the perspective from their reality, and although we live very comfortably here, it's really important for me to try to have experiences of seeing the reality of some other folks. (William's life-story)

Peace and Conflict Studies Research: A Qualitative Perspective, pp. 137–160
Copyright © 2014 by Information Age Publishing

It should come as no surprise that we begin our chapter on narrative inquiry with a story. It is one of the many "stories we live by" (McAdams, 1993). William, the storyteller, was born in 1950 in Pennsylvania into a wealthy Evangelist family.[1] When he told his life story in 2009, William was a long-term nonviolent peace activist.

William's activist engagement started with conscientious objection and was part of the anti-Vietnam War movement. He had also volunteered for inner city projects in the 1960s and since that time had been very concerned about issues of racism. William had a long-term engagement with the antinuclear movement and antiarms movement. Another concern was the U.S. intervention in Latin America, Christian-Muslim relations, and the Middle East conflict, including the Iraq Wars. For his activist engagement, William served two prison sentences, one which lasted six months. The words of Dan McAdams (2006), an expert in narrative research, help us understand the significance of William's story: "Understanding why people do what they do is essential, you can imagine, for social life" (p. 82). In only a few lines of William's life story, we learn about his experience that ties into concepts that are central to peace and conflict studies: structural violence, power, privilege, otherness, us versus them, and injustice.

Over the years, narrative inquiry has become increasingly important in qualitative research. Sociology, psychology, social-psychology, education, anthropology, communication studies and cultural studies have adopted narrative inquiries (Andrews, Sclater, Squire, & Treacher, 2000; Andrews, Squire, & Tamboukou, 2008; McAdams, 2008; Trahar, 2011).

The academic disciplines of conflict analysis and resolution and peace and conflict studies can also benefit from narrative inquiry. As Johnston (2005) states, "the study of protracted, seemingly unresolvable conflicts requires an in-depth method of research and analysis" (p. 278). The author argues that the stories reflect the conflicting parties' perception of a dispute, i.e. their perception of the reality. And as Denzin (2000) reminds us, "we have no direct access to experience as such. We can only study experience through its representations, through the stories we are told" (p. xi). It is, therefore, surprising that there are relatively few studies of social conflict that deal with the stories and experiences of people.

In this chapter we focus on narrative inquiry and its application in peace and conflict studies. We begin with an overview of and brief history of narrative inquiry and then discuss some of the key approaches, while focusing our attention on the life history methodology. By presenting several examples of narrative research in peace and conflict studies, we provide ideas concerning the broad potential of this approach across several areas in the field. As our contribution to the methodological nature of this book, we lead the reader through methodological considerations of a life history study on nonviolent activists in the United States.

We purposefully mesh the theoretical with actual application and examples from the study that we will present, allowing the reader to envision his/her own applied research design. At the end of the chapter, we share a few "researchers' notes," that offer reflections on our roles as researchers, our expectations and our opportunities for creativity. We conclude by reemphasizing the tremendous potential of narrative inquiry in conflict resolution studies.

Overview and Brief History of Narrative Inquiry

Narrative inquiry can be understood as a method and phenomena of study (Pinnegar & Daynes, 2007). It can be defined as "any study that uses or analyzes narrative materials" (Lieblich, Tuval-Mashiach, & Zilber, 1998, p. 2). Narrative inquiry is far from a footnote in contemporary social sciences. In its briefest form, narrative inquiry is a method that allows researchers to collect, analyze and interpret the stories people tell about their lives.

In narrative inquiry, researchers record and explore peoples' stories based on the presumption that their realities are shaped through the narratives (Marshall & Rossman, 2010). Narrative inquiry offers ways of understanding experience and is based on collaboration between the researcher and participants, over time.

From a qualitative research perspective, "narrative is understood as the spoken or written text giving an account of an event/action or series or events/actions, chronologically connected" (Creswell, 2012, p. 70). Narrative research, as a method, examines the experiences expressed in the lived and told stories of individuals (Clandinin & Connelly, 2000; Creswell, 2012). Narrative researchers assume that that the narratives are fundamental for understanding human experience (Pinnegar & Daynes, 2007) and that they are chronological, meaningful and social products (Wells, 2011).

Person-centered case studies, biographies and life histories developed as responses to positivist empiricism. Other antecedents of narrative inquiry included structuralist, poststructuralist, postmodern, psychoanalytic, and deconstructionist approaches (Squire, Andrews, & Tamboukou, 2008). As a result of its background, narrative inquiry is interdisciplinary; its many uses evolved in humanist sociological and psychological research in the second half of the 20th century.

While we acknowledge the complex nature of narrative inquiry, Creswell's (2012) outline of its defining features is most helpful:

- Narrative researchers collect stories from individuals about individuals' lived and told experiences.

- Narratives tell about individual experiences and shed light on identities and self-perceptions.
- Narrative stories are collected in multiple ways, with interviews being the primary form of data collection.
- Narratives stories often contain turning points.
- Narratives occur within specific places or situations.

Our overview is intentionally brief; others have done great work in explaining and placing narrative research within the social sciences. For more information on the ideas we briefly reviewed above, we refer the reader to the complete works by Andrews et al. (2008), Bruner (1991) , Elliot (2005), Lieblich et al. (1998), Wells (2011) and Clandinin (2007).

Key Approaches to Narrative Inquiry

Within the broad tradition of narrative inquiry there are several popular approaches. We will begin by pointing out that the terminology used is at times ambiguous: the terms biography, life history and oral history are often interchanged, due to epistemological and methodological features. Thus we suggest that when choosing a tradition, one should be clear on how s/he will be using the terms and be consistent in this use.

The most commonly used forms of narrative inquiry include the following. In *biographical* studies the experiences of a person's life are written and/or recorded by a researcher. In *autoethnography*, individuals who are the subject of the study, write and record data about themselves, examining their personal stories within the larger sociocultural context (Creswell, 2012). *Oral history* is a method of collecting narratives from individuals who experienced important historical-social-political events (Leavy, 2011, p. 4) and can include stories and personal reflections of events of families, communities and societies (Creswell, 2012; Thompson, 1978).

The remainder of this section will examine some of the theoretical underpinnings of the *narrative life history approach*, which are rooted in sociology, anthropology, history, education, religion, philosophy and other disciplines (Atkinson, 2007).

Life histories focus on the lives of individuals and are particularly useful when studying processes of social identity formation (Holstein & Gubrium, 2000; Lieblich et al., 1998). Work by Erikson (1950/1963, 1959) is considered a foundation for contemporary concepts of personal identity. Erikson's psycho-social perspective recognizes individual psychological factors as well as social structural factors in the development of human identities within a life-course, considered by Côté and Levine (2002) to be a "rich theoretical understanding of the relationship between identity formation, social structure, culture, and history" (p. 30). Jenkins (2008) states that identity is a multidimensional classification, a mapping of the human world and our (individuals and collectives) place in it, a process— that is—not a thing, and a basic cognitive mechanism for humans to sort out themselves and others, both individually and collectively.

McAdams (1988, 2001, 2006) extends the literary cannon on identity formation by exploring how one's life story provides an identity and a sense of meaning and purpose. McAdams's life-story model of identity offers a compelling rationale for narrative inquiry in conflict resolution and beyond:

> Life stories are based on biographical facts, but they go considerably beyond the facts as people selectively appropriate aspects of their experience and imaginatively construe both past and future to construct stories that make sense to them and to their audiences, that vivify and integrate life and make it more or less meaningful. Life stories are psychosocial constructions, coauthored by the person himself or herself and the cultural context within which that person's life is embedded and given meaning. As such, individual life stories reflect cultural values and norms, including assumptions about gender, race, and class. Life stories are intelligible within a particular cultural frame, and yet they also differentiate one person from the next. (McAdams, 2001, p. 101)

In sum, we see that life stories and personal narratives not only tell us a great deal about the individual, but also about his/her collective and his/her perception of the social reality. The use of narrative inquiry in research spans a number of different disciplines. While narrative research has been used in studies that look at individual processes, we find that it is a good vehicle for studies emanating from the conflict resolution and peace studies field. This is the topic to which we now turn.

The Roles of Narratives in Peace and Conflict Studies

In this section we share several examples in which narrative inquiry has been used in peace and conflict related research.[2] This is by no means a comprehensive overview, but it aims to provide a summary of the broad opportunities for use of narrative inquiry. Narrative research is especially relevant for studies of peace and conflict since narratives often contain contradictory layers of meaning, dialogical interaction and the growing understanding about individuals and social change, political change, violence, trauma and genocide and particularly social identity in such contexts (Andrews, 2007; Andrews et al., 2008; Bar-On, 2006; Chaitin, Awwad,

& Andriani, 2009; Fujii, 2010; Hammack, 2010; McAdams, Josselson, & Lieblich, 2006).

In *Women, War and Peace in South Asia*, Manchanda (2001) presents narratives of women negotiating violent politics in their everyday lives. By examining narratives of six Palestinians in the Gaza Strip in their study, *Beyond Intifada*, Gordon, Gordon, and Shriteh (2003) connect Palestinian life-stories to crucial events of the Intifada. In *Seasons of Captivity*, Lieblich (1994) uses a narrative approach to describe facets of life of Israeli POWs held captive in Egypt, during the War of Attrition fought between Egypt and Israel from 1969 to 1970. In *When Blood and Bones Cry Out*, Lederach and Lederach (2010) focus on stories on metaphors with interviewees from a number of conflict arenas, including child soldiers in West Africa who are both victims and perpetrators of violence, and the disappeared in Columbia.

The use and potential of narratives in peace and conflict studies is virtually unlimited. It has been used for: learning about "the other" or identities in the Israeli-Palestinian conflict (Chaitin et al., 2009; Kamel & Huber, 2012); the impact of traumatic testimony in Chile (Cornejo, Rojas, & Mendoza, 2009); sex trafficking and exploitation (Kara, 2009); testimonies of war and violence in Rwanda (Fujii, 2010); ethnicity and belonging among refugees/immigrants to the United States (Chaitin, Linstroth, & Hiller, 2009), narrative of Israeli youth in connection to the Middle East conflict (Hammack, 2009); traumatic memories of Holocaust survivors (Langer, 1991); working through the past and present-day conflict among Germans, Jews and Palestinians (Albeck, Adwan, & Bar-On, 2002); Palestinian autobiographical memory (Nets-Zehngut, 2011); Maya identities in exile (Linstroth, 2009); and the interplay between narrative and healing in postapartheid South Africa (Young, 2004)

In order to demonstrate how narrative inquiry can be used in peace and conflict studies, we will now present an overview of research that explored the life trajectories of nonviolent peace activists in the United States.

TRAJECTORIES TOWARD NONVIOLENCE ACTIVISM—AN ILLUSTRATION OF CONDUCTING NARRATIVE RESEARCH

Brief Overview of the Study

The life-story study explored the psychological and social meanings given to the experiences of long-time nonviolent peace and social justice activists in the United States.[3] The research question was: How do nonviolent peace activists construct and negotiate their identities? Special emphasis was placed on the meaning of nonviolence for these activists;

the intersection of the individual's personal life with family, social, cultural, political, ideological, and economic norms; the influence of the social context on the development of a nonviolent orientation; the themes of "obedience" and "disobedience" developed; and the role of religion in their decisions to devote their lives to activism.

Nonviolent peace activism has primarily been investigated using quantitative methods. Certainly these studies were helpful in creating specific categories, and pointing out commonalities and differences of motives and issues. However, the weakness in approaching nonviolent peace activism solely from a quantitative perspective lies in the fact that the personal meanings attached to the actions are left unexplored. With this in mind, it was possible to determine that narrative research was extremely relevant for a study of peace and social justice activists.

The study applied life story methodology to expand the narrative, in-depth interviews (Chaitin, 2002, 2004; Lieblich et al., 1998; Rosenthal, 1993), and was based on Chaitin's (2002) reasoning concerning the use of life-stories in social-science research. The study aimed: (1) to learn about and understand the complex human and social phenomena inherent to being an individual dedicated to nonviolent peace activism; (2) to expand knowledge concerning the meaning nonviolent peace activists give to their actions; and (3) to learn about the experiences of nonviolent peace activists, in order to find out what events were of importance to them in the development of their identities.

Chaitin (2004) identifies three elements/assumptions central to life story methodology. (1) Every person has a unique story to share and gives his/her own personal meaning to the story. (2) Although the stories are unique by themselves, they are rooted in specific social and cultural settings. (3) Individuals do not tell random stories; everything that they share in such narratives has meaning for their lives. Moreover, it is invaluable to explore people's own representations of their lives by allowing them to frame their stories and emphasize those aspects of their lives meaningful to them without direction by the researcher.

Since narrative inquiry helps understand an individual's inner world as well as uncovers change, development and growth (McAdams et al., 2006), the life story approach was chosen since it could help explain why activists willfully transgress social norms and, at times, even risk personal injury and imprisonment.

In addition to the life stories, additional data collection included documentary research (Marshall & Rossman, 2010; May, 2001) obtained from local and national newspapers and from a myriad of flyers, stickers, posters, articles, and books often created by activist groups. This allowed me (Patrick) to place the activists' live stories into the historical and current context of their actions. By using multiple methods and sources—a process called triangulation—qualitative research approaches were strengthened (Creswell, 2012; Denzin & Lincoln, 2005).

We will now present the methodological approach to the study, hoping to help clarify how theory and method interact with one another.

Choosing a Sample Population

Sixteen individuals (6 women, 10 men), who regularly engage in activities pertinent to nonviolent peace activism and who define themselves as nonviolent peace activists, were interviewed. A number of sampling strategies described by Miles and Huberman (1994, as cited in Marshall & Rossman, 2010) came into play.

Criterion sampling involved a selection process by which individuals in the United States with a long-term commitment to nonviolent peace activism were chosen. Snowball or chain sampling then expanded this population, as informants provided contact information and acted as gatekeepers for individuals who fit the criteria of the desired study population. This approach was somewhat similar to convenience sampling procedures, which allows researchers to locate participants suitable for a study avoiding time consuming research.

The participants had diverse demographic backgrounds. Their ages ranged from 45 to 89 years at the time of the interviews. The levels of formal education ranged from high school degrees to postgraduate. Professionally, participants were engaged in a variety of activities ranging from employment directly related to activism, in higher education, in the insurance sector or in ticket sales. Some participants were in full or semi-retirement, concentrating their efforts on volunteer work in the realm of their activist commitment.

Often, (young) researchers ask: How many people do we have to interview? This is a question that cannot be easily answered. We certainly have to display sound judgment in terms of feasibility and do-ability (Marshall & Rossman, 2010) when selecting a sample size, but it is important to refrain from setting a fixed number at the study's initial phase. We gather data while simultaneously engaging in data analysis and find that we can stop interviewing when we reach theoretical saturation (Glaser & Strauss, 1967). This concept, derived from the tradition of grounded theory, refers to the situation in which the researcher sees similar patterns emerging for the data, and determines that a point of saturation, i.e. no new information is to be won, has been reached (Glaser & Strauss, 1967). As practical advice for dealing with institutional review boards and ethics committees, we suggest proposing to interview a larger number of interviewees than expected in order to avoid the need to reapply for approval to conduct the research.

The Life-Story Method of Interviewing

The life-story interview is one type of narrative inquiry methodology that seeks to gain life-as-a-whole narrative, respecting the subjective meaning making of individuals. By examining first person narratives, we better understand the subjective meaning of a person's life. Interview participants are asked to tell the story of their lives as a whole, without being interrupted by the interviewer (Flick, 2007; Rosenthal, 1993). These are unstructured interviews that allow respondents to talk at length about their lives as they set their own frames of reference. It allows respondents to give meaning to events in their own way and provides better understanding of their point of view. The main assets of unstructured interviews are their flexibility and the discovery of meaning (May, 2001).

Elicitation of a life-story requires several guidelines. First, we focus our attention on the interviewee. While we may be tempted to "jump into" respondents' stories, correct factual inaccuracies, commend the respondents' actions or share our own point of view, we need to refrain from doing so (Chaitin, 2004). In life-story interviews, the narrators are considered to be the only experts on their own lives. Therefore, as researchers, we do not impose our knowledge, but are respectful and show interested attention (Czarniawska-Joerges, 2004; Elliott, 2005). Second, the underlying values and ethics of qualitative research require us to be completely transparent about our research agenda (Christians, 2003). In addition, the information gathered in the interview cannot be shared with others, unless the interviewee gives her/his approval.

Life-story interviews tend to be very personal; therefore, appropriate warm-up and follow-up is essential. In general the life-story interview has four stages: (1) making contact; (2) getting acquainted; (3) the interview; (4) saying good bye and keeping in touch. For a more in-depth overview of the methodology, we recommend Rosenthal (1993, 2007) and Chaitin's (2002, 2004) work on life-story interviewing.

We now turn to the specific process applied in the study of nonviolent peace activists in the United States.

For those nonviolent peace activists that were identified and agreed to be interviewed, the following process took place. Through e-mail and phone conversations, the project was explained in detail and any questions that potential interviewees had were answered. The interviews were held during one or two sessions, depending on scheduling and fatigue of the interviewees or the researcher. The interviews lasted from a little more than

1 hour to 9.5 hours. They were held at homes, offices or quiet public places mutually agreed upon previously with the participants. After warming up and getting acquainted with the respondent, the interview followed the sequences of a narrative interview as outlined by Rosenthal (2007). All interviews were recorded digitally.

In the initial narrative question, the interviewee was asked tell his/her life story, sharing whatever s/he felt as relevant. During the main narration, the interviewee provided a self-structured biographical self-presentation, while the researcher listened actively and took some notes. An open-ended question period followed the main narration. First there were intrinsic questions (Rosenthal, 1993), related to the main narrative, that were also based on Della Porta's (1992) suggestion that the individuals' social processes can be examined through questions concerning the family background, education, and adolescence.

The key factors addressed in the questions were phases in the interviewees' lives (e.g., the time at college during the anti-Vietnam War movement), particular themes that came up (e.g., the exposure to unfamiliar contexts), and specific situations already mentioned in the narrative (e.g., the experience of participating in lunch-counter sit-ins during the Civil Rights Movement). Extrinsic questions—that is questions prepared ahead of time that dealt specifically with the topic of experiences of being a peace activist – focused on the activists' phases of life directly related to their political involvement. For example: How do you define nonviolence? How do you define activism? Can you tell me about your most meaningful experience as an activist?

Asking questions during the life-story interview process is as much a learned art as it is a planned qualitative research approach. It is important that the interview questions be framed in straightforward, everyday language and not in sociological terms (Elliott, 2005). Most importantly, we want to elicit stories in the respondents' own words. Atkinson (1998) provides a list of more than 200 questions which can focus on the life course or on a given thematic framework. Preparing a large set of questions should be seen as a repertoire from which we can draw rather than a list that must be followed in all interviews. In narrative inquiry, which looks to elicit in-depth recounting of personal experiences, less is often better.

Analyzing Narrative Life History Data

Narrative analysis utilizes a set of interpretive tools that allows us to *"examine phenomena, issues, and people's lives holistically"* (Daiute & Lightfoot, 2004, p. xi, original emphasis). Moreover, narrative analysis generates insights into the dynamic relations between self and society (Daiute &

Lightfoot, 2004). The fundamental goal of narrative analysis is to reveal information concerning the "actual lived life, termed the life history, and the meanings that the individual attaches to the lived life, termed the life story. The life story exists on two levels—the told story and the untold (latent) story" (Chaitin, 2002, p. 14).

Eight basic steps for analyzing data in life story studies were followed in this research project:

Steps 1 and 2—Listening, Transcribing and Reading the Interview

All interviews were transcribed and printed out in a way that allowed writing notes, marking words and/or paragraphs. We recommend first reading the entire interview several times. As Lapadat and Lindsay (1999, p. 82) state, understandings of the data "are derived through the process of constructing a transcript by listening and re-listening, viewing and re-viewing" the material.

Step 3—Chronological Analysis

Based on the transcript, a chronology of the interviewee's life was constructed (Rosenthal, 2007). Commonly presented in a table, the main objective of a chronological sketch is to identify life-course stages or experiences such as childhood, marriage, employment, residence, siblings, and so on (Creswell, 2012). In this and other analytical stages, we try to manage and reduce the vast amount of data so that we can make progress in our interpretations (Marshall & Rossman, 2010). This is particularly important in life history interviews, in general, and in this study as well—for example, in the chronological analysis of one of the interviewees whose interview that lasted 9.5 hours covered many years of the 89-year old respondent's life—from high school all the way to his present involvement in peace activism.

In this study, life histories were also examined in relation to an historical timeline. Multilayered chronological charts were created in order to enrich the visualization of a temporal connection between personal and social events, based on the categories of personal life, education, occupation, activist engagement and history emphasizing events, periods and social movements that were significant for nonviolent activism. These charts aided the analysis of the interview data, as it placed them into a social-political context.

It was important to juxtapose the respondents' life histories with the his-torical-social-political events that occurred over time, especially since many of the interviewees shared experiences of significant times such as the Civil Rights Movement, the anti-Vietnam War Movement or the ongoing move-ments opposing the wars in Iraq and Afghanistan (Hiller, 2011). Regardless of the format used to record the chronologies, the goal of life-story research is to connect the life history with the narrated life (Rosenthal, 2007).

Step 4—Global Analysis

The global analysis addresses four main points: (1) a description of the interview context that describes how hard/easy it was making contact with the participant, the interview setting, the manner/dress of interviewee, how the interviewer felt, length of the interview, and so forth; (2) an overall summary of the interview including first-identified themes, style of speech (questions, arguments, stories, hesitations, etc.), emotional atmosphere, and so forth; (3) first hypotheses concerning possible meanings the experiences have had for the interviewee; and (4) a critical examination of the interview process in respect to the positive/negative aspects, the necessity of follow-up interviews and/or ideas/ concerns for future interviews.

In this study the global analysis looked at: (1) general impressions, (2) major life themes, (3) formative events/turning points, (4) the construction of identity, (5) the perception of nonviolence and activism, (6) the main issues and groups of activist involvement and (7) metaphors.

Step 5—In-Depth Thematic Analysis

Thematic analysis aims to understand the life-story by identifying major themes that reoccur and are emphasized by the interviewees. This overall analytical approach is relatively similar to the holistic-content perspective or narrative analysis explained by Lieblich and colleagues (1998). Here the material is read several times until patterns can be identified.

There are a number of ways to identify themes: by the space devoted to them in the text, their repetitive nature and the details provided by the biographer. Lieblich and colleagues (1998) remind us to be aware of the first and last appearance of the theme; the transitions between the themes, the context of each theme, and their relative salience in the text—all good clues concerning the importance of a theme to an interviewee. In general, we suggest looking for no more than six main themes for each interviewee and to decide on a name for each theme. From a research technical perspective, we suggest to either number or color-code the identified themes for easier analysis.

The major themes that emerged in the activists' lives covered a broad range from "justice/Injustice," "creativity," "Bethlehem," "education" and "curiosity." For example, the theme of Bethlehem (in the West Bank, Palestine) in the life of one female participant stood out in that her 5 years of work in that city had a formative influence on her life. That period of her life provided her with a sense of belonging and being needed, she obtained firsthand knowledge of injustice and she realized how she had led a privileged life. She not only said that the time spent in Bethlehem was the best part of her life, but she also shared positive emotions related to places, companions and her own role in fighting injustices against the Palestinian people. At the time of the study, her activism mainly concentrated on the Middle East conflict and the majority of her work related to the rights of the Palestinian people, even though more than 20 years had passed since she lived in Bethlehem.

It should be noted, that the overall research agenda influences how deeply the actual language of the narrative will be studied. While it is very useful to undertake in-depth thematic analyses in life story interviews, the researcher should also examine additional details of the conflict narrative, such as pauses, false starts and utterances (Johnston, 2005), since such analyses help us recognize conflict dynamics including emotional experiences of conflict or individual conflict styles.

Step 6—Looking for Metaphors

Life story interviews tend to be long, multifaceted and complex. Whereas the previous analysis helps us examine major themes in the interviewees' lives, it is helpful to take a step back and to approach the interpretation in a holistic manner. Metaphors do this by helping capture the participants' lives in general. Metaphors are creative ways to translate/convert the entire life-narrative into brief meaningful descriptions. While there are endless ways to create metaphors, we often use movie/song titles or proverbs in this stage. All metaphors we develop are then supported by one or two explanatory sentences.

The following examples serve as illustrations. For one interviewee, the metaphor of "still waters run deep" described his strong and powerful acts of civil disobedience which led to several prison sentences. A unique aspect of the interviewee's conduct was his quiet, respectful manner and spirituality, as well as his aversion to public recognition. "Allegro for peace" was a metaphor devised for another participant. In classical music vocabulary, the different speeds and moods of music are expressed in different tempi. Allegro connotes speed, but more importantly joy. The participant, a dedicated violinist who holds a degree in music, also is dedicated to social action and oftentimes derives immense joy out of its creativity and successes.

It is important for us to note here our ethical obligations. While it might be evident, it is crucial that researchers refrain from suggesting derogatory metaphors, and there is a danger that more subtle forms of ridiculing or judgmental metaphors may find their way into the analysis. We must remain aware of the potential hierarchical (researcher-biographer) power relations that are associated with gender, class, ethnicity, race, nationality, and so forth (Christians, 2003; Fine, 1998) and remember, at all times, to be respectful of the interviewees who donated their time to our study.

Step 7—Creating a Summary

A summary ties together all of the previous steps and answers the research questions. In the study described here, the main question was: How does the interviewee appear to construct his/her identity as a nonviolent peace activist? The summary reviewed the chronology, the global analysis, the themes and the metaphors. These summaries enabled me (Patrick) to identify the common themes of religion, faith and spirituality, experiencing the unfamiliar, significant influences and education in the lives of the activists.

In the next section, we discuss how the tremendous amount of narrative data and the results of the analytical steps can be reported.

Reporting Results From Life Stories

By writing a narrative report, we bring the threads of the entire study together (Creswell, 2012). Structurally we shift away from a chronological reporting to two embedded rhetorical structures (Creswell, 2012): (1) an extensive discussion of the major themes identified in the study; and (2) a focus on epiphanies/turning points which often are considered crucial elements in processes of identity formation. McAdams, Josselson, and Lieblich's (2001) *Turns in the Road* provides excellent examples of narrative studies with the focus on turning points or central experiences in people's lives.

In the study discussed above, the main body of the narrative report consisted of the chapters "religion, faith and spirituality and the construction of activist identities," "experiencing 'the unfamiliar and the construction of activist identities," "significant influences and the construction of activist identities," and "the role of education and the construction of activist identities." In the writing stage, it is extremely important to use (long) direct quotes from the narrative interviews that demonstrate the analyses and themes and present the "flavor" of the interview. In this study, several long quotes from the life story interviews were cited so that the reader could follow the reasoning concerning how the themes contributed to the development of the activists' identities. While long quotes might be problematic due to space limitations in many publications, especially academic journals, it is not recommended to compromise the main asset of a narrative study—the participants' own words. With the growing proliferation of peer-reviewed electronic journals and publications focusing on qualitative research, there are more opportunities for researchers to adequately report their findings.

In our writing, we need to reflect on why the identified themes turned out to be so meaningful. We need to show the different threads and how they weave together into an individuals' life perspective.

Looking at the major themes that emerged from the interviews and the analyses, it was possible to construct a theory of the process (Mertens, 2009). The theoretical results of this study were the development of a trajectory of development in individuals committed to long-term peace and justice activism and developed understandings of psycho-political development, self-actualization through altruism and integrative worldviews that were labeled as "peace-scapes."

RESEARCHERS' NOTES

From our experiences in conducting life-story and narrative interviews in the context of conflict resolution and peace studies, we share some reflections on our roles as researchers, our expectations, our emotions and opportunities for creativity.

On Our Expectations From the Interview

As Atkinson (2007) states, we cannot anticipate the outcome of a life-story interview. We conduct interviews with high expectations and despite our best preparation, intent and training in gathering stories, the interview falls short with regard to time and depth. Then we must remind ourselves that we are not responsible for what the interviewee says. We should ensure that we create an interview atmosphere where the respondent feels respected and safe (Brounéus, 2011). If, however, we feel that the interview did not go as we had hoped, because we did not hear what we wanted to hear in the life story, we are on the wrong track. As mentioned earlier, the interviewees are the experts on their lives, and if we expect them to provide us with certain information or understandings, we are shutting ourselves off from gaining important new insights into unchartered fields. This is not only arrogant, but is also a waste of precious participant and researcher time.

On the Emotions That Arise in an Interview

The experience of conducting interviews itself can be powerful regardless of how seasoned we are as researchers. This is especially so when dealing with life-stories in the realm of peace and conflict studies, since we might be overwhelmed emotionally, find it hard not to be judgmental, be disturbed by the participants' expression of ideology or political views which contradict ours, or have difficulties accepting other realities and perspectives. Therefore, one should not try to shut down emotions that arise during the interview, as the research participant tells his/her story, but we must also take care not to let these emotions become overwhelming. If we become engulfed in negative emotions—such as sadness or fear—we run the risk that the interviewee will stop talking—so as not to disturb *us*—and we will be unable to remain opening to hearing and understanding how the interviewee understands his/her life in a complex, conflict situation.

Narrative inquiry requires openness and a basis of trust between researcher and participant (Marshall & Rossman, 2010). This can only be accomplished when the researcher is honest about the emotions that s/he is experiencing. Trust is constructed through a joint process of hearing different voices in a collaborative exploratory manner that allows for a new examination of a conflict-laden story. This form of broadening possibly allows conflicting parties to experience new perceived realities and, perhaps, move toward the development of a conflict-free narrative.

On the Discomfort of Approaching Potential Interviewees

It seems like we are asking much from strangers to share their live stories with us—especially those who have lived through/ or continue to live through violent times. However, we have found that most people want to share their story and are happy to be given the opportunity to do so (Atkinson, 2007). When we *do* face reluctant interviewees, we can tell them of possible benefits (raised by Atkinson, 2007) that can come from narrating one's life story. These include gaining a clearer perspective of one's own life, greater self-knowledge, inner peace, validating personal experience, creation of community, inspire others, helping others understand herself/himself better, or creating goals for the future.

While it may not be easy to ask people to talk about their experiences connected to conflict and social injustice, by letting potential respondents understand the importance of their contribution to research, while being very sensitive to their needs and fears, we have the opportunity to learn much about what it is like to live through violent times, and/or fight for freedoms and justice, and as a result of our study, perhaps help bring about some (small) social-political changes. However, it must be stressed that a potential interviewee should *never* be coerced into participating in our research. Badgering an individual to share their life story is not only disrespectful, it can also cause psychological, and in extreme cases, physical, harm. Therefore, such insistence is not only disrespectful; it is potentially dangerous, and hence highly unethical.

On the "Truth" in Life Stories

The recollection of personal experiences connected to historical events reflects the individual's present stance in a conflict situation or his/her sociopolitical viewpoints. Memory is "not a passive depository of facts, but an active process of creation of meanings" (Portelli, 1991, p. 52). In other words, when people relate their life stories, there is either a conscious or unconscious interpretive manipulation of history. Researchers are well aware of reliability concerns, especially when they are dealing with traumatic issues such as genocide. Fujii (2010) argues that the value of narratives in such cases does not solely lie in their truthfulness, but in metadata such as rumors, silences, evasions, denials and invented stories.

We maintain that in conflict resolution, we need to approach the conflicting parties with the understanding they are arguing from their respective truths. The stories represent those reconstructions of the truths.

In the study discussed above on nonviolent activists, for example, one should not view the narratives as providing testimonial eyewitness accounts of U.S. history, but rather as accounts of the *meanings* that individuals give to their life stories, including their social activism. Moreover, the narratives should not be perceived as factual accounts of the participants' lives or the events they experienced; they are stories that the participants *chose* to tell in a certain way. The importance does not lie in their accuracy but in what they mean for these particular participants and perhaps can be modestly generalized to other social activists as well.

On Our Roles as "Neutral" Researchers

While often advocated as neutral, the field of conflict analysis and resolution is one where theorists and practitioners play a role in not only examining unjust power structures, but also in transforming them. As conflict resolution researchers we are educated, privileged individuals. The studies we conduct evolving around different forms of social conflict address indirect —yet powerful—forms of violence such as structural, cultural or symbolic violence. Our researchers' privileges come with the moral obligation to confront forms of invisible violence rather than hide behind the curtain of neutrality. As Squire and colleagues (2008) posit, narratives tend to be "modes of resistance to existing structures of power" (p. 4).

THE RELEVANCE OF
NARRATIVES FOR CONFLICT RESOLUTION

In this chapter we showed how narrative inquiry is intrinsically connected to peace and conflict studies. We are not the first ones to make these connections, but we hope that our ideas presented here will be helpful for the reader. The multidisciplinary nature and applicability of narratives was expanded to conflict resolution and peace studies, which are interdisciplinary fields in themselves.

We briefly discussed different forms of narrative approaches, but focused on the life history approach which we have used in our own studies covering topics such as ethnicity and sense of belonging of Cuban, Haitian and Guatemalan immigrants in South Florida, Palestinian and Israeli identities in conflict and nonviolent peace activists in the United States.

Studying nonviolent peace activists with the life history approach provided theoretical understandings of individuals' psycho-political development, and brought out untold stories of ordinary people doing extraordinary things in American society. The study also recognized the importance of nonviolent actors in the field of conflict resolution, and can hopefully be useful for policymakers and civil society concerning how we knowingly or unknowingly contribute to structural and cultural violence.

The discipline of conflict analysis and resolution can benefit from the life story methodological approach. Narratives in conflict can be considered frameworks for action and explanation of identity groups in conflict (Ross, 2002). Narratives allow conflicting parties to develop a higher quality of communication, and to create deeper understanding and forms of deconstructing presumptions, biases and stereotypes based on previously learned reified understandings of otherness.

Qualitative research, particularly narrative inquiry certainly is more than an "add-on" to quantitative peace and conflict studies. Quantitative studies will approach topical themes such as worldviews, conflict attitudes, perceptions of "the other," emotional responses, victim-offender relations, casualties of war, and so forth, by categorizing and quantifying those complex processes of human action, experience and identity formation. A solely quantitative approach when dealing with complex social, psychological and cultural human phenomena leaves the personal meanings attached to human experiences and behaviors unexplored.

To make our point, we offer two perspectives on the human costs of war. Quantitatively measuring war casualties, more specifically civilian versus military casualties, is a controversial issue in public, organizational and academic discourse. Numerous peace researchers and humanitarian organizations argue that the majority of war casualties are civilians (see, e.g., Clemens & Singer, 2000; Sivard, 1996). Others argue that the civilian versus military death ratio is an overestimate (see, e.g., Goldstein, 2011; Human Security Center, 2005; Pinker, 2011). The difficulties begin with ambiguities in defining what constitutes war casualties and we are warned to make statistical generalizations about war (Roberts, 2010).

According to the Peace Research Institute Oslo, battle deaths are defined "as deaths resulting directly from violence inflicted through the use of armed force by a party to an armed conflict during contested combat," excluding "the sustained destruction of soldiers or civilians outside of the context of any reciprocal threat of lethal force" (http://www.prio.no). The Correlates of War Project (http://www.correlatesofwar.org/), which "seeks to facilitate the collection, dissemination, and use of accurate and reliable quantitative data in international relations," also points to the complexity of gathering fatality figures.

Now let us use a completely different lens to understand what it means to be a casualty of war by returning to William's life story with which we began this chapter. Recalling a 2002 trip to Iraq with a Christian Peacemaker Team, he said:

> *I got to go down to Basra to visit at the children's hospital and water treatment plants, and we specifically had permission to go to the area where depleted uranium was used, because of our work at Alliant Tech,[4] and the government gave us special permission to do that for 20 minutes as long as the wind wasn't blowing and we didn't touch anything, so we saw all the tanks, but also the cars and trucks and other civilian vehicles that had been shot with depleted uranium munitions during the 91 war, and the whole area still was very radioactive, and then we went to the children's hospital and we saw all the kids, we saw, we didn't see any of the kids with birth defects, but we saw three notebooks full of pictures from that hospital and talked with the head of the head of the OB-GYN department, and then met with the head of the pediatric oncology department, and then Dr. Nasser took us up to the cancer ward introduced us to Shehad, who is a 6 year old girl who was in the terminal stages of leukemia and Amara, she was a 15 year old girl with a plastic anemia and others, that he as an oncologist was convinced that their cancers were a result of their exposure to depleted uranium.*

We hope our point is clear. Hearing and studying personal narratives of people whose lives have been touched by structural conflict, helps us understand conflict perception, conflict motivation, conflict behavior and conflict dynamics from a unique angle. This angle, we believe, opens pathways to nonviolent, sustainable and just conflict transformation.

NOTES

1. The name has been changed to maintain his anonymity.
2. A distinction between the role of narratives in the study and analysis of conflict, and the role of narratives in actual conflict resolution/transformation

needs to be made. The Center for the Study of Narrative and Conflict Resolution at George Mason University (http://scar.gmu.edu/cncr) is a needed addition to the field. Their mission is to "advance the theory, practice and research on narrative processes in conflict dynamics." Applied uses of narratives in conflict resolution include: reconciliation in postconflict settings from the interpersonal to the international level, dialogue programs and the narrative approach to mediation.

3. The study was Patrick Hiller's doctoral dissertation titled: *Trajectories toward Nonviolent Identities: Development, Negotiation and Maintenance of Integrative Worldviews of a Selected Group of Peace and Social Justice Activists in the United States.*

4. William has been very involved in a campaign against the military contractor Alliant Techsystems Inc.

REFERENCES

Albeck, J., Adwan, S., & Bar-On, D. (2002). Dialogue groups: TRT's guidelines for working through intractable conflicts by personal storytelling in encounter groups. *Peace and Conflict: Journal of Peace Psychology, 8*(4), 301–322.

Andrews, M. (2007). *Shaping history: Narratives of political change.* Cambridge, NY: Cambridge University Press.

Andrews, M., Sclater, S. D., Squire, C., & Treacher, A. (2000). *The uses of narrative. Explorations in sociology, psychology and cultural studies.* New Brunswick, NJ: Translation.

Andrews, M., Squire, C., & Tamboukou, M. (2008). *Doing narrative research.* Los Angeles, CA: Sage.

Atkinson, R. (1998). *The life story interview.* Thousand Oaks, CA: Sage.

Atkinson, R. (2007). The life story interview as a bridge in narrative inquiry. In D. J. Clandinin (Ed.), *Handbook of narrative inquiry: Mapping a methodology* (pp. 224–247). Thousand Oaks, CA: Sage.

Bar-On, D. (2006). *Saper et chayeicha: Yitzirat dialog ben yehudim v'germanim, yisraelim u'falistinim* [Tell your story: Creating dialogue between Jews and Germans, Palestinians and Israelies]. Beer Sheva, Israel: Ben Gurion University of the Negev Press. [in Hebrew]

Brounéus, K. (2011). In-depth interviewing: the process, skill and ethics of interviews in peace research. In K. Höglund & M. Öberg (Eds.), *Understanding peace research: Methods and challenges.* New York, NY: Routledge.

Bruner, J. S. (1991). The narrative construction of reality. *Critical Inquiry, 18*, 1–21.

Chaitin, J. (2002). How do I ask them about the war? Collecting and understanding the stories of soldiers and victims of war. *Social Science Research Network Electronic Library.* Retrieved from http://ssrn.com/abstract=304580

Chaitin, J. (2004). My story, my life, my identity. *International Journal of Qualitative Methods, 3*(4). Retrieved from http://www.ualberta.ca/~iiqm/backissues/3_4/html/chaitin.html

Chaitin, J., Awwad, E., & Andriani, C. (2009). Belonging to the conflict: Collective identities among Israeli and Palestinian immigrants to the United States. *Social Identities: Journal for the Study of Race, Nation and Culture, 15*(2), 207–225.

Chaitin, J., Linstroth, J. P., & Hiller, P. (2009). Ethnicity and belonging: An Overview of a Study of Cuban, Haitian and Guatemalan Immigrants to Florida. *Forum Qualitative Sozialforschung / Forum: Qualitative Social Research, 10*(3). Retrieved from http://www.qualitative-research.net/index.php/fqs/article/view/1363

Clemens, W. C., Jr., & Singer, D. J. (2000). The human costs of war. *Scientific American, 282*(6), 56–57.

Christians, C. G. (2003). Ethics and politics in qualitative research. In N. K. Denzin & Y. S. Lincoln (Eds.), *The landscape of qualitative research* (2nd ed., pp. 208–243). Thousand Oaks, CA: Sage

Clandinin, D. J. (2007). *Handbook of narrative inquiry: Mapping a methodology*. Thousand Oaks CA: Sage.

Clandinin, D. J., & Connelly, F. M. (2000). *Narrative inquiry: Experience and story in qualitative research* (1st ed.). San Francisco, CA: Jossey-Bass.

Cornejo, M., Rojas, R. C., & Mendoza, F. (2009). From testimony to life story: The experience of professionals in the Chilean National Commission on Political Imprisonment and Torture. *Peace and Conflict: Journal of Peace Psychology, 15*(2), 111–133.

Côté, J. E., & Levine, C. (2002). *Identity formation, agency, and culture: A social psychological synthesis*. Mahwah, NJ: Erlbaum Associates.

Creswell, J. W. (2012). *Qualitative inquiry and research design: Choosing among five approaches* (3rd ed.). Los Angeles, CA: Sage.

Czarniawska-Joerges, B. (2004). *Narratives in social science research*. Thousand Oaks, CA: Sage.

Daiute, C., & Lightfoot, C. (2004). *Narrative analysis: Studying the development of individuals in society*. Thousand Oaks, CA: Sage.

Della Porta, D. (1992). Life histories in the analysis of social movement activists. In M. Diani & R. Eyerman (Eds.), *Studying collective action* (pp. 168–193). Newbury Park, CA: Sage.

Denzin, N. K. (2000). Foreword. In M. Andrews, S. D. Sclater, C. Squire & A. Treacher (Eds.), *The uses of narrative: Explorations in sociology, psychology and cultural studies*. New Brunswick, NJ: Translation.

Denzin, N. K., & Lincoln, Y. S. (2005). *The SAGE handbook of qualitative research* (3rd ed.). Thousand Oaks, CA: Sage.

Elliott, J. (2005). *Using narrative in social research: Qualitative and quantitative approaches*. Thousand Oaks, CA: Sage.

Erikson, E. H. (1959). *Identity and the life cycle; selected papers*. New York, NY: International Universities Press.

Erikson, E. H. (1963). *Childhood and society*. New York, NY: W. W. Norton. (Original work published 1950)

Fine, M. (1998). Working the hyphens: Reinventing self and other in qualitative research. In N. K. Denzin & Y. S. Lincoln (Eds.), *The landscape of qualitative research: Theories and issues* (2nd ed., pp. 130–155). Thousand Oaks, CA: Sage.

Flick, U. (2007). *Designing qualitative research*. Thousand Oaks, CA: Sage.

Fujii, L. A. (2010). Shades of truth and lies: Interpreting testimonies of war and violence. *Journal of Peace Research, 47*(2), 231–241.

Glaser, B. G., & Strauss, A. L. (1967). *The discovery of grounded theory; strategies for qualitative research.* Chicago, IL: Aldine.

Goldstein, J. S. (2011). *Winning the war on war: The decline of armed conflict worldwide.* New York, NY: Penguin Group.

Gordon, H., Gordon, Ri., & Shriteh, T. (2003). *Beyond intifada: Narratives of freedom fighters in the Gaza Strip.* Westport, CT: Praeger.

Hammack, P. (2009) Exploring the reproduction of conflict through narrative: Israeli youth motivated to participate in a coexistence program. *Peace and Conflict, 15,* 49–74.

Hammack, P. (2010) Identity as burden or benefit. Youth, historical narrative, and the legacy of political conflict. *Human Development, 53,* 173–201.

Hiller, P. (2011). Visualizing the intersection of the personal and the social context: The use of multi-layered chronological charts in biographical studies. *The Qualitative Report, 16*(4), 1018–1033.

Holstein, J. A., & Gubrium, J. F. (2000). *The self we live by: Narrative identity in a postmodern world.* New York, NY: Oxford University Press.

Human Security Center. (2005). *Human security report: War and peace in the 21st century.* New York, NY: Oxford University Press.

Jenkins, R. (2008). *Social identity* (3rd ed.). New York, NY: Routledge.

Johnston, L. M. (2005). Narrative analysis: Doing research. In D. Druckman (Ed.), *Doing research: Methods of inquiry for conflict analysis* (pp. 276–292). Thousand Oaks, CA: Sage.

Kamel, L., & Huber, D. (2012). The de-threatenization of the other: An Israeli and a Palestinian case of understanding the other's suffering. *Peace & Change, 37*(3), 366–388.

Kara, S. (2009). *Sex trafficking: Inside the business of modern slavery.* New York, NY: Columbia University Press.

Langer, L. L. (1991). *Holocaust testimonies: The ruins of memory.* New Haven, CT: Yale University Press.

Lapadat, J. C., & Lindsay, A. C. (1999). Transcription in research and practice: From standardization of technique to interpretive positionings. *Qualitative Inquiry, 5*(1), 64–86.

Leavy, P. (2011). *Oral history.* New York, NY: Oxford University Press.

Lederach, J. P., & Lederach, A. J. (2010). *When blood and bones cry out: Journeys through the soundscape of healing and reconciliation.* New York, NY: Oxford University Press.

Lieblich, A. (1994). *Seasons of captivity: The inner world of POWs.* New York, NY: New York University Press.

Lieblich, A., Tuval-Mashiach, R., & Zilber, T. (1998). *Narrative research: Reading, analysis and interpretation.* Thousand Oaks, CA: Sage.

Linstroth, J. P. (2009). Maya cognition, memory and trauma. *History and anthropology, 20*(2), 139–182.

Manchanda, R. (2001). *Women, war, and peace in South Asia: Beyond victimhood to agency.* Thousand Oaks, CA: Sage.

Marshall, C., & Rossman, G. B. (2010). *Designing qualitative research* (5th ed.). Thousand Oaks, CA: Sage.

May, T. (2001). *Social research: Issues, methods and process* (3rd ed.). Buckingham; Philadelphia, PA: Open University Press.

McAdams, D. P. (1988). *Power, intimacy, and the life story: Personological inquiries into identity.* New York, NY: Guilford Press.

McAdams, D. P. (1993). *The stories we live by: Personal myths and the making of the self.* New York, NY: Guilford Press.

McAdams, D. P. (2001). The psychology of life stories. *Review of General Psychology, 5*(2), 100–122.

McAdams, D. P. (2006). *The redemptive self: Stories Americans live by.* New York, NY: Oxford University Press.

McAdams, D. P. (2008). Personal narratives and the life story. In O. P. John, R. W. Robins & L. A. Pervin (Eds.), *Handbook of personality: Theory and research* (3rd ed., pp. 241–261). New York, NY: Guilford Press.

McAdams, D. P., Josselson, R., & Lieblich, A. (2001). *Turns in the road: Narrative studies of lives in transition* (1st ed.). Washington, DC: American Psychological Association.

McAdams, D. P., Josselson, R., & Lieblich, A. (2006). *Identity and story: Creating self in narrative* (1st ed.). Washington, DC: American Psychological Association.

Mertens, D. M. (2009). *Transformative research and evaluation.* New York, NY: Guilford Press.

Nets-Zehngut, R. (2011). Palestinian autobiographical memory regarding the 1948 Palestinian exodus. *Political Psychology, 32*(2), 271–295

Pinker, S. (2011). *The better angels of our nature: Why violence has declined.* New York, NY: Viking.

Pinnegar, S., & Daynes, J. (2007). Locating narrative inquiry historically: Thematics in the turn to narrative. In D. J. Clandinin (Ed.), *Handbook of narrative inquiry: Mapping a methodology* (pp. 1–34). Thousand Oaks, CA: Sage.

Portelli, A. (1991). *The death of Luigi Trastulli, and other stories: Form and meaning in oral history.* Albany, NY: State University of New York Press.

Roberts, A. (2010). Lives and statistics: Are 90% of war victims civilians? *Survival, 52*(3), 115–136.

Rosenthal, G. (1993). Reconstruction of life stories. Principles of selection in generating stories for narrative biographical interviews. In R. Josselson & A. Lieblich (Eds.), *The narrative study of lives* (Vol. 1, pp. 59–91). London, England: Sage.

Rosenthal, G. (2007). Biographical research. In C. Seale, G. Gobo, J. F. Gubrium & D. Silverman (Eds.), *Qualitative research practice* (pp. 48–65). London, England: Sage.

Ross, M. H. (2002). The political psychology of competing narratives: September 11 and Beyond. In C. Calhoun, P. Price, & A. Timmer (Eds.), *Understanding September 11* (pp. 303–320). New York, NY: New Press.

Sivard, R. L. (1996). *World military and social expenditures 1996.* Washington, DC: World Priorities.

Squire, C., Andrews, M., & Tamboukou, M.. (2008). Introduction: What is narrative research. In M. Andrews, C. Squire, & M. Tamboukou (Eds.), *Doing narrative research* (pp. 1–22). London, England: Sage.

Thompson, P. (1978). *The voice of the past: Oral history.* New York, NY: Oxford University Press.

Trahar, S. (2011). *Learning and teaching narrative inquiry: Travelling in the Borderlands.* Philadelphia, PA: John Benjamins.

Wells, K. (2011). *Narrative inquiry.* New York, NY: Oxford University Press.

Young, S. (2004). Narrative and healing in the hearings of the South African Truth and Reconciliation Commission. *Biography, 27,* 145–162.

CHAPTER 8

"TOGETHER WE CAN DO SO MUCH"

Conducting Action Research Projects in Peace and Conflict Studies

Terry Morrow and Laura Finley

As the partial quote in the title says, action research (AR), also called participatory action research (PAR), is carried out in schools, communities, organizations, medical institutions, churches and anywhere where people are collectively working toward common goals. AR or PAR have been used in a wide array of disciplines, including sociology, criminal justice psychology, peace and conflict studies, labor and unions, social work, human resources, medicine, women's studies and more (Hynes, Coghlan, & McCarron, 2012; Huzzard & Bjorkman, 2012; Rai, 2012). It is most often used in education (Ferrance, 2000). AR or PAR have been used as a means of helping address environmental conflicts (Moeliono & Fisher, n.d.), to repair war-torn societies (Johansen, 2001), and to develop peace education programs (Conley-Tyler, Bretherton, Halahoff, & Nietschke, 2008). The intent of action research is to collaboratively generate knowledge and create theories of practice that drive collective outcomes. One of the hallmarks of action research is progressive problem solving; a focus on continuous improvement, understanding and adaptive change in which researchers and stakeholders are both deeply involved. Emerging from Dewey's valuing of the integration between theory and action, Freire's pedagogy of conscientization, feminist critiques, and other concerns about power and ethics in conventional research AR or PRA are methodological tools used to develop social change plans, generally focused on a specific organization in which the researcher participates (Dick, Stringer, & Huxham, 2009; Smith, Bratini, Chambers, Jensen, & Romero, 2010). AR can result in knowledge that does not reproduce the interests or perspectives of the status quo (Smith et al., 2010).

Partnerships are central to AR. It is far different from the typical top-down approaches that objectify research subjects, failing to consider their knowledge and input into the very social issues impacting them. As Reason and Bradbury (2008) put it: "Action Research is only possible *with, for* and *by* persons and communities, ideally involving all stakeholders both in the questioning and sense making that informs the research, *and* in the action which is its focus" (p. 2). A basic premise, according to Argyris and Schön (1996) is that "[P]eople are more likely to accept and act on research findings if they helped to design the research and participate in the gathering and analysis of data" (p. 44).

Morrow (2011) used appreciative inquiry research (Reed, 2007), a strength-based approach to action research, to explore the process of developing the National Peace Academy (NPA). Using a mixed-method survey and interview approach, she explored the life-giving force of the NPA, factors that promoted success in building the organization and movement, and opportunities for the continued development of the NPA. She cites the importance of key leaders' and stakeholders' ownership and investment in the development of the research questions, implementation, and participation as pivotal to the success of the research process and the overall quality of the findings.

Put simply, action research is designed to improve practice (Kitchen & Stevens, 2008). Practice involves both the behaviors and actions that take place as well as the implicit and explicit knowledge or understanding which underlies those actions. Action research uses iterative cycles including diagnosis of the issue, data gathering, discussion and analysis, designing plans of action based on the emergent knowledge, carrying out the planned action, and evaluating the action with a new round of data gathering (Levin, 2012; Conley-Tyler et al., 2008).

LEVELS OF ACTION RESEARCH

Personal	Organizational/ Community	Scholarly

Action research outcomes occur on a personal level, organizational or community level, and at a scholarly level. At the personal level, the researcher(s) look inward to reflect on the knowledge, skills and identity insights they are gaining through the research experience. Action researchers must be reflective or mindful (Langer, 1997). Such mindfulness

> requires patience and courage to continually observe what happens without evading unwelcome or unexpected events or responding by re-enacting habitually formed patterns.... Although organizational problems and power issues will not be resolved immediately, it helps the researcher to deal with differences and her own feelings more constructively. (Snoeren, Niessen, & Abma, 2012, p. 199)

Margaret Riel (2010) notes that the researcher uses a "systematic set of methods for interpreting and evaluating one's actions with the goal of improving practice" (para. 12). At an organizational or community level, the researcher(s) gain insight regarding the factors that are driving or restraining change which can lead to new behaviors and processes. According to Riel (2010), "Action research goes beyond self-study because, outcomes, goals and assumptions are located in complex social systems" (para. 13). On a scholarly level, the researcher uses a process to validate findings and shares them with others through publications and conference presentations. Individuals are often engaging in organizational learning in their workplace and communities, but researchers value the process of sharing and building on one another's knowledge through the ongoing cyclical process of dialogue, reflection and application (Riel & Lepori, 2011).

AR is consistent with peace education and peace pedagogy (Conley-Tyler et al., 2008). That is because peace education is not just about what is taught but rather about the methods of doing so, which are participatory in the same way as is action research (Conley-Tyler et al., 2008; Snoeren, Niessen, & Abma (2012) refer to action research as a "participative and democratic process," asserting that it "contributes to the empowerment of people" (p. 190). In particular, scholars have noted that action research can give voice to marginalized groups and encourage equality through rebalancing power (Boog, 2003; Brantmeier, 2007; Fals-Borda & Rahmann, 1991; Snoeren, Niessen, & Abma, 2012). Brantmeier (2007) demonstrated how action research can assist educators in understanding peace and in implementing peace education practices. Action researchers utilize dialogue to challenge all participants. Rather than working toward consensus, action researchers recognize that disagreement helps identify differences and is thereby essential in moving toward solutions (Snoeren, Niessen, & Abma, 2012). Huang (2010) noted that AR helps to promote the voices of students, who are so often silenced.

The promotion of participation requires the creation of open, trustworthy and reciprocal spaces. Wicks and Reason (2009) called these "communicative spaces." Such spaces are developed in three phases. First, the inclusion phase, in which first contact is made and the tasks and meaning of the inquiry are elucidated. Second, the control phase, in which power issues and differences related to the project and processes may emerge and thus must be collectively navigated. Third, the intimacy phase, in which participants find ways that their identities can exist in harmony with others in the group, allowing for effective carrying out of essential tasks.

Action researchers recognize that the dialogue that is so essential to the methodology can come in a variety of forms. As Snoeren, Niessen, and Abma (2012) explain, dialogue

> should not be sought solely in spoken communication, but also in physical forms: by doing and working together. Dialogue in the latter sense takes the role of performance, in which understanding each other is initiated through working hands and embodied performance. (p. 200)

This ability to use multiple methods of dialogue helps further the connection with the field of peace and conflict studies, as it utilizes Galtung's (1996) concept of "peace by peaceful means."

Key Considerations of the Action Research Process

In considering action research, it is important to understand some key terminology. These include epistemology, methodology, and ontology. Epistemology refers to our theory of knowledge and knowledge creation. Action researchers work on the epistemological assumption that the purpose of academic research and discourse is not just to describe, understand and explain the world but also to change it (Reason & Torbert, 2001). This approach is focused on self- and collective-reflexivity as a tool for revealing interests and promoting emancipation (Coghlan & Brannick, 2009). Action researchers recognize that reflexivity and thus the knowledge that emerges is rooted in social, historical and political contexts and is, therefore, not neutral. In order for action research to produce change, it must be guided by principles of deliberative dialogue, democratic engagement, and a commitment to positive change. The gaze is toward what could be and can be, and according to Reason and Bradbury (2008), collective values and beliefs emerge through the process of consciousness-raising and conscientization.

Methodology refers to how things are done. There are a range of methodologies, including more systematic methodologies and haphazard methodologies. The specific method selected is less important than the process for selecting them. Ideally, research participants should be involved in diagnosing or defining the situation and defining the goals of the action research. They should be involved in deciding how the data is collected and the process of collecting the data. Stakeholders should be involved in the reflexive analysis of the data and the decisions about the improvements and changes that will be planned and implemented as a result of the findings. Finally, they should remain involved through multiple iterations of this cyclical and ongoing process.

Ontology refers to how one see's oneself in relation to others. Our ontological perspective will influence our sense of meaning and purpose. Action researchers believe people can craft their identities and walk alongside others as they create their identities. They recognize the reality of multiple perspectives, values, and experiences and look for ways to accommodate the disparate and conflicting aspects of each. Action researchers work alongside others to find new ways of living with one another in community while wrestling with, and ultimately through, these multiple realities (Reason & Bradbury, 2008). This requires compassion, reflection, and the suspension of judgment. They hold a vision of the future that is better than the present and they engage others in multiple cycles of reflection, dialogue, and action with the intent of improving actions, structures and relationships within their collective community.

Action researchers can and should begin their practice in their own lives as individuals, practitioners and researchers. They accept responsibility for the honest, ongoing assessment of their actions, thoughts, and beliefs. As a researcher or practitioner, what are your strengths? Where are opportunities for you to further develop or hone your skills, actions, or understanding? What are your values and how do you embody them? How do others answer these questions? A great exercise for your first action research study could be the Reflected Best Self Exercise, a great tool developed by the Center for Positive Organizational Development at the University of Michigan (Center for Positive Organizational Development, 2011). A brief overview of this exercise is as follows:

Step 1: Identify the research question. For the purpose of this exercise, we will identify an appreciative question such as "What attitudes, behaviors, characteristics, knowledge and skills lead me to be most successful?"

Step 2: Identify 10 friends and coworkers who know you well. Conduct an in-person interview or send an e-mail questionnaire asking the following questions:

- What do believe are my top five strengths?
- Please give two or three examples of a time when you have seen my at my best.
- In your examples, what was I doing that was particularly valuable or effective?
- What was the context of the situation? What was it about the context (people, places, problem, and process) that contributed to my success?

Tip: When you send the e-mail or do the interview, open the conversation or e-mail with an introduction explaining what you are doing and why it is valuable. See Appendix A for a sample e-mail. Your goal here is to engage a group of stakeholders who are impacted by your performance and behaviors to play a role in helping you to improve, and thereby, enhance your contribution to the system you share.

Step 3: Conduct the in-person interviews or send out the e-mail questionnaires.

Step 4: Analyze the data. Look for categories that emerge from the interviews. You will have numerous stories and statements from your participants. A small subset of your feedback (data) might include:

- "You seem very comfortable when you are talking in front of a lot of people."
- "you are articulate and always seem to have the right words when you speak to groups"
- "You tell good stories that help people understand the topic or issue better."

As you continue to sift through the data, you find that a pattern is emerging and you create a category entitled "effective at speaking in public." Congratulations! You have identified your first category in the analysis process. This category, like the process of action research itself, is not static, and may evolve throughout the analysis process as you read through the data. Let's say, for example, that the data also includes quotes such as "you are a good listener and people tend to trust you" and "you tend to stay calm in the midst of difficult situations and this helps others feel calm, too." And "I've noticed that you're good at helping people see both sides of an issue and find common ground" Another category here might be "Effective in bringing people together to address difficult situations."

This abbreviated example of two categories shows how a theme might emerge. The theme might be "Effective at working with small and large groups of people to lead them in constructively resolving a conflict." The questions about context and specific behaviors will provide also likely lead to categories and add further dimension to the themes.

DATA

- "You seem very comfortable when you are talking in front of a lot of people."
- "You are articulate and always seem to have the right words when you speak to groups."
- "You tell good stories that help people understand the topic or issue better."
- "You are a good listener and people tend to trust you."
- "You tend to stay calm in the midst of difficult situations and this helps others feel calm, too."
- "I've noticed that you're good at helping people see both sides of an issue and find common ground"

Category 1	Category 2
Effective at public speaking	**Helps people resolve conflict**

- "You seem very comfortable when you are talking in front of a lot of people."
- "You are articulate and always seem to have the right words when you speak to groups."
- "You tell good stories that help people better understand the topic or issue."

Theme 1
Effectively works with small and large groups

- "You are a good listener and people tend to trust you."
- "You tend to stay calm in the midst of conflict and this helps others feel calm, too."
- "I've noticed that you're good at helping people see both sides of an issue and find common ground"

Another example might be:

DATA SUBSET

- I remember the time when you sat with Anne and helped her reflect on where she finds meaning and in what areas she generally excels. This helped her to get a better grasp on her possible career paths."

(List continues on next page)

DATA SUBSET
(continued from previous page)

• "You seem to 'get' young adults"

• "You seem to come alive when you are leading peace building experiences with young people."

• "You give people hope by helping them see the possibilities rather than the problems."

• "You helped me learn how to plan a great event that raised over $1,000 for Amnesty International."

• "You help students focus on their strengths and identify the strengths of others in their organization.

Category 3	**Category 4**
Works well with young adults	**Encourages and develops others**

• "I remember the time when you sat with Anne and helped her reflect on the issues she is most passionate about and how she can make a difference in the world.

• "You seem to 'get' young adults."

• "You seem to come alive when you are leading peace building experiences with young people."

Theme 2

Excels at developing and influencing young adults to lead

• "You give people hope by helping them see the possibilities rather than the problems."

• "You helped me learn how to plan a great event that raised over $1,000 for Amnesty International."

• "You help students focus on their strengths and identify the strengths of others in their organization."

Step 5: Write up your findings so that others can understand what you learned and how you came to these conclusions. Why did you select these certain people to give you feedback? How did you choose them? What process or method did you use to generate the information? How did you arrive at the understandings you did? For example, you are reporting that you excel at teaching and training college students and developing and mentoring college students. What led you to this belief? Where there any areas where the data seemed to conflict? How did you handle that? As an outside expert (on yourself), do you agree with these conclusions? Can you provide any other information or data sources (awards, letters of recommendations, performance evaluations, etc.) that might validate these findings? Did you send your findings back to your participants to ask them if they believe you have correctly analyzed the information they shared and allow them to provide additional insight or feedback? You could also ask a colleague who also does action research to check your data and she if see would come to the same conclusions. This is a form of member-checking.

Step 6: Write an action plan. What will you do with the findings of your study? What is your plan for reflection on this newfound knowledge? How will you adjust the actions, processes, systems, and focuses in your personal and professional life to maximize your strengths and live fully as your "best self"? Be specific. Decide how you will measure the effects of your actions. Ensure that your plan is attainable. Make sure that your plan is relevant or connected to your findings. Finally, create a timeline. When do you hope to go through this cycle again and assess how your plan is working? Action research is cyclical. It begins with action, moves to reflection, into learning, on to planning, and back to action.

You can do this on your own since the research is specifically about you, but consider taking the more challenging, but rewarding route and involve your participants. Action researchers recognize that we are never an island unto ourselves. We are part of a larger community and our actions impact and influence the people and places with which we are connected. Therefore, it is recommended that you invite your participants to join you in analyzing your data and looking for emerging categories and themes. You can invite all participants to join you for a two hour dialogue about the data or you could send it out to them and ask them to do the work on their own and send it back. Another route would be just to include the two to three people that you believe know you best or are willing to do it.

Now that we've considered a small-scale personal action research project that you might undertake consider how this action research approach might be utilized to research an organization, community, classroom, workgroup or project.

Exercise 1: Identify an organization, group or initiative that you could study using the action research approach. Why do you believe this would be valuable? For instance, educators or professors may be interested in studying the interest and capacity of their school or university in developing a peace education program (Conley-Tyler et al., 2008). Organizations or nonprofits may wish to use AR or PAR to assess needs and develop or expand programs.

As you begin to craft your action research project, it is important to understand the research process. In this section, we will explore some of the methodological approaches and tools. The major components of any action research study include the following:

1. Identify the research question by diagnosing the intent of the action research.
2. Choose your sampling method to select who you want to participate in the study.
3. Design a data collection method and carry out the process.
4. Choose a data analysis method and generate findings
5. Reflect on the findings, plan the next steps for continuous improvement and write up the report.
6. Carry out the action plan and repeat this cycle again.

IDENTIFY A RESEARCH QUESTION

Many emerging researchers make the mistake of trying to change the world with their action research study. Particularly for those who are just beginning their research career, it is important to focus on a specific issue within a contained context. For example, let's consider the Reflected Best Self exercise discussed earlier. The context is you and your performance. We didn't focus on every area of your performance. Since the literature shows that it is more fruitful to zero in and build on our strengths rather than focusing on our weaknesses, we chose to ask "When am I at my best?" and "What are the specific behaviors, contexts and characteristics that seem to lead to success?" The intent of this research is to identify what you at your best looks like so you can expand upon, increase the frequency, and develop those areas.

Your question should be a higher-order question. In other words, it should require some depth of understanding rather than a yes or no answer. Make sure that the research question is clear. There is no need to use complex language or jargon. What exactly needs to be understood more completely? Possible research questions include:

- What practices support student learning for first-year college students living on campus?
- What are the barriers to forgiveness among those who are participating in restorative justice processes?
- What influences college students voting behaviors on our college campus?
- How can we promote peace in our school?

- How can our team be more effective in achieving our mission?
- What challenges does our nonprofit face in acquiring funding for peace work?

Finally, it is important that your research question is researchable and your action research group has the ability to influence the process or situation. For example, let's consider the first question. Do you have access to college students to invite them to be part of the inquiry process? If so, do you have any influence to be able to apply the new knowledge created with the college students? Concerning the second question, do you have access to those participating in the restorative justice process and the ability to adjust or develop the system? While many research methods are intended to create knowledge for knowledge sake, Action Research is specifically designed to create knowledge that will influence action. It is rooted in action and designed to influence action.

Exercise 2: Develop a research question for your action research study. Remember to make sure that it is a higher-order question that is focused, clear, researchable and meaningful to your organization, community, or group.

Sampling

The first step in designing your action research study is to select your research participants. These individuals have the best insight into the issue and they will be your partners in this research. Other more positivist approaches see participants as "subjects" who will provide you with pieces of data that the researcher, the expert, will piece together and interpret (Lincoln & Guba, 1985). Action research is rooted in social constructionism, which is more focused on "power to" rather than the "power over" (Gergen, 1995) positivist approach. The researchers are "joining with" the participants to coconstruct a reality in which each is invested and by which all are impacted to move towards collaborative action (Dachler & Hosking, 1995; Gergen, 1995; Hosking, 1995; Hosking & Bass, 1998; Pearce, 1992). The process of collaborative inquiry leads to knowledge creation and influence as the individuals share and coconstruct their collective reality. This relational process is an intervention into the organization, work group or community in itself. The process raises individuals' and groups' collective consciousness through the knowledge creation process. As groups use the knowledge to reflect, plan and act, the research has the potential to change behavior and outcomes.

With this in mind, you will select the individuals with whom you want to partner on your action research project. Action researchers generally employ what is known as purposive sampling (Jupp, 2006) among qualitative researchers. Purposive sampling is a type of sampling that uses certain criteria to decide who will participate in the research. Since the intent of action research is to do research that improves action, the goal is to include those individuals in the study that are in some way knowledgeable about and involved with the research question. They also must be willing to participate at some level in the data collection, analysis, planning and action processes. These people are often considered stakeholders, or persons who have an interest in a particular issue or organization.

If you were studying the practices that support learning among first year college students, it would be important to include first-year college students and those individuals who are designing and facilitating the learning practices such as faculty, the residence hall director, resident assistants, and peer leaders. It would also be important to consider aspects of your target audience such as race, gender, socioeconomics, spiritual or religious beliefs, residence hall community, and age to ensure that your team is bringing multiple viewpoints to the research process and is able to identify with and engage a variety of different groups in the action phase of your study. If there are others that are particularly interested in the research topic, you would want to include them as well. These individuals would all have first-hand knowledge of the topic and would likely have influence to make change or act on the findings of the findings. If you were studying barriers to forgiveness among restorative justice participants, you might want to include persons who have recently gone through a restorative process and others who did it some time ago. You would also want to ensure that a diverse group of participants was selected. You might also want to include some restorative justice facilitators to gain their input.

Exercise 3: Consider your action research project. Who might be included as participants in your study?

ROLE OF THE RESEARCHER

The role of the researcher is to implement the action research method in a way that promotes collective learning and investment so that the project can be continued and maintained by them. The researcher should help facilitate dialogue and reflection among the participants, assist in writing reports and developing the final analysis. It is also important that the researcher support and mentor the group leaders (formal or informal) to so they can facilitate the cyclical process as they continue forward with the initiative.

STANDARD DATA COLLECTION METHODS

The next step in the action research process is data collection. This is the point in which you will be gathering information to answer your research question. There are a variety of approaches to data collection and it is best to employ two or three approaches to ensure the validity of your findings. There are numerous approaches to gathering data. We have provided an abbreviated list of some of the most common.

Direct Observation

Direct observation involves observing, taking notes and recording the specific actions witnessed, such as spatial interactions, verbal and nonverbal communications, or exclusions. It can be focused on people and/or processes as people go through certain spaces, interventions, or experiences. Many organizations do this through observing meetings of staff or reviewing records of meetings.

Interviews

Interviews involve personal contact with stakeholders either over the phone or in person. There are structured and semistructured interviews. Structured interviews adhere to a strict protocol in which specific questions are asked and the interviewer asks the same questions in the same way to all participants. Unstructured interviews generally have specific questions but the interviewer has much more flexibility regarding how they are asked. For reliability purposes, interviewers should identify a minimum standard regarding the core of the inquiry across interviews.

Activity Interviews

An activity interview is designed to identify the perceptions that participants have about a certain intervention's overall process and impact. Interviews are semistructured and generally take place a couple weeks after the activity. This feedback is combined with that of the staff responsible for the intervention and the findings are compiled in a short report. This is a great tool for ongoing program monitoring, as well as research.

Participant Diaries

Participant diaries record participants' narrative experiences. They can be open-ended with participants recording anything that was important to them during that week or day. They can also be more structured and focused toward specific attitudes, behaviors, thoughts, and experiences during a specified period of time.

Photography/Video

Individuals can be invited to take pictures or videos of people, places, and symbols that relate to the topic being studied. This can be done individually or in groups. You might consider your overarching theoretical framework when you make this decision. For example, if you are working from a constructivist perspective, you would likely have individuals take their own pictures and write or share about why they selected that scene. If you are working from a social constructionist perspective, you would have groups select the scenes based on their collective understanding about the meaning. Interpeace, a documentary film company, promotes video footage as a way of making observations that can be used for peacebuilding purposes (Interpeace, 2005).

Project Document Review

Project Document Review involves gathering important documents relevant to your study, such as annual reports, student evaluations or samples of the work, donor reports, proposals, assessments, and meeting minutes.

Questionnaire

A questionnaire uses a set of targeted questions relevant to the information you are attempting to gather. They can be administered in paper or electronic form to which participants will respond in narrative form. It is important that the questions are constructed while considering cultural and language differences that could impact participants' understanding of the questions.

Focus Groups

Focus groups generally are composed of six to eight participants and are designed to understand how people feel or think about an issue, process, initiative or product. Participants are selected based on their connection to the element being studied. Focus groups have a specific process and require a skilled moderator.

Venn Diagrams

Venn diagrams are done using circular cards of different colors and sizes that represent an issue. Each card represents a different issue and the size of the card represents the issue's importance in the conflict. The larger the card, the greater the importance. The cards are placed in relation to one another to reflect the interrelationships of the issues within the conflict. For example, two cards may lie next to each other with an inch between them to show that they are separate and unrelated issues. On the other hand, they may overlap one another to show that the issues are connected and intertwined. Venn diagrams are an active and visual way for stakeholders to share their perspective. It also removes some of the potential for power imbalances that can emerge from differences in educational levels or language proficiencies.

Pairwise Ranking

Pairwise ranking is a technique used to determine the relative importance of various options to stakeholders. Two options are compared at a time and participants identify the reasons for selecting one option over the other. As groups systematically compare each of the different options, they create results that provide criteria for assessing current and future options.

Drawing

Drawing a visual depiction of the conflict is another tool for collecting data. It provides another medium for individuals to communicate beyond language. Pictures can be focused toward emotions, situations, visions for the future, metaphors, or memorable moments that define the conflict for the parties.

Affinity Diagrams

Using post-its, group members individually brainstorm ideas regarding the question being studied. Each writes individual insights or ideas on the post-its during a three to five brainstorming session and the group works together to connect ideas under certain categories and themes. Similar to the constant comparative method in grounded theory (Glaser & Strauss, 1967, Strauss &Corbin, 1990), the themes will constantly morph as the group continues to sort through the post-its. This process includes both data collection and data analysis phases.

Cause and Effect Diagrams

These diagrams are similar to the Fishbone models typically used in organizational development. Here, different areas of the research question are identified (i.e., people, processes, external influences, resources, practices) and the group works together to identify the issues that are impacting the research questions and what interventions would improve functions or outcomes. The data collection process occurs during structured group dialogue about the different issues on each area. The analysis process occurs as the group looks at the categories and themes that emerge in each area and across areas. Upon analyzing the data, the group then decides the next steps and priorities for collectively moving forward.

Conflict Mapping

Conflict mapping is used as a tool to help stakeholders develop a better understanding of a particular situation. It helps identify levels of power distribution across parties and allows for relationships, and provides a forum for parties to reflect upon and discuss the elements of the conflict through the experience of coconstructing a visual representation of the situation.(Wehr, 1979). Bringing people with different perspectives on the conflict helps the group explore the issues that are creating conflict between individuals from a more systemic perspective.

Search Conference

The search conference is an organizational development tool that can be utilized as an action research process that engages large groups of people to consider the past and present realities of the organization with the intention toward crafting a preferred future of the organization. It involves stakeholders in the process of identifying issues, looking at possibilities, considering obstacles, and developing an action plan for moving in the direction of the preferred future. As with all action research methods, the process is cyclical.

Exercise 4: Selecting the best data collection method for your action research study.

Identify the data collection methods that will be most valuable for your action research study. Which ones are most feasible? Which are most relevant? How might you use multiple methods to triangulate your data to promote the validity of your group's findings?

Data Analysis

According to Bruner, Goodnow, and Austin (1972), "To categorize is to render discriminably different things equivalent, to group the objects and events and people around us into classes, and to respond to them in terms of their class membership rather than their uniqueness" (p. 16). Sorting items, ideas, thoughts, values or beliefs, for example, into categories decreases entropy and complexity while creating clarity, organization and direction. "Categorizing, therefore, is a crucial element in the process of analysis" (Dey, 1990, 112). The act of creating a category demonstrates that some similarities or commonalities have been identified within the data. The data analysis experience is an ongoing exercise in proving that a certain category indeed exists through the process of continuing to add additional pieces of data to it. As the data is analyzed, the categories may adjust slightly to reflect the emerging conceptual message that the data is attempting to convey.

Content analysis, or analyzing the content of interviews and observations, is the process of identifying, coding, and categorizing the primary patterns in the data (Patton, 1990). "The qualitative analyst's effort at uncovering patterns, themes, and categories is a creative process that requires making carefully considered judgments about what is really significant and meaningful in the data" (Patton, 1990, p. 406).

Action researchers generally utilize inductive analysis (Patton, 1990). This type of analysis is rooted in the idea that the categories, themes, and patterns "emerge out of the data rather than being imposed on them prior to data collection and analysis" (p. 390). While the data should drive the process of category generation, according to Dey (1993), "inferences from the data, initial or emergent research questions substantive policy and theoretical issues and imagination, intuition and previous knowledge" are important resources upon which to draw (p. 100). Dey goes on to point to the importance of the action researchers' familiarity with the data and its context. The researchers should be willing to discard or amend categories that no longer fit, reflect on different ways of understanding and categorizing the data, and clarify and note the criteria that has is being used to make category decisions (p. 100). Lincoln and Guba (1985) encourage researchers to "devise rules that describe category properties that can ultimately be used to justify the inclusion of each data bit that remains assigned to the category as well as to provide a basis for later tests of replicability" (p. 347).

After the action researcher(s) have identified categories, the goal is to look for themes within those categories. For example, in the Reflected Best Self example, we identified "Effective at training and teaching college students and young adults" and "Excels at developing and mentoring college students and young adults" as themes that emerge from the data. After reading through the data multiple times, categories emerged and the data bits or quotes were connected with their corresponding categories. As you read and reflect on the data bits within each category, themes and patterns will emerge. It is important, as exemplified in the exercise above, that the researchers also consider the themes and patterns that exist across categories. While it is natural to focus on the similarities within and between categories, it is also important to look for disparate data bits.

Exercise 5: Since many of the action research data collection methods toward the bottom of the list have roots in organizational development processes, many include a data analysis phase built into the process. You may choose to select from one of the pure data collection methods provided toward the top of the list and use the inductive analysis process which uses open coding, axial coding and selective coding to identify categories and themes within the data. An annotated look at this process was briefly described in the exercise at the beginning of this section. You may choose to use one of the practice-based models described toward the end of the data collection methods list that incorporates data analysis in the process.

Step 6: Carry out your action plan and begin the cycle again.

CHALLENGES IN CONDUCTING ACTION RESEARCH

Because action research is holistic and utilizes a systems-based understanding of social issues, and because it based on the participation of all relevant actors, action research is not constrained by the normal disciplinary boundaries in higher education (Levin, 2012). Greenwood (2012) asserted that this makes action research problematic to some, as it is not considered to be rigorous.

Reason and Bradbury (2001) suggest five guiding questions to ensure rigor in action research.

1. Does the action research clearly promote relational participation? The study should be designed to foster a partnership between the action researcher and the stakeholders.
2. Is there an ongoing focus on reflection related to the practical outcomes of the research? In other words, is there consistent and iterative reflection infused into the continuous improvement process? If the stakeholders are involved in all aspects of the action research processes, this can be built into each phase. If not, researchers can use member-checking to make sure that data reflects their intended message and the analysis of the information they shared correctly represents their collective insights.
3. Does the research include multiple ways or sources of gathering and analyzing information that ensures the integrity of the findings and recommendations for change? Also, is the methodology appropriate for the intent of the study?
4. Is the action research study significant? Does it add value to the individuals involved, the organization or community being studied, and the larger research community?

5. Does sustainable change or infrastructures occur as a result of the action research study? What is the enduring value of the work?

In action research, rigor is based on how data is generated, gathered, analyzed and interpreted and how it is recorded. It is also important to make it clear how researchers challenged and reflected on their own assumptions and interpretations regarding the content of the data, the process undertaken, and the premise or findings so others can understand the path the researcher(s) took to come up with the findings, planned next steps and actions. Researchers should also demonstrate how they invited participation from those with disparate views to provide a range of perspectives. This is often done through triangulation and/or purposive sampling. Finally, good action research is grounded in scholarly theory. The process should be informed by and contribute to the larger research community and a discussion of how the outcomes supported, disconfirmed or challenged existing theory is an important aspect of the action research (Coghlan & Brannick, 2009).

Greenwood (2012) and Levin (2012) also identified the challenge of intellectual property rights with respect to action research.

> Copyrights to unique and personal property are the common currency of academic research. But in action research, many of the research directions, hypotheses, and interpretations of the results are the work of collaborative large groups. The resulting analysis is clearly not the sole intellectual property of the postgraduate researcher and yet it must be represented as such to be accepted as a thesis, a dissertation, or a manuscript submitted to a journal for peer review. (Greenwood, 2012, p. 127)

Working with groups who are experiencing challenges is not always easy. The action researcher must be careful to remain what Greenwood and Levin (2007) called "the friendly outsider." As Snoeren, Niessen, and Abma (2012) explained,

> The researcher is challenged to keep a balance between distance and proximity, to approach situations with an open mind and to value and see clearly the beliefs and values of oneself and those of others. Such attentiveness is also needed to cope adequately with internal struggles and organizational and political pressures and differences. (p. 190)

The action researcher, albeit offering collaborative assistance, does not "own" the problem, the people do (Levin, 2012).

Facilitating dialogue can be challenging, especially in certain types of organizations (Wicks & Reason, 2009).

> Particularly difficult seems to be promoting bottom-up processes in top-down organizations like health care organizations, which are typically characterized by top-down structures, bureaucratic control and hierarchical working orders. An unsupportive organizational culture and little support from management can also hinder participation and engagement: a flattened organizational structure and supportive management can be accommodating. (Snoeren, Niessen & Abma, 2012, p. 191)

Further, because action research is collaborative and thus not under the total control of the researcher, it is difficult to manage the timeline of the project. As Greenwood (2012) explains, "It is ethically incoherent and methodologically impossible to order a group of people to do an AR project and to do it in a particular time framework" (p. 128).

CONCLUSION

In sum, action research is a valuable tool for scholars engaged in peace and conflict studies, as well as activists and organizations doing peace-related work. It is a method that integrates multiple voices and that offers benefits at the personal, institutional and societal level. Through critical reflection, dialogue and analysis, AR is an important way to address social issues and to help build more just and humane organizations and systems.

While action research has been used in educational settings (e.g., Brantmeier, 2007), we hope to see it utilized to a greater degree as educators seek to implement classroom and whole school peace education initiatives. We see great potential for action research to help answer pivotal questions about the effectiveness of conflict resolution, peer education, and other K–12 school-wide programs, as well as for individual teachers to assess their classroom methodologies. Further, action research can assess the effectiveness of peace education in teacher education programs and among college faculty who are evaluating their service learning and other programs.

APPENDIX A: SOLICITATION LETTER FOR INVOLVEMENT IN YOUR ACTION RESEARCH PROJECT

Dear [Insert Name],

As part of my [academic program or professional development], I am learning to do action research. Action research is a type of research that involves learning through action and reflection. I have chosen you because we interact with one another often and thus you are well-qualified to comment on my strengths. Please consider partnering with me on my first action research project by simply answering the questions below. All feedback received will be compiled and my research partners and I will develop themes from the strengths and examples you share. I will use this information to reflect on how I can continue to leverage my strengths in my professional and personal life. Thank you for your participation. If you would like to receive the findings of this study and my action plan, I would be happy to share them with you. Also, it would be an honor to have you join me and participate in the analysis and planning process. Please let me know if you are willing to participate. It will require approximately 3 hours of your time during the next 4 weeks.

Thank you for your support and feedback.

Sincerely,

[Your Name]

REFERENCES

Argyris, C., & Schön, D. (1996). *Organizational learning II: Theory, method and practice,* Reading, MA: Addison Wesley.

Boog, B. (2003). The emancipatory character of action research, its history and the present state of the art. *Journal of Community and Applied Social Psychology, 13*(6), 238–245.

Brantmeier, E. J. (2007). Everyday understandings of peace & non-peace: Peace-keeping and peacebuilding at a U.S. Midwestern high school. *Journal of Peace Education, 4*(2), 127–148.

Bruner, J. D., Goodnow, J. J., & Austin, G. A. (1972). Categories and cognition. In J. P. Spradley (Ed.). *Culture and cognition* (pp. 168–190). New York, NY: Chandler.

Center for Positive Organizational Development. (2011). Reflected Best Self Exercise (2nd ed.). Retrieved from http://www.centerforpos.org/the-center/teaching-and-practice-materials/teaching-tools/reflected-best-self-exercise

Coghlan, D., & Brannick, T. (2009). *Doing action research.* Thousand Oaks, CA. Sage.

Conley-Tyler, M., Bretherton, D., Halafhoff, A., & Nietschke, Y. (2008). Developing a peace education curriculum for Vietnamese primary schools: A case study of participatory action research in cross-cultural design. *Journal of Research in International Education, 7*(3), 346–368.

Dey, I. (1993). *Qualitative data analysis: A user-friendly guide for social scientists.* New York, NY: Routledge.

Dachler, H. P., & Hosking, D. M. (1995). The primacy of relations in socially constructing organizational realities. In D. M. Hosking, H. P. Dachler, & K. J.

Gergen (Eds.), *Management and organization: Relational alternatives to individualism* (pp. 1–28). Aldershot, England: Avebury.

Dick.B., Stringer, E., & Huxham. C. (2009). Theory in action research. *Action Research, 7*(1), 5–12.

Fals-Borda, O., & Rahman, M. (Eds) (1991). *Action and knowledge: Breaking the monopoly with participatory action research.* New York, NY: The Apex Press.

Ferrance, E. (2000). Action research. Brown University Themes in Education. Retrieved September 9, 2012 from, http://www.lab.brown.edu/pubs/themes_ed/act_research.pdf

Galtung, J. (1996). *Peace by peaceful means: peace and conflict, development and civilization.* Thousand Oaks, CA: Sage.

Gergen, K. J. (1995). Social construction and the educational process. *Constructivism in Education* (pp. 17–39). Hillsdale, NJ: Lawrence Erlbaum.

Glaser, B. G., & Strauss, A. L. (1967). *The discovery of grounded theory: Strategies for qualitative research.* New York, NY: Aldine De Gruyter.

Greenwood, D. (2012). Doing and learning action research in the neo-liberal world of contemporary higher education. *Action Research, 10*(2), 115–132.

Greenwood, D., & Levin, M. (2007). *Introduction to action research: Social research for social change.* Thousand Oaks, CA: Sage.

Hosking, D. M. (1995). Constructing power: Entitative and relational approaches. In D. M. Hosking, H. P. Dachler, & K. J. Gergen (Ed.), *Management and organization: Relational alternatives to individualism.* Aldershot, England: Avebury.

Hosking, D.M., & Bass, A. (1998). Constructing changes through relational dynamics. *Aston Business School Research Paper Series*, RP9813.

Hynes G., Coghlan, Coghlan, D., and McCarron, M. (2012). Participation as a multi-voiced process: Action research in the acute hospital environment. *Action Research, 10*(3), 293–312.

Huang, H. (2010). What is good action research? Why the resurgent interest? *Action Research, 8*(1), 93-109.

Huzzard, T., & Bjorkman, H. (2012). Trade unions and action research. *Work, Employment & Society, 26*(1), 161–171.

Interpeace. (2005). The uses of video in a participatory action research process for peacebuilding: The Interpeace experience. Retrieved March 8, 2013 from, http://dmeforpeace.org/sites/default/files/2005_IP_The_Uses_of_Video_In_Participatory_Action_Research.pdf

Jupp, V. (2006). *Purposive sampling. The SAGE dictionary of social research methods.* London, England: Sage.

Kitchen, J., & Stevens, D. (2008). Action research in teacher education: Two teacher-educators practice action research as they introduce action research to preservice teachers. *Action Research, 6*(1), 7–28.

Langer, E. J. (1997). *The art of mindful learning.* Reading, MA: Addison-Wesley.

Levin, M. (2012). Academic integrity in action research. *Action Research, 10*(2), 133–149.

Lincoln, Y. S., & Guba, E. G. (1985). *Naturalistic inquiry.* Beverly Hills, CA: Sage.

Moeliono, I., & Fisher, L. (n.d.). Research as mediation: Linking participatory action research to environmental conflict management in East Nusa Tenggara,

Indonesia. Retrieved September 17, 2012 from, ftp://ftp.fao.org/docrep/fao/005/y4503e/y4503e10.pdf

Morrow, T. (2011). *Toward a National Peace Academy: Leading positive organizational development and change* (Unpublished doctoral dissertation). Fort Lauderdale-Davie, FL, Nova Southeastern University

Patton, M. Q. (1990). *Qualitative Evaluation and Research Methods* (2nd ed.). Newbury Park, CA: Sage.

Pearce, W. B. (1992). A "camper's guide To constructionisms." *Human Systems: The Journal of Systemic Consultation and Management, 3,* 139–161.

Rai, R. (2012). A participatory action research training initiative to improve police effectiveness. *Action Researcher, 10*(3), 225–243.

Reason, P., & Bradbury, H. (Eds.). (2008). *The SAGE Handbook of Action Research. Participative Inquiry and Practice* (2nd ed.). London, England: Sage

Reason, P., & Torbert, W. (2001). The Action turn: Towards a transformational social science. *Concepts and Transformation, 6*(1), 1–37.

Reed, J. (2007). *Appreciative inquiry: Research for change.* Thousand Oaks, CA: Sage.

Riel, M. (2010). Understanding Action Research. *Center For Collaborative Action Research.* Pepperdine University. Retrieved September 27, 2012 from, http://cadres.pepperdine.edu/ccar/define.html

Riel, M., & Lepori, K. (2011, April). *A meta-analysis of the outcomes of Action Research.* Paper presented at the American Educational Research Association conference, New Orleans.

Smith, L., Bratini, L., Chambers, D., Jensen, R., & Romero, L. (2010). Between idealism and reality: Meeting the challenge of participatory action research. *Action Research, 8*(4), 407–425.

Snoeren, M., Niessen, T., & Abma, T. (2012). Engagement enacted: Essentials of initiating an action research project. *Action Research, 10*(2), 189–204.

Strauss, A., & Corbin, J. (1990). *Basics of qualitative research: Grounded theory procedures and techniques.* Newbury Park, CA: Sage.

Wehr, P. (1979). *Conflict regulation.* Boulder, CO: Westview.

Wicks, P., & Reason, P. (2009). Initiating action research: Challenges and paradoxes of opening communicative spaces. *Action Research, 7*(3), 243–262.

CHAPTER 9

"WE'LL HAVE TO RESCHEDULE THE INTERVIEW; THE AIR RAID SIREN JUST WENT OFF AGAIN"

Undertaking Qualitative Research in Conflict Zones

Julia Chaitin

Living through a long-term and violent social-political conflict is extremely difficult. Studying such contexts raise a host of issues not usually encountered in 'normal' situations, especially when the researcher belongs to the society that is experiencing the violence. Given that researchers have a choice of what to study, it can be asked why any/some of them would choose to research a topic that is not only unstable and unpredictable, but also often physically (and psychologically) dangerous.

This question is especially relevant for qualitative research, which by its nature, is a long-term endeavor, one that often involves prolonged immersion in the field and complex processes of data collection, interpretation, and representation. Many questions arise concerning such a research

Peace and Conflict Studies Research: A Qualitative Perspective, pp. 185–204
Copyright © 2014 by Information Age Publishing

process: How does the researcher know when it is 'safe' to begin research? What events are stable enough to explore? How can the researcher ensure that s/he will find enough people to discuss the impact of the conflict on their lives, especially when it is a traumatic topic? And once a topic of inquiry is chosen, and reality "on the ground" abruptly and significantly changes, how does the researcher deal with these rapid changes—changes which might result in a severe revision, or even worse, the end of the planned research?

In this chapter, I focus on methodological topics central to qualitative research undertaken in conflict areas. My examples will come from the Israeli-Palestinian conflict, a conflict with which I live on a daily basis, since I am Israeli, and which I have also studied for years. However, I believe that the topics raised here are relevant for qualitative researchers who live in other conflict zones. Therefore, it is my hope that this chapter will shed some light on these issues in a more general sense.

When a researcher chooses to study individuals, groups or communities who are living in a conflict area, s/he is often faced with questions that, as a rule, do not concern researchers from peaceful areas whose topics do not relate to structural violence. The work becomes even more difficult when the researcher studies his/her own volatile "backyard," such as in my case. In my region of the Middle East, there is intense political life, which takes place in a small geographical area. The conflict is connected to a myriad of social, political, and economic issues that directly affect the everyday life of every person who lives here.

I am not alone in this endeavor; there are many researchers from the area who have studied the Israeli-Palestinian conflict from "close up." The main topics which psychologists, sociologists, social workers, education specialists and anthropologists have study include: the trauma that results from continuous living in a war zone, different psycho-social impacts of the war on the victims, dialogue experiences and other peace-building activities between Jews and Arabs, the different historical narratives of the two peoples, and perception of self and other as related to the conflict (e.g., Abdeen, Qasrawi, Shibli Nabil, & Shaheen, 2008; Adwan & Bar-On, 2001, 2004; Bar-On, 2006, 2008; Bar-Tal & Teichman, 2005; Chaitin, 2011; Chaitin, Awwad, & Andriani, 2009; Dekel & Nuttman-Shwartz, 2009; El Sarraj, 2002; Elbedour, Onwuegbuzie, Ghannam, Whitcome, & Abu Hein, 2007; Maoz, 2011; Nuttman-Shwartz, Dekel, & Tuval-Mashiach, 2011; Solomon, 1995; Steinberg & Bar-On, 2002).

This chapter will look at five main issues characteristic of qualitative research undertaken in conflict zones, when the researcher is part of that conflict. These topics include: (a) different impacts of the conflict on the researcher; (b) reflexivity; (c) relationships with others (researchers and participants) in the research process; (d) deciding what topics to study; and

(e) standards for assessing the quality of the work, generalization or transference to other populations in conflict, and challenges in publishing. I will combine theoretical discussions of these issues with some of my experiences from the field, that help demonstrate the complexity of dealing with the issues that arise, as well as some ways of dealing with them.

1. *The impact of the conflict on the researcher and the research design*

When the researcher is exploring his/her own society, especially the difficult aspects of life, s/he must be able to gain access to the population and site under study, while simultaneously keeping enough of a distance in order to see needed, different, and nuanced perspectives concerning the topic of inquiry. Although in the follow excerpt Vidich and Lyman (2003) refer to ethnographic research, their assertion holds true for researchers working in other qualitative traditions as well:

> qualitative ethnographic social research ... entails an attitude of detachment toward society that permits the sociologist to observe the conduct of self and others, to understand the mechanisms of social processes, and to comprehend and explain why both actors and processes are as they are. (p. 56)

Being part of the context that one is studying has advantages and disadvantages. On the one hand, the researcher "knows" the context and therefore, possesses insider information concerning the language, rites and symbols to which an external researcher might not be privy. On the other hand, this prior knowledge can, at times, be a disadvantage in that it may keep local researchers from approaching the context from a fresh angle in order to gain new insights concerning what might still be hidden from understanding.

How does the often-changing and often violent social-political context influence the researcher during the study? Researchers who are studying their own societal conflict face the same objective dangers and fears, at least to some degree, that face their research participants. For example, during a life-story research study of elderly people who have lived in rural communities along the Gaza-Israeli border (Chaitin et al., 2012)—an area that has known violent conflict for decades, and massive rocket attacks for over a decade—I was brought face-to-face with the many tensions which face the interviewees, both as a researcher and as a resident of the area that I was studying. Whenever there were eruptions in the violence (and they unfortunately occurred every few months), our research schedule had to be revised and I often wondered if living in such a region hindered my ability to be open to examining the different perspectives raised by the interviewees concerning life in a region that posed physical and psychological dangers.

Connected to this challenge is the issue of the relationship between qualitative work and political stances (Denzin & Lincoln, 2003; Fine, Weis, Weseen, & Wong, 2003; Gergen & Gergen, 2003). As Gergen and Gergen (2003) note, "sound" research has traditionally been conceived as being politically and value-neutral. However, as qualitative researchers know, it is impossible to truly separate method from ideology. The authors state:

> If inquiry is inevitably ideological, the major challenge is to pursue the research that most deeply expresses one's political and valuational investments … [i]f science is politics by other means, then we should pursue the inquiry that most effectively achieves our ends. (p. 594)

Punch (1986) also notes that it is impossible to disentangle politics from much of social science research and that the political views of a researcher, as well as the ideologies espoused by societal institutions, which often impact what will be studied, since they fund and/or approve the research plan, critically influence every stage of the research process (p. 13).

Gergen and Gergen (2003) assert that researchers should explore all of the different voices within a given research setting and problem, including voices of the privileged. This stance differs from that of Fine et al. (2003) who stress the need to focus on populations that traditionally have been marginalized and as a result also underresearched. However, Gergen and Gergen *do* press for honesty on the part of the researcher concerning his/her political and ideological stands. As these researchers see it, one way to take a clear political stance and also be open to documenting dissenting voices is through the use of polyvocality—by making sure that the different voices of the different parties—in our case Israelis and Palestinians from different social-political standings and different political views—are (re) presented in the publications of our findings.

However, when a researcher's life is spent in the conflict context, we can ask if this is a realistic demand? For example, can I, a self-defined left-wing peace activist, who believes that the siege on Gaza is very wrong, *really* listen and give voice to right-wing Israeli nationalist extremists who believe that all Gazans are potential terrorists who must be kept from entering Israel? This is one of the challenges that I have faced often in my work —and perhaps one reason why I have tended to shy away from engaging in research that will bring me face-to-face with people who hold extremely divergent political perspectives from mine, even though I could be quite surprised by what they have to say.

Undertaking field research in unstable and conflict-ridden areas can also, at times, put the researcher in physical danger. As Padgett (1998) and Creswell (1998) note, qualitative research is enhanced by "prolonged engagement" in the field. However, this may be difficult, if not impossible, when the field is fraught with dangers (Daniel, 1996). Daniel (1996), an anthropologist originally from Sri Lanka, who immigrated to the United States, experienced similar concerns when he undertook fieldwork in his native homeland:

> My project was a benign one: to collect folk songs sung by Tamil women ... When I wrote my proposal, I was on a quest for an alternative narrative ... about the history of labor and displacement.... Little did I expect to find *another alternative* narrative, one that defied my expectations and plans. I had no idea that by the time I reached Sri Lanka ... I would arrive on the heels of the worst anti-Tamil riots known in that island paradise to find that none of my singers were in a mood to sing, and to find my best singer rummaging for what she could salvage from the shell of her fire-gorged home.... Before I knew it, defying all research designs and disciplinary preparations, I was entangled in a project that had me rather than I it.... The challenge was to understand a state of utter discordance that had begun to be sustained by the relentless ... violence. The ... standard practice in anthropology, of staying put in one location for a certain length of time ... had become impossible. I was urged to move on ... to move away from where my continued presence could have spelled trouble for both my informants and me. (pp. 3–4)

Israeli researchers, studying their own society, cannot retreat from the field. The country is small, events come quickly one after another, and incidents that occur in one part of the country can easily also "hit close to home" as Israelis often have friends or family who are hurt by the violence. Since borders between the political and the research are not always clear-cut, the closer one is to one's fieldwork—both emotionally and professionally—the more difficult it becomes to gain clarity. As Schratz and Walker (1995) state: "The degree to which political issues saturate the research process is not always understood, especially by those directly involved" (p. 135).

2. *Reflexivity during the research process.*

This leads to the second aspect addressed in this chapter, briefly touched on above: How does the study of one's conflictual backyard impact the process of reflexivity? Reflexivity is multilayered and never easy; it requires one to deeply consider one's beliefs and understandings, pushing toward acute self-consciousness (Chaitin, 2011). Lincoln and Guba (2003) note that reflexivity:

> is the process of reflecting critically on the self as researcher ... [it] forces us to come to terms not only with our choice of ... problem and with those with whom we engage in the research process, but with our selves and with the multiple identities that represent the fluid self in the research setting ... Reflexivity demands that we interrogate ourselves concerning the ways in

which research is shaped and staged around the contradictions and paradoxes of our own lives. (p. 283)

Other researchers have stressed the histories, culture, and meanings
that researchers bring to their studies and the effects that these have on
their abilities to attain deep levels of self-understandings (e.g., Gergen
& Gergen, 2003; Scheper-Hughes, 1992). As Gergen and Gergen (2003)
stated:

> investigators ... demonstrate ... their historical and geographical situated-
> ness, their personal investments in the research, various biases they bring to
> the work, their surprises and "undoings" in the process of research ... and the
> ways in which they have avoided or suppressed certain points. (pp. 579–580)

During the reflective process, investigators look at ways in which their
personal histories saturate their inquiry. Here is an example that comes
from a study on Israeli and Palestinian NGOs (nongovernmental organizations) that focused on environmental issues, which I undertook with
Palestinian colleagues (Chaitin, Obeidi, Adwan, & Bar-On, 2004). This
project was interrupted when the second *Intifada* erupted (the Palestinian
uprising that began in September 2000)

When the uprising began, I did not understand why they had resorted
to war, when it seemed that we were on the threshold of finally reaching a comprehensive peace agreement (the violence came on the heels
of attempts to reach a final agreement at Camp David in the previous
summer). In spite of the fact that I was very worried about my Palestinian colleagues, and remained in ongoing e-mail and phone contact with
them, I was furious with their people, who I saw, as once again, choosing
war, instead of peace.

I remember those first few days; I spent hours tending my garden in
order to calm the overwhelming tension that I was feeling. In addition, I
used another technique that helps me deal with stress: I wrote about my
hard feelings. I sent the piece to a number of people, including my Palestinian colleagues and was shocked when I received their answers.

One of my colleagues was furious: How could I (an Israeli) write about
pain and destruction, when I was working in my garden? As he let me know,
the Palestinians were under siege, had no water, no electricity, and were
being bombed day and night by the Israeli air force! And I was complaining
that things are tough while I watered and pruned my flowers?! My colleague wrote that instead of feeling sorry for myself—unjustifiable from his
perspective—I should actively demonstrate against the Israeli aggression,
that he saw as being responsible for the atrocities against innocent people.

During those days, I did not accept his point of view; in fact, I was hurt and insulted. I did not believe that they *actually* expected *me* to demonstrate against my army and government when it seemed clear that it had been the Palestinians who were to blame for this round of violence.

It took me a number of months to reflect on the situation and to see the unfolding of the war from a more complex point of view. I began to understand that the changes that we Israelis had felt during the "peace" years had been barely felt by the other side. I began to understand why the Palestinians were insulted during the rounds of negotiations, and that they increasingly felt that the injustices were never going to end. I also began to understand that my Palestinian colleagues saw joint research as one (small) part of a greater joint action, and that they really *did* expect me to stand with them while the war was going on. They did/could not listen to my worries when I was safe in my home, with my running water, electricity, and well-kept garden.

I did not demonstrate against the Israeli actions during that time, but I did begin to think more critically about my views and to listen more closely to the voices of my colleagues. The insult dissipated. Even though I had considered myself fairly knowledgeable about Palestinians—certainly more than most Israelis—I realized that I had much more to learn about life in the Occupied Territories. I managed to gain a deeper understanding of the frustrations and pain that they felt on a daily basis. I better understood that since I was an Israeli, my colleagues saw me as a representative of the more powerful side that was occupying them. Therefore, I had to be prepared to contain much of their pain and not demand, and not expect that they would respond kindly when I wrote of my own pain and fear. I understood that this process was not separate from our joint academic research. I also saw that I would neither be capable of deeply analyzing the data nor be able to count on our research coming to fruition, as long as I kept my un-empathetic blinders on.

As researchers reflect on their ongoing work, these reflections grow into rigorous representations of their participants and research site. Therefore, it is important for researchers to be as honest as they can with themselves about the topic chosen for study (Rossman & Rallis, 1998) and to modify the study as they proceed in order to deepen the level of their insights.

In sum, then, reflexivity is a conscious act, one that demands that the researcher situate him/herself clearly within the social and cultural context of conflict. The researcher must be willing to openly confront the self and to challenge previously-held "truths" and understandings, in order to engage in in-depth inquiry, even when such a process is painful.

3. *Relationships with others, including the "enemy" and (potential) participants*

The ideas discussed above also tie into notions addressed by Shifra Sagy, an Israeli psychologist (and peace activist) who has spent years studying issues connected to the conflict—on her own, with Israeli researchers and with Palestinian scholars (e.g., Braun-Lewensohn, Sagy, & Roth, 2010; Sagy, 2002; Sagy & Adwan, 2006; Sagy & Antonovsky, 1986; Sagy, Orr, Bar-On, & Awwad, 2001; Sagy, Steinberg, & Diab, 2006; Sagy, Steinberg, & Fahiraladin, 1999). Sagy and I have often talked about relationships with Palestinian colleagues, since we have both had these experiences. For example, when discussing a collaborative study that she worked on during the Oslo years, Sagy spoke about the good personal and working relationship she had with her colleagues, stating that, at that time, she believed that peace between Palestinians and Israelis was imminent. According to the researcher, her close relationships with the Palestinian researchers prevented her from seeing one clear trend that was emerging from questionnaire and interview data: neither the Palestinian nor the Israeli participants expressed empathy toward the other side. After the second *Intifada* began and the peace years ended, and Sagy had distanced herself from the research, she was able to objectively "see" what she had missed before. She had, indeed "avoided or suppressed certain points" (Gergen & Gergen, 2003, p. 580).

Another aspect concerning the relationship between the researcher and his/her field of qualitative inquiry is the notion of the researcher as the instrument (Rossman & Rallis, 1998). As Rossman and Rallis (1998) have noted, the researcher's biography shapes his/her work in many ways and it is through the biography that "she makes sense of the setting and how the people she studies make sense of her" (p. 38).

There is always a relationship between the researcher and the participants, the researcher and his/her audience (after the article/book has been published or the lecture at the conference given), and ultimately, between the researcher and society. This point has been stressed by Gergen and Gergen (2003) who note that researcher-participant relationships are "dialogical and co-constructive" and that the relationship of researchers to their audiences is "interdependent ... [with] the negotiation of meaning within any relationship as potentially ramifying outward into the society" (p. 603). Therefore, the ways in which the researcher presents him/herself to potential interviewees and colleagues, the ways in which s/he poses interview questions and listens to the answers, and the ways in which s/he writes about the study, create and influence relationships that ultimately impact how the data collection process proceeds, how well the collaborative researchers work together and how the written work is perceived by its readers.

According to Padgett (1998), researchers need to maintain critical distance from the participants/site under study, to manage one's emotions, and to "go with the flow" (p. 20) if they are to produce creative scholarship.

As Padget notes, "Because we are engaged in the same emotionally intense encounters as our respondents, it would be impossible to avoid experiencing ups and downs during fieldwork" (p. 41). Therefore, Padget advises us to "practice bracketing" (p. 41) so that we can put aside prior understandings and emotions in order to allow new emotions and understandings of the topic under inquiry to emerge.

How do researchers, who like their participants, are living through the vicissitudes of the structural violence that characterizes their society, practice such bracketing? How can we demand that a researcher keeps emotions in check when s/he is studying a conflict that has numerous personal and familial influences on daily life? And how can we refrain from harboring negative thoughts about potential interviewees who do not see the world as we do? In many ways, such demands are impossible. Perhaps an example from my work can provide some insights into this quandary.

In 2002 I was the head Israeli researcher in a joint Palestinian-Israeli study that was undertaken under the auspices of the Peace Research Institute in the Middle East (PRIME). The study documented the experiences of present-day and former refugees, and aimed to learn their perspectives on the Israeli-Palestinian conflict, especially concerning the issue of Palestinian refugee return. The Palestinian team interviewed Palestinians who became refugees in 1948, and remained living in refugee camps, and we Israelis talked to Jews who came to the country after World War II as refugees from the Holocaust or from Northern Africa and became citizens of the State. We interviewed Israelis who had established communities in areas where there had once been Arab villages, and that were destroyed after the 1948 war.

This study provided new challenges for me since I encountered a problem that I had never encountered before: I had a very hard time recruiting Israeli participants. For weeks I tried to build a sample, phoning different communities that were situated in places when Palestinian villages had once existed and where former Jewish refugees had settled. I met with numerous refusals and did not understand what was keeping people from agreeing to be interviewed. Eventually I reached a Holocaust survivor who wanted to be interviewed. After the interview, she told me that her son, who lived in the same community, might also like to be interviewed since he was very interested in the Holocaust and in his family's roots. I was very excited since we also wished to get intergenerational perspectives as well.

I phoned the man, introduced myself, and asked him if he would be interested in participating in the study. He obviously was expecting my call since he said that he had talked to his mother about her interview, and she had told him how well it had gone. I began explaining the study and mentioned that the research was a joint Israeli-Palestinian undertaking. At that point, the man cut me off and literally began screaming at me:

Do you think that I am going to collaborate with you on this, that I am going to take part in something that is Palestinian-Israeli? You are a traitor! They want to kill us and you want me to participate in such a joint project? You must belong to the left-wing or to *B'Tselem*." (an Israeli watchdog organization that documents violations of human rights, mostly in the West Bank)

I tried to reassure him that I would let him say whatever he wanted; promising him that he could choose to speak about whatever he wanted. I explained the importance of documenting different voices, his as well. However, the response I got was that the son of the survivor slammed down the phone, putting an end to our talk.

It took me quite a while to get over that call; I was literally speechless after our "conversation." While, before, I had worried about my relationships with my Palestinian colleagues, I now understood how fragile relationships could be with interviewees from my *own* Israeli side. This is not an experience that most researchers face in their academic work, but one that can be encountered by researchers who are studying conflicts gripping their own country, especially ones that create divisions within the society. I learned from the experience that I could not take researcher-participant relationships for granted in the kind of studies I was conducting.

My failed attempt to recruit as many interviewees as we had originally planned for showed me very clearly that the idea of participating in a joint Palestinian-Israeli venture was threatening, and undesirable, for many Israelis. I repeatedly heard: "I am not interested"; "Why should I get involved in something so complicated?" or simply, "No thanks." When I interpret the refusals, I reach the understanding that among Israelis there is a general distrust and suspicion toward Israeli researchers who are working with Palestinian researchers, as well as suspicion about what might happen with their interviews. Potential participants asked me: What are you going to do with the results of the study? How can you promise me that the Palestinian researchers will not exploit what I said for their propaganda? How can you promise me that the study will not fall into the wrong hands, such as the Hamas?

To be honest, I could *not* make such promises. I could *not* promise that the results of the research would not be used for purposes of Palestinian "propaganda." All I could do, which turned out not to be enough, was assure the potential participants that *I* had no intention of distorting what had been told to us, or to knowingly "arm" hostile others with "weapons" against us This fear of misuse of the data, which of course, is completely understandable given the hostile reality in which we live, certainly decreased the number of people who agreed to be interviewed

From the above, we can summarize that the typical guidelines, such as theoretical sampling (Glasser & Strauss, 1967) that can aid the researcher in choosing a sample for his/her qualitative inquiry are problematic for the scholar who lives in and studies a dangerous and contentious "backyard." Relationships between researcher and participants, or between researchers and their colleagues, if they come from the "enemy" side, can impact who will be interviewed, what they will be asked, how the relationship between the participant and researcher develops, how the data will be understood, and/or if the relationships between the researchers succeed in withstanding the tests of the violence.

4.   *What topics should I choose for my study?*

Another issue to consider concerns choosing a relevant research question for one's work. How does the researcher know that the decided-upon research question that seems pertinent today will remain relevant over time? This issue is connected to the demands often put on researchers by universities and funding sources to choose a topic that has "academic" and "social" importance. Perceptions of "importance," however, often differ between formal institutions and minority or social justice groups, or researchers that also wish to further certain social-political agendas (Fine et al., 2003; Greenwood & Levin, 2003). As Fine et al. (2003) and Greenwood and Levin (2003) have noted, universities tend to be conservative and slow-moving bureaucracies, thus they do not easily support nonmainstream research. Furthermore, they often tend to reflect the political-social status quo; as a result, topics that are considered "hot" or reflecting "nonmainstream political/ideological views" may find themselves without backing or approval.

A timely example comes from the joint Israeli-Palestinian research endeavor entitled "Victims of Our Own Narratives?" Portrayal of the "Other" in Israeli and Palestinian School Books (initiated by the Council of Religious Institutions of the Holy Land and funded by the United States Department of State, Bureau of Democracy, Human Rights and Labor). The head researchers of this study, Daniel Bar-Tal from Israel, Sami Adwan from Palestine and Bruce Wexler from Yale University, all considered to be world-class scholars, came under fire when results of the study—which showed that the Palestinian textbooks did *not* demonize Israelis—were reported in the Israeli press (the Palestinian governmental responses were much less critical). Readers might find this response to the findings surprising. After all, if the results showed that the Palestinian textbooks did not demonize Israelis, then this would be a sign that peace between the peoples *is* possible. However, in order to understand why the results and the researchers came under attack, it is important to understand that the present government is a self-defined right-wing government that continuously avers that "there is no partner for peace." Therefore, such a finding could be seen as undermining the government.

According to an article, written by Friedson and Gradstein (2013), which appeared in the *Jewish Journal*:

> A ... study on Israeli and Palestinian textbooks ... set-off a wave of insults, charges and counter-charges. Israel's Ministry of Education called the detailed report "biased and unprofessional" .... The three-year study ... found that textbooks on both sides present one-sided narratives of the Israeli-Palestinian conflict but rarely resort to demonization of the other side. The researchers analyzed 74 Israeli and 94 Palestinian textbooks in-depth....The Israeli Ministry of Education declined to help the researchers and leveled some serious charges against both the researchers and their methods. "The report is biased and unprofessional," ... [a] spokeswoman for the Ministry of Education, said in a statement. "The conclusion of this 'research' was known before it was carried out, and it certainly does not reflect reality.... The Ministry of Education chose not to cooperate with those elements who are interested in maliciously slandering the Israeli education system and the state of Israel. The results of the 'research' show that the decision not to cooperate was correct." Israel's Ministry of Strategic Affairs was even more harsh, saying that the study "omits important examples of incitement and delegitimization found in official Palestinian Authority textbooks".... The response from the Palestinian Authority was far more positive. Prime Minister Salam Fayyad welcomed the results.

From this example, we see that when results of a study, even one undertaken by researchers who are considered to be at the top of their fields, do not reflect official governmental lines of a society embroiled in an intractable conflict, the researchers can be denigrated and their study vilified. Under such circumstances, it is easy to understand why many academics might shy away from posing a research question that is bound to draw fire, and perhaps seriously harm their careers and reputations.

Vidich and Lyman (2003) discuss difficulties in selecting pertinent research questions under "normal" conditions: "(what is) meaningful about the world ... for one person, is not necessarily meaningful for another." (p. 58). And, as Daniel (1996) asks us, the question of whether or not our research interest will make it into a "second edition" is one that tends to preoccupy those interested in stability, but may be less relevant for those who see the world through the lens of dynamics and change.

In sum, researchers who live in a conflict region and choose to study that conflict have far from an easy time decided what to study. As events unfold, mainstream ideologies that support the ongoing violence are strengthened, especially when "dangerous" research results are found. Academics who engage in such work must think long and hard about how far they are willing to go and what social and professional price they are willing to pay for challenging the status quo.

5. *Standards, transference to other populations, and publishing opportunities*

There is no doubt that collaboratively exploring a conflict that grips the society in which one lives, with colleagues from the "enemy" side, will influence the quality of the work being carried out. Therefore, it is important to ask: are the accepted standards devised for research in "normal" times relevant for joint Israeli-Palestinian (or other conflicts) research, and if not, what can be done?

It is often *very* difficult for Palestinian and Jewish-Israeli researchers, who are working together, to produce a study that meets accepted standards of quality in social science research. This is not because they are less professional than their colleagues from other places in the world, but because they face numerous objective challenges. The challenges include: (1) difficulties in meeting—since borders are often closed and relations are tense between the peoples, (2) differences in status—since Israelis have freedom of movement and citizenship while Palestinians are restricted in their movement and under occupation, (3) uncertainties about the future of the study during violent times, (4) difficulties in recruiting participants, and (5) difficulties in finding academic and/or financial support for the research. All of this means that people who are intent on undertaking such work need to continually figure out how to meet the standards when much of their work is impacted by events outside of their control.

If existing criteria do not take into account the difficulties of doing research in a war zone, we can ponder whether researchers who live in such social-political situations should relinquish their desire to work together on a collaborative study. As perhaps can be expected, my answer is that if relevant criteria do not exist, we should construct criteria that are relevant for the social-political world in which we are living and working.

I am often asked by Israeli academics: "If it is so complicated, why not wait for quieter times before entering into such collaborations?" I always respond that research is a part of life, and that we could ask that question about all other aspects of life. For example, I sometimes sarcastically ask, how can discouraging dialogue encounters between Israelis and Palestinians hasten peace? What good can come from telling Israeli and Palestinian entrepreneurs to put off creating joint economic endeavors that can be of service to both societies until the political problem is solved? It is clear to me that if we wait, nothing will ever change. And in spite of the fact that our work is full of virtual and concrete landmines, giving up is not the answer. The opposite is true: I hold that scholars who believe that everyone who lives in the region has a role to play in helping end the conflict, must do their part by reaching out to colleagues from the other side, especially when the signs point to a mountain of obstacles.

This way of thinking connects to discussions on the overarching objectives of social science research. Researchers agree that the main goal of research is to further knowledge (Delanty & Strydom, 2003). However, this is not its only aim. Scholars that adhere to critical and feminist perspectives (e.g., Haraway, 2003) or who undertake participatory action research (such as Kemmis & McTaggart, 2003) aver that an additional objective of social science research is to bring about change in an unequal, racist, chauvinistic, and ethnocentric environment that characterizes many social and political contexts, such as the Palestinian-Israeli context.

The new question, therefore, becomes *how* can we design and undertake quality research in the context of an "intractable" conflict? It appears to me that the best place to start is with the goodwill and fervent desire of the partners who have decided to engage in a joint study, since they are committed to constructing a new, nonviolent reality. Courageous thinking can lead to the birth of creative research ideas (Lederach, 2005) and innovative insights and solutions often appear when the individual (researcher) finds him/ herself stuck and then, almost miraculously, finds a way to solve the problem that beforehand appeared to have no solution.

However, we must return to reality and note that there are a number of obstacles that Palestinian and Israeli researchers face when attempting to work according to traditional standards of rigorous research.

First, when working together on a study, these researchers need to be able to continue on with their work even when external events keep them for meeting face-to-face. In such times, therefore, they must move from joint work to parallel work. Under such circumstances, each researcher works on his/her side of the border and they "meet" periodically by phone, Skype, or via e-mail. Of course, this is far from optimal, but it cannot be helped.

For example, in the refugee study for **PRIME** briefly presented above, the Palestinians and Israelis decided to use different types of interviews since we could not meet together to undergo joint training in the life-story methodology. On the Israeli side, we used biographical interviewing (Rosenthal, 1993), while our Palestinian colleagues used semistructured interviews (Creswell, 1998). Because we were unable to sit together in order to devise an agreed-upon interview strategy and guide, and to train those who had never used biographical methods, we settled on writing questions that concerned the experiences of the participants from the different sides, including how they viewed the conflict. I am not claiming that this was the ideal solution; it was simply the only option that we had at the time, since we were caught in the middle of the Second *Intifada*. Parallel work, which also translates into differences in the ways data are collected, also impacts the ways in which the data can be interpreted.

Another challenge facing researchers working together is integrating the differences in styles of writing, especially since they come from different cultures. Multivoice writing (Gergen & Gergen, 2003) is not a phenomenon that is unique to Palestinian and Jewish-Israeli researchers; when members of any research team write up their findings, we will hear different voices in their text. However, when the researchers are "enemies," who also come from different cultural backgrounds, this diversity becomes even more conspicuous and creates new challenges.

The result of all of these phenomena is that we cannot expect a high level of uniformity in such a research study. And when there is little uniformity, there is a greater risk that the quality of the research will suffer. Unfortunately, I am still unable to offer tried and true solutions to the problems noted above; these challenges demand more thinking, practice and reflection.

What can further be noted is that the obstacles facing collaborative researchers do not stop at the writing stage; they continue on to the publication stage as well. If editors/publishers of academic journals and books be unwilling to accept unconventional manuscripts from scholars pursuing peace, that, at times, do not completely meet conventional standards of research—be they quantitative or qualitative—then joint research faces even more problems. However, if they are open to accepting different kinds of research, and interested in promoting new knowledge and "peace academics," there is a chance that collaborative research will succeed. The researchers will be able to show others in Palestinian and Israeli societies, as well as in other parts of the world, that joint research in a war zone is not only possible, but also publishable

The final issue addressed here looks at the question of generalization or the transference (Lincoln & Guba, 1985) of findings from a study undertaken in one particular unstable context to "similar" contexts. This issue has often been debated among qualitative researchers, and there is little consensus concerning whether or not it is possible, or even desirable, to generalize findings from one qualitative research to other contexts and populations (Greenwood & Levin, 2003; Stake, 1995). Here, I will adopt Greenwood and Levin's (2003) notion of generalization in qualitative research:

> Given ... that knowledge is context-bound, the key to utilizing this knowledge in a different setting is to follow a two-step model. First, it is important to understand the contextual conditions under which the knowledge has been created. This contextualizes the knowledge itself. Second, the transfer of this knowledge to a new setting implies understanding the contextual conditions of the new setting, how these differ from the setting in which the

knowledge was produced, and involves reflection on what consequences this has for applying the actual knowledge in the new context. Hence generalization becomes an active process of reflection in which involved actors must make up their minds about whether or not the previous knowledge makes sense in the new context. (p. 152)

From the above, concern with generalizing understandings from our research in our conflictual and unstable backyard to other conflict arenas, or other populations, has come (almost) full circle—back to the issue of reflexivity in research and to the relationship between the researcher and the field and the researcher and the reader. While I do hold that results from qualitative research studies of intractable conflicts can be modestly generalized to larger populations facing the same or similar challenges, or to other intractable conflicts, I leave it up to the reader to decide if generalization is an issue that concerns him/her in his/her particular qualitative study. The methodological conflict surrounding the issue of generalization may be yet another intractable conflict in a long line of conflicts that plague our world

Some final remarks—Create research opportunities and build the peace

This chapter focused on issues connected to undertaking qualitative research in an unstable and violent social and political context, especially when one lives in such a society. While most of the chapter focused on difficulties, I believe that it is also important to see the positive aspects of conflict, and not only as obstacles to be overcome. Attempting to understand how the dynamics of the society impact individuals, communities and societies can be a fascinating topic for research, one far from depressing. Furthermore, the researcher who is in the middle of such "action" has much to offer his/her society, as well as audiences from other places around the world, who wish to gain deeper understandings of conflicts that appear too complex to untangle.

A case can be made that it is easier for qualitative research to study conflictual and dynamic contexts then it is for quantitative research, since qualitative work not only looks at outcomes, but more importantly, examines processes. Therefore, this may be one of the special contributions that qualitative research can make to the sister disciplines of conflict and peace studies. Avoiding studying such contexts, because this is difficult, will only lead to a continued lack of knowledge concerning such contexts.

As noted above, researchers who study their own conflictual backyard are constantly confronted with their (changing and developing) relationships to themselves, to their participants, to their colleagues, to others in their societies and to others outside of the region. Therefore, qualitative researchers can help develop complex understandings concerning these relationship trajectories. Researchers can encourage their participants to think together with them about their lives and the conflict, and thus simultaneously help themselves and others consider new insights. Or, additionally, researchers can provide information to participants concerning what others, from the "enemy camp" or outside of the area, think and feel about the conflict. Such sharing of knowledge and insights can be one of the benefits we can offer interviewees who agree to participate in the study.

Researchers who are studying the conflict area in which they live also have unique opportunities to identify dynamic changes happening in the field, before others may become aware of what has developed. This can make them research "pioneers." However, in order to be a pioneer, the researcher needs to be sensitive to the social-political changes taking place, in order not to miss them, and also be highly reflexive in order to understand the impact that these changes are having on her/his "knowledge" and belief systems. Such knowledge is invaluable for theory, practice and methodology.

Based on my experiences, and on the examples from the Palestinian-Israeli context presented above, it is clear that undertaking joint studies with others—especially when some/all of these others come from the "enemy camp"—has numerous potential pitfalls. I have found that while this work comes with tension and uncertainty, it is do-able (Marshall & Rossman, 1999) *because* of these collaborations. This is because colleagues offer needed moral and academic support. That is, somewhat paradoxically, researching the conflict alone is more difficult than working with the "enemy," since when one works alone, s/he has to confront the difficulties of researching "undesirable" or "dangerous" territory without support and counsel from others. Having partners in dialogue means that we can help one another deal with the hard times since we are committed to not only completing the academic task, but to making a political statement as well, that Palestinians and Israelis *can* work together and produce something of value.

The last points I will raise connect to the issues of choosing relevant questions for research and the ability to generalize/transfer knowledge from one context to another. In contexts which are characterized by conflict and rapid change, it is difficult to know if an event under study is a "one time" and very local event or if it reflects something more stable in that context or something more universal within human experience. Experience has shown that researchers do not really need to give into the fear that their topic will not have relevance beyond the specific study. For example, Sagy and Antonovsky's (1986) study of the impact of the dismantling of Yamit—an Israeli settlement formerly located in the Sinai that was dismantled after a peace treaty was signed between Israel and Egypt—on

the children of that town, a one-time and local Israeli event, was later used
to inform research on the impacts of the disengagement on Israeli settlers
from the Gaza Strip that took place in 2005 (Nuttman-Shwartz, Dekel, &
Tuval-Mashiah, 2011). Another way to look at these issues, and to see what
can be learned from one context to the next, is by undertaking longitudinal studies that situate these one-time events as points along an unfolding
social process. If we take such a stance, we can be more confident that we
will be able to transfer the theoretical and methodological insights that we
gained in our local studies to other projects, sites, cultures, and groups that
are characterized by conflict. And no less importantly, we can transfer our
understandings that we gained through our hard work, to our new research
projects that aim to delve even deeper into the conflicts that continue to
tear apart our societies and our lives.

REFERENCES

Abdeen, Z., Qasrawi, R., Shibli Nabil, S., & Shaheen, M. (2008). Psychological reactions to Israeli occupation: Findings from the national study of school-based
screening in Palestine. *International Journal of Behavioral Development, 32*(4),
290–297.

Adwan, S., & Bar-On, D. (2001). *Victimhood and beyond: The Bethlehem encounter.* Beit
Jala, PNA: Peace Research Institute in the Middle East.

Adwan, S., & Bar-On, D. (2004). Shared History Project: A PRIME Example of
Peace Building Under Fire. *International Journal of Politics, Culture and Society,
17*(3), 513–522.

Bar-On, D. (2006). *Tell your story: Creating dialogue between Jews and Germans, Palestinians and Israelis.* Beer-Sheva: Ben Gurion University of the Negev Press.
(in Hebrew).

Bar–On, D. (2008). *The "others" within us: Constructing Jewish-Israeli identity.* New
York, NY: Cambridge University Press.

Bar-Tal, D., & Teichman, Y. (2005), *Representations of Arabs in Jewish Israeli Society.*
Cambridge, England: Cambridge University Press, .

Braun-Lewensohn, O., Sagy, S., & Roth G. (2010). Coping strategies as mediators of the relationships between sense of coherence and stress reactions:
Israeli adolescents under missile attacks. *Anxiety, Stress & Coping.*
doi:10.1080/10615806.2010.494

Chaitin, J. (2011). *Peace Building in Israel and Palestine: Social Psychology and Grassroots
Initiatives.* New York, NY: Palgrave-Macmillan.

Chaitin, J., Awwad, E., & Andriani, C. (2009). Belonging to the conflict: Collective
identities among Israeli and Palestinian émigrés to the United States. *Social
Identities: Journal for the Study of Race, Nation and Culture, 15*(2), 207–225.

Chaitin, J., Obeidi, F., Adwan, S., & Bar-On, D. (2004). Palestinian and Israeli
NGOs: Work during the "Peace Era." *International Journal of Politics, Culture
and Society, 17*(3), 523–542.

Chaitin, J., Sternberg, R., Arad, H., Barizili, L., Drey, N., & Shinhar, S. (2012). "I may look 75 but I'm really a pioneer": Self-perception and resilience among Israeli elder adults living in a war zone. *Journal of Happiness Studies.* doi: 10.1007/s10902-012-9398-3

Creswell, J. W. (1998). *Qualitative inquiry and research design: Choosing among five traditions.* Thousand Oaks, CA: Sage.

Daniel, E. V. (1996). *Charred lullabies: Chapters in an anthropology of violence.* Princeton, NJ: Princeton University Press.

Dekel, R., & Nuttman-Shwartz, O. (2009). Posttraumatic stress and growth: The contribution of cognitive appraisal and sense of belonging to the country. *Health and Social Work, 34,* 87–96.

Delanty, G. & Strydom, P. (Eds.) (2003). *Philosophies of social science: The classic and contemporary readings.* Maidenhead, England: Open University Press.

Denzin, N. K., & Lincoln, Y. S. (2003) The seventh moment: Out of the past. In N. K. Denzin & Y. S. Lincoln (Eds.), *The landscape of qualitative research* (2nd ed., pp. 611–640). Thousand Oaks, CA: Sage.

El Sarraj, E. (2002). Suicide bombers: Dignity, despair, and the need of hope. *Journal of Palestine Studies, 4,* 71–76.

Elbedour, S., Onwuegbuzie, A. J., Ghannam, J., Whitcome, J. A., & Abu Hein, F. (2007). Post-traumatic stress disorder, depression, and anxiety among Gaza Strip adolescents in the wake of the second Uprising (Intifada). *Child Abuse and Neglect, 31*(7), 719–729.

Fine, M., Weis, L., Weseen, L., & Wong, L. (2003). For whom? Qualitative research, representations and social responsibilities. In N. K. Denzin & Y. S. Lincoln (Eds.), *The landscape of qualitative research* (2nd ed., pp. 167–207). Thousand Oaks, CA: Sage.

Friedson, F., & Gradstein, L. (February 4, 2013). Israeli-Palestinian textbook study sparks controversy. *The Jewish Journal.* Retrieved from http://www.jewishjournal.com/israel/article/israeli_palestinian_textbook_study_sparks_controversy

Gergen, M. M., & Gergen, K. J. (2003). Qualitative inquiry: Tensions and transformations. In N. K. Denzin & Y. S. Lincoln (Eds.), *The landscape of qualitative research* (2nd ed., pp. 611–640). Thousand Oaks, CA: Sage.

Glasser, & Strauss, A.L. (1967). *The development of grounded theory.* Chicago, IL: Aldin.

Greenwood, D. J., & Levin, M. (2003). Restructuring the relationships between universities and society through action research. In N. K. Denzin & Y. S. Lincoln (Eds.), *The landscape of qualitative research* (2nd ed., pp. 131–166). Thousand Oaks, CA: Sage.

Haraway, D. (2003). Situated knowledges: The science question in feminism and the privilege of partial perspective. In G. Delanty & P. Strydom (Eds), *Philosophies of social science: The classic and contemporary readings* (pp. 410–415). Maidenhead, England: Open University Press.

Kemmis, S., & McTaggart, R. (2003). Participatory action research. In N. K. Denzin & Y. S. Lincoln (Eds), *Strategies of qualitative inquiry.* (2nd ed., pp. 336–396). Thousand Oaks, CA: Sage.

Lederach, J. P. (2005). *The moral imagination: The art and soul of building peace.* New York, NY: Oxford University Press.

Lincoln, Y., & Guba, E. G. (1985). *Naturalistic inquiry.* Newbury Park, CA: Sage.

Lincoln, Y. S., & Guba, E. G. (2003). Paradigmatic controversies, contradictions and emerging confluences. In N. K. Denzin & Y. S. Lincoln (Eds.), *The landscape of qualitative research* (2nd ed., pp. 253–291). Thousand Oaks, CA: Sage.

Maoz, I. (2011). Contact in protracted asymmetrical conflict: Twenty years of planned encounters between Israeli Jews and Palestinians. *Journal of Peace Research, 48*(1), 115–125.

Marshall, C. & Rossman, G.B. (1999). *Designing Qualitative Research* (3rd ed.). Thousand Oaks, CA: Sage.

Nuttman-Shwartz, O., Dekel, R., & Tuval-Mashiach, R. (2011). Post-traumatic stress and growth following forced relocation. *British Journal of Social Work, 41*(3), 486–501.

Padgett, D. K. (1998). *Qualitative methods in social work research: Challenges and rewards.* Thousand Oaks, CA: Sage.

Punch, M., (1986). *The politics and ethics of fieldwork. Qualitative research methods series.* Beverly Hills, CA: Sage.

Rosenthal, G. (1993). Reconstruction of life stories. Principles of selection in generating stories for narrative biographical interviews. In R. Josselson & A. Lieblich (Eds.), *The narrative study of lives* (Vol. 1, pp. 59–91). London, England: Sage,

Rossman, G. B., & Rallis, S. F. (1998). *Learning in the field: An introduction to qualitative research.* Thousand Oaks, CA: Sage.

Sagy, S. (2002). Intergroup encounters between Jewish and Arab students in Israel: Towards an interactionist approach. *Intercultural Education, 13*, 259–274.

Sagy, S. & Adwan, S. (2006). Hope in times of threat: The case of Palestinian and Israeli-Jewish youth. *American Journal of Orthopsychiatry, 76*, 128–133.

Sagy, S., & Antonovsky, H. (1986). Adolescents' reactions to the evacuation of the Sinai settlements: A longitudinal study. *Journal of Psychology, 120*, 543–557.

Sagy, S., Steinberg, S., & Diab, K. (2006). Between peace talks and violent events: The impact of the political context on discourse characteristics in Jewish-Arab encounters in Israel. *Intercultural Education, 17*, 341–358.

Sagy, S., Steinberg, S., & Fahiraladin, M. (1999). Self in society and society in self: An evaluation study of small group encounters between Jews and Arabs in Israel. *Babylon, 19*, 48–67. (in German).

Scheper-Hughes, N. (1992). *Death without weeping: The violence of everyday life in Brazil.* Berkeley, CA: University of California Press.

Schratz, M. & Walker, R. (1995). *Research as social change: New opportunities for qualitative research.* London, England: Routledge.

Solomon, Z. (1995). *Coping with war-induced stress: The Gulf War and the Israeli response.* New York, NY: Plenum Press.

Stake, R. E. (1995). *The art of case study research.* Thousand Oaks, CA: Sage.

Steinberg, S., & Bar-On, D. (2002). An analysis of the group process in encounters between Jews and Palestinians using a typology for discourse classification. *International Journal of Intercultural Relations, 26*(2), 199–214.

Vidich, A. J., & Lyman, S. M. (2003) Qualitative methods: Their history in sociology and anthropology. In N. K. Denzin & Y. S. Lincoln (Eds.), *The landscape of qualitative research* (2nd ed., pp. 55–130). Thousand Oaks, CA: Sage.

CHAPTER 10

CONCLUSIONS AND LOOKING FORWARD

Laura Finley and Robin Cooper

In Chapter 2 of this book, Finley explains that the development of grounded theory was motivated in part by the perception of Glaser and Strauss that some forms of qualitative research were "impressionistic, anecdotal, unsystematic and biased" (Charmaz, 2006, p. 5). We hope that the preceding chapters have illustrated for readers the remarkable rigor applied in the qualitative methodologies described in this text. In addition, we hope readers find the detailed description of the data collection, data analysis, and reporting conventions associated with each methodology helpful as they design and conduct studies of their own related to peace studies, conflict resolution, or peace education. Above all, we hope the examples and illustrations included by the authors in this book will inspire readers to feel empowered and motivated to contribute to positive social change through their own qualitative studies in this field.

The preceding chapters show that each qualitative methodology has its own unique objectives and focus. As Cooper notes in Chapter 4,

> The names of qualitative methodologies often suggest their primary focus: case study is primarily focused on describing and explaining factors related to a particular case or set of cases; narrative research is primarily focused on

Peace and Conflict Studies Research: A Qualitative Perspective, pp. 205–213
Copyright © 2014 by Information Age Publishing

exploring individuals' narratives; grounded theory research is primarily focused on development of theory; and so forth. Phenomenology, as the name
suggests, is primarily focused on a particular phenomenon, or experience.
(pp. 71–72, this volume)

Just as there are particular objectives associated with each qualitative methodology, there are also unique terms related to each approach, such as
"horizonalization" in transcendental phenomenology, "theoretical saturation" in grounded theory, and the "thick description" of ethnography.

In spite of these distinctions, the chapters in this book also show that
there are some common characteristics of qualitative inquiry that contribute
to its value and impact for those working to analyze and resolve conflict and
those addressing structural and cultural violence through peace education.
One helpful characteristic highlighted by the chapter authors is the flexibility provided by the emergent and iterative nature of qualitative inquiry.
This flexibility in the design stage is noted by Muvingi and Duckworth,
who explain in their chapter on case study research that the definition of
the "case" under study may evolve during the research process. The flexibility available in data collection is illustrated in grounded theory research,
whereby the use of theoretical sampling guides the researcher to identity
new sources of data based on initial data analysis. And such techniques
as employing the hermeneutic circle in phenomenological data analysis builds a holistic, fluid approach to the analysis process in qualitative
research as well.

Another important characteristic of qualitative research discussed by all
of the authors in this text is that of researcher reflexivity. In some cases,
reflexivity is built right into the methodology, such as the bracketing and
epoche process of phenomenology. But whether or not it is noted overtly
in the research procedures, in each qualitative methodology, researcher
reflexivity is a critical element of the research process from start to finish. In
describing this aspect of ethnographic research, Welty thoughtfully shares
her reflections on the power dynamics of being a White woman conducting
research in East Africa, as well as her insider and outsider status in light of
her research topic. Chaitin likewise reflects on being an Israeli researcher
studying aspects of the Israeli-Palestinian conflict. As Chaitin observes in
Chapter 9,

> In sum, then, reflexivity is a conscious act, one that demands that the re-
> searcher situate him/herself clearly within the social and cultural context of
> conflict. The researcher must be willing to openly confront the self and to
> challenge previously-held "truths" and understandings, in order to engage
> in in-depth inquiry, even when such a process is painful. (p. 191, this volume)

One of the greatest contributions of qualitative research highlighted throughout this text is the emphasis on participants' voice. As Finley notes, qualitative approaches provide opportunities to hear the voices of people who have been historically silenced. Hiller and Chaitin point out,

> While we may be tempted to "jump into" respondents' stories, correct factual inaccuracies, commend the respondents' actions or share our own point of view, we need to refrain from doing so (Chaitin, 2004). In life-story interviews, the narrators are considered to be the only experts on their own lives. Therefore, as researchers, we do not impose our knowledge, but are respectful and show interested attention (Czarniawska-Joerges, 2004; Elliott, 2005). (p. 145, this volume)

Participant voices are included not only in the data collection stage of research but also in research reports in qualitative studies through the inclusion of participant quotes. Participants are also given voice through the process of member checking, where participants are invited to review and comment upon transcripts or preliminary findings as a method of ensuring the trustworthiness of a study's findings.

These characteristics of rigor, flexibility, and participant voice all contribute to enhancing the role of qualitative research in bringing about positive social change. This objective is explicit in such approaches as action research, as explained by Morrow and Finley. Those engaged in critical approaches to research, whether critical ethnography or grounded theory, also focus on social change, especially for those marginalized or silenced by dominant social structures. Hiller and Chaitin observe,

> As conflict resolution researchers we are educated, privileged individuals. The studies we conduct evolving around different forms of social conflict address indirect—yet powerful—forms of violence such as structural, cultural or symbolic violence. Our researchers' privileges come with the moral obligation to confront forms of invisible violence rather than hide behind the curtain of neutrality. (p. 153, this volume)

Other chapter authors note that the nature of the research process in many forms of qualitative inquiry may lead to change as a by-product of the research process. Muvingi and Duckworth point out that through direct interaction with research participants, the qualitative research process itself is an intervention. Welty shares the comment by a participant in her ethnographic study that she wanted to thank Welty for the interview as she felt benefitted by the opportunity to think about the issues being researched and what they mean to her. This is a sentiment qualitative researchers often hear from participants regarding in-depth interviews.

Qualitative Methods Appropriate for Peace and Conflict Studies Research

In light of these characteristics of qualitative research, we hope readers will agree with us that qualitative methods are ideally suited for research in peace and conflict studies and peace education. This is a theme that runs throughout the preceding chapters. For example, speaking specifically of qualitative case study research, Muvingi and Duckworth observe,

> Case study research is therefore suitable for investigating complex social phenomena such as conflicts and the efforts to resolve them. Conflicts take place in the real world in which the researcher has little to no control over the behaviors of parties to the conflict, and where invariably numerable and contested factors are involved. The field of conflict analysis and resolution is concerned with understanding the causes of conflicts and their processes so as to find appropriate ways of resolving them. Why and how are thus questions that are core to the field, but to these two would have to be added a search as well for the disputed narratives regarding "what" happened in a particular conflict. (pp. 95–96, this volume)

Welty likewise argues "that ethnography is particularly suited for peace and conflict studies because of its careful attention to power dynamics, focus on the local/grassroots level and tendency to seek understanding rather than simply explanation." (p. 112, this volume). She notes,

> Canonical peace studies professor and scholar John Paul Lederach (1996) describes the in situ and emic approach of ethnography as particularly well-suited to the field due to its "enormous respect for how people in a given setting understand themselves and events" and "careful attention to everyday talk and taken-for-granted meaning" (p. 30). (p. 112, this volume)

Hiller and Chaitin refer to the ability of narrative research to explore "contradictory layers of meaning" (p. 141, this volume) associated with social change, violence, and trauma. As they note, "the weakness in approaching nonviolent peace activism solely from a quantitative perspective lies in the fact that the personal meanings attached to the actions are left unexplored" (p. 143, this volume).

Issues Related to Publishing Qualitative Research in Peace and Conflict Studies

Once researchers conduct their qualitative studies in this field, they look forward to publishing their findings. There are some unique issues related to publishing peace and conflict research. As several chapters in this book noted, it is sometimes challenging to move past ownership issues when it comes to joint research. That is, the traditional academic model is that the researcher "owns" the results of his/her study and can use them for publications and presentations without further discussion. When research is conducted jointly, however, coupling an organization with a researcher, the scholar is no longer the sole owner of the work. Further, as Chaitin notes in her chapter on research in conflict zones, it is imperative that the journals in the field recognize that qualitative research in peace and conflict studies may differ methodologically than studies conducted in other fields. Editors should be prepared to accept nontraditional research methodologies as the field grows.

Keeping qualitative research reports creative and engaging to readers remains challenging for many, as most scholars are taught and encouraged to write in very prescriptive ways, including repetitious use of passive voice (Caulley, 2008; Cheney, 2001). Using interesting titles prompts curious readers to continue reading. Cheney (2001) recommends that scholars begin seeing their writing as "creative nonfiction," which

> tells a story using facts, but uses many of the techniques of fiction for its compelling qualities and emotional vibrancy. Creative nonfiction doesn't just report facts, it delivers facts in ways that move the reader toward a deeper understanding of the topic. (p. 1)

Narrative analysis, as described in the chapter by Patrick Hiller and Julia Chaitin, can give voice to those who are often silenced and can help researchers assess how people experience particular phenomenon through participants' use of metaphors and other themes. Hiller and Chaitin also issue an important reminder to researchers, noting the emotional difficulty that can occur when approaching participants to ask them to share important life stories. In addition, Chaitin notes in her chapter on research in conflict zones that ensuring all the voices are heard is a challenge when participants are speaking or writing from different cultural contexts.

Further, authors of qualitative research in peace and conflict studies sometimes struggle to find appropriate outlets to publish their work. Thankfully, a growing number of journals are devoted to qualitative research in general, such as *The Qualitative Report* and *Forum: Qualitative Social Research*, and to specific forms of qualitative research (e.g., *Grounded Theory Review* and *Action Research*). Likewise, peer-reviewed print and online journals in peace and conflict studies continue to emerge, while there has also been an increase in peace and conflict studies blogs and websites that can be vehicles for disseminating research studies. The references cited in each of the chapters in this book provide a great starting point for persons interested in where they might publish their work.

Issues Related to Funding Qualitative Research in Peace and Conflict Studies

Scholars and practitioners wishing to conduct research in peace and conflict studies often find obtaining financial support for their work to be a challenge. Although some universities may have funds for which a researcher can apply, these are often very small and not available to those working outside of academe. Obtaining funding for any research can be a challenge, but it might be even more difficult in qualitative studies. As Phillips (1997) notes, the reason may be a combination of the quality of proposals as well as the lack of standards for evaluating qualitative proposals. Further, funders may be more prone to support quantitative research (Phillips, 1997). The field should continue to develop funding support for scholars and practitioners seeking to conduct research that will advance peace. The United States Institute of Peace (USIP) currently offers funding for peace research. It provides funding for students at U.S. universities completing dissertations on topics related to peace, conflict and international security. Through its annual grant program, USIP "supports academic and applied research, the identification of promising models and effective practices, and the development of practitioner resources, tools, and training programs related to conflict management, international peace and security and peacebuilding." USIP's priority grant program "supports nonprofit organizations working in or on Afghanistan, Iraq, Pakistan, and Sudan, Arab World Political Transformation, and projects related to the theme of communication and peacebuilding."

Finally, the Jennings Randolph Senior Fellowship Program funds "scholars, practitioners, policy analysts, and other experts for the opportunity to spend 10 months in residence at the Institute, reflecting and writing on pressing international peace and security challenges" (http://www.usip.org/grants-fellowships). The International Peace Research Association Foundation (IPRA) also provides funding to support "systematic observation or study of conflict phenomena and peace strategies," with special consideration for studies conducted in the developing world (http://iprafoundation.org/peace-research-grants-instructions/). The Berghof Foundation for Conflict Studies provides funds in three focus areas: (1) Peacebuilding and reconciliation in postwar societies; (2) Transformation processes of nonstate armed groups into political actors; and (3) Interactions between state and nonstate actors in conflict transformation processes (http://www.berghof-foundation.org/en/).

Several fellowships are available for scholars in peace and conflict studies. The Herbert Scoville Jr. Peace Fellowship funds a stipend, health insurance and travel costs to Washington, D.C. for college graduates who work on research and public policy regarding arms control and international security (http://scoville.org/). The Kroc Institute for International Peace Studies provides funding for Notre Dame faculty members but also a Visiting Research Fellowship (http://kroc.nd.edu/research/grants-and-fellowships). Fulbright-Hays Fellowships may also be used for peace and conflict studies research and course development. Compilations of funding and related programs can be found at Idealist (www.idealist.org), the Peace and Justice Studies Association (www.peacejusticestudies.org) and the Peace and Conflict Development Network (PCDN) (http://www.internationalpeaceandconflict.org/).

In the 2000s, crowdsourcing has become a popular means for obtaining funding for special topics. Crowdsourcing sites like Kickstarter (www.kickstarter.com), Indiegogo (www.indiegogo.com) and Good Two (www.goodtwo.com) allow people with unique ideas to present their proposals and let people from around the world contribute to funding the project. Although these sites are often used for programs, researchers may find them useful to fund studies as well.

Areas for Further Exploration and Research

As researchers obtain funding and plan future research, we encourage them to consider qualitative studies in some emerging areas. These include virtual arenas. Virtual worlds may be the site of research or the sources of data collection (such as blogs, social media sites), the topic of research (such as virtual peace education, cyberbullying), and virtual technologies may also support the research process (such as interviews conducted in Second Life using avatars). Muvingi and Duckworth note that case study research has expanded the boundaries of the case to encompass virtual domains. And Welty points to the growing number of web-based ethnographies. While not addressed in depth in this text, the virtual arena holds tremendous potential for research in our field.

Another arena for additional research is that related to the arts. Again, arts-related topics may serve as the subject of research (such as performance-based peace education, or the role of theater in peacebuilding); or arts-based methods may be incorporated into qualitative research designs. Hiller and Chaitin referred to the use of metaphors in biographical narrative research. Cooper noted the use of collage in bracketing within phenomenological studies. She also uses found data poetry in narrative thematic analysis. Morrow and Finley mention the use of photography, video, or drawing in action research to engage participants in the research process. While this text has not focused on this important area within qualitative inquiry, this is an area that merits further development and discussion.

Another form of research that warrants further attention for peace researchers and peace educators is community-based research (CBR). Strand et al. (2003) define CBR as "collaborative, change-oriented research that engages faculty members, students, and community members in projects that address a community-identified need" (p. 5). The goal is to engage multiple voices in assessing a local need and developing and implementing a research strategy that will help improve the community. CBR is often incorporated as a form of service learning, whereby undergraduate and graduate students are involved in the design, implementation, and dissemination of research, all with the collaboration of a community group or organization. Peace educators can utilize CBR, which is a tremendous form of active learning to help local groups conduct needs assessments and evaluate their work (O'Donnell, 2011). This can serve as a form of mentorship of students, not just in terms of understanding local peace-related organizations but also in understanding research methodologies.

Finally, it is our hope that peace educators at all levels continue to see the importance of researching the impact of their work. While academics are perhaps more prepared to understand why this type of research matters so much, we predict that increasing numbers of K–12 peace educators will utilize critical ethnography and other qualitative methods to assess their work and to identify best practices.

In conclusion, there is no doubt that research plays a critical role in peacemaking, peacebuilding, and peace education. Qualitative forms of research are particularly well-suited to assess these efforts and will continue to build a knowledge base that can help build a more peaceful and just world.

REFERENCES

Caulley, D. (2008). Making qualitative research reports less boring: The techniques of creative nonfiction. *Qualitative Inquiry, 14*(3), 424–449.

Charmaz, K. (2008). Grounded theory in the 21st century. In N. Denizin & Y. Lincoln (Eds.) *Strategies of qualitative inquiry* (3rd ed., pp. 203–241). London, England: Sage.

Cheney, T. (2001). *Writing creative nonfiction: Fiction techniques for crafting great nonfiction.* Berkeley, CA: Ten Speed Press.

Czarniawska-Joerges, B. (2004). *Narratives in social science research.* Thousand Oaks, CA: Sage.

Elliott, J. (2005). *Using narrative in social research: Qualitative and quantitative approaches.* Thousand Oaks, CA: Sage.

O'Donnell, K. (2011). Feminist social justice work: Moving towards solidarity. *Societies Without Borders, 6*(2), 51–67.

Phillips, B. (1997). Qualitative methods and disaster research. *International Journal of Mass Emergencies and Disasters, 15*(1), 179–195.

Strand, K., Marullo, S., Cutforth, N., Stoecker, R., & Donohue, P. (2003, Spring). Principles of Best Practice for Community-Based Research. *Michigan Journal of Community Service Learning,* 1–15.

ABOUT THE AUTHORS

EDITORS

Robin Cooper is assistant professor of conflict resolution and ethnic studies and director of doctoral programs in the Department of Conflict Analysis and Resolution at Nova Southeastern University's School of Humanities and Social Sciences. She is editor-in-chief of *Peace and Conflict Studies Journal*, senior editor of *The Qualitative Report*, and associate editor of *Forum: Qualitative Social Research*. She conducts research and teaches courses in conflict analysis and resolution, as well as qualitative research design, collection, and analysis and has multiple publications in these fields.

Laura Finley is assistant professor of sociology and criminology at Barry University. She is the author or coauthor of 11 books and numerous book chapters and peer-reviewed journal articles. Dr. Finley is also an activist for peace, justice, and human rights. She serves on a number of local, state, and national boards, including the Peace and Justice Studies Association, Floridians for Alternatives to the Death Penalty, No More Tears, and the Humanity Project.

AUTHORS

Julia Chaitin, PhD, is a resident of Kibbutz Urim, located in the Eshkol regional council, which is near the border with the Gaza Strip. She is a scholar-practitioner, and her background is in social psychologist, with an expertise in qualitative research and peace-building. Her academic research focuses on the long-term psychosocial impacts of the Holocaust and the Palestinian-Israeli conflict—including topics such as personal narratives, collective identity, and dialogue—and she has published articles and books on these topics. Dr. Chaitin is a Senior Lecturer in the Social Work Department at the Sapir College, and teaches in the Masters Conflict Management Program at the Eilat campus of Ben Gurion University. Dr. Chaitin is also active in grassroots peace and social justice work. She is a board member of Other Voice—a volunteer organization that calls for a non-violent end to the conflict in the Gaza-Sderot region, a member of Friendship across Borders—a joint German, Israeli and Palestinian peace education NGO, and a member of Circles in Eshkol—a group comprised of secular and Orthodox Jews.

Robin Cooper is Assistant Professor of Conflict Resolution and Ethnic Studies and Director of Doctoral Programs in the Department of Conflict Analysis and Resolution at Nova Southeastern University's School of Humanities and Social Sciences. She is Editor-in-Chief of *Peace and Conflict Studies Journal*, Senior Editor of *The Qualitative Report*, and Associate Editor of *Forum: Qualitative Social Research*. She conducts research and teaches courses in conflict analysis and resolution, as well as qualitative research design, collection, and analysis and has multiple publications in these fields.

Cheryl Duckworth is Assistant Professor of Conflict Resolution at Nova Southeastern University. A peace-building program leader and conflict resolution policy analyst, she has served such organizations as the Institute for Multi-Track Diplomacy and the Center for International Education. She has lived in Zimbabwe and Paraguay, and published and presented globally on her two passions, peace education and peace economics, exploring ways to transform the economic, political, social and psychological root causes of war and violence. Her more recent publications include her book which explores the role of dignity in social movements, Land and Dignity in Paraguay, and an article on her implementation of critical peace education curriculum in a juvenile detention home. A proponent of engaged scholarship, she also recently co-edited *Conflict Resolution and the Scholarship of Engagement: Partnerships Transforming Conflict*, which examines how engaged scholarship can enhance the field of conflict resolution.

Laura Finley is Assistant Professor of Sociology and Criminology at Barry University. She is the author or co-author of eleven books and numerous book chapters and peer-reviewed journal articles. Dr. Finley is also an activist for peace, justice, and human rights. She serves on a number of local, state, and national boards, including the Peace and Justice Studies Association, Floridians for Alternatives to the Death Penalty, No More Tears, and the Humanity Project.

Patrick T. Hiller holds a PhD in Conflict Analysis and Resolution from Nova Southeastern University and a MA in Human Geography from the Ludwig-Maximilians-University in Munich, Germany. He is the Executive Director of the War Prevention Initiative by the Jubitz Family Foundation and teaches in the Conflict Resolution Program at Portland State University. His writings and research are almost exclusively related to the analysis of war and peace. He contributes on a regular basis to mainstream media through op-ed commentaries promoting nonviolent conflict transformation approaches. In his work he also focuses on social injustice, most often identified through structural violence and power dynamics, with an emphasis on human dignity, solidarity among all peoples, equal participation of all peoples, the role of the governments and the promotion of peace. Patrick is member of the editorial team for the Peace and Conflict Studies Journal, member of the Governing Council of the International Peace Research Association, member of the Advisory Council of the organizations International Cities of Peace, PeaceVoice and PeaceVoiceTV, member of the Board of Directors of the Oregon Peace Institute, as well as member of the Peace and Justice Studies Association.

Terry Morrow, PhD, is currently the Assistant Dean of Student Affairs and Assistant Professor in the College of Health Care Sciences at Nova Southeastern University. She holds a PhD in Conflict Analysis and Resolution and is a Certified Florida Supreme Court Mediator. Currently, she serves on the editorial boards of the Journal of Peace and Conflict Studies, The Qualitative Report and the Journal of Leadership Education. Dr. Morrow served on the Florida Board of the National Association of Student Personnel Administrators (NASPA) as the Co-Chair of the Student Leadership Programs Knowledge Community for five years and is the founder and former co-chair of the South Florida Diversity Alliance. She is passionate about researching and practicing the art of leveraging human and organizational capital to cultivate the potential of individuals and systems. Dr. Morrow has lobbied for HR 808, a bill in Congress that will create a platform for peace in our communities, schools, families and world. She is also a founding member of a nonprofit ministry to empower the Christian community to address domestic abuse and leads the Peacemakers Ministry at her local church.

Ismael Muvingi is an Associate Professor in Conflict Resolution and African Studies at Nova Southeastern University, Florida, United States. He is a native of Zimbabwe and during Zimbabwe's war for liberation from colonial rule, he worked for the Catholic Commission for Justice and Peace going into war zones and recording the stories of the unarmed civilians caught in the middle of the war. After Zimbabwe's independence, Muvingi practiced law both in the private and the public sectors for close to twenty years and also lectured in law on a part time basis at the University of Zimbabwe. In North America, Ismael has worked for a US based NGO as a legislative advocacy campaign manager on conflict resolution and HIV/AIDS issues in Africa. Thereafter, Ismael taught conflict resolution at Menno Simons College, University of Winnipeg for seven years before joining Nova Southeastern University. His research interests include transitional justice, human rights, extractive industries and social movements with an area focus on Sub-Saharan Africa.

Claire Michèle Rice, PhD, is Associate Professor and serves as Chair of the Department of Conflict Analysis and Resolution at School of Humanities and Social Sciences, Nova Southeastern University. For over 13 years, Rice had served as a consultant in poverty alleviation, diversity training, and conflict management to businesses, civic organizations, and institutions of primary to higher education in the Caribbean and in the United States. She received a PhD at Florida International University (FIU) in Comparative Sociology with concentrations in race and ethnicity, sociolinguistics and cultural analysis. She also earned a Master's of Arts degree in Linguistics and Bachelor of Arts degree in Spanish, with a minor in French at FIU. Rice's research activities have focused on conflict resolution training, community organization, group dynamics, poverty alleviation/economic empowerment, diversity training, collaborative problem-solving and mentoring as viable tools for human resource and community development. Dr. Rice has also authored, co-authored and edited several journal articles, monographs, book chapters, training manuals, and newsletters on her work. She teaches courses in conflict resolution and research methods, with a focus on qualitative methodologies.

Emily Welty, PhD, is the Director of Peace and Justice Studies and an Associate Professor of Political Science at Pace University in New York City. She is the co-author of Occupying Political Science: the Occupy Wall Street

Movement from New York City to the World and Unity in Diversity: inter-faith dialogue in the Middle East. She researches religion, peacebuilding, development, reconciliation and nonviolence.

Made in the USA
Monee, IL
16 July 2022

99810727R00125